INTEGRATED
ACCOUNT
MANAGEMENT

INTEGRATED
ACCOUNT
MANAGEMENT

How Business-to-Business Marketers Maximize Customer Loyalty and Profitability

Mark A. Peck

AMACOM
American Management Association

New York • Atlanta • Boston • Chicago • Kansas City • San Francisco • Washington, D.C.
Brussels • Mexico City • Tokyo • Toronto

This book is available at a special
discount when ordered in bulk quantities.
For information, contact Special Sales Department,
AMACOM, a division of American Management Association,
1601 Broadway, New York, NY 10019-7420.

This publication is designed to provide accurate and authoritative
information in regard to the subject matter covered. It is sold with the
understanding that the publisher is not engaged in rendering legal,
accounting, or other professional service. If legal advice or other expert
assistance is required, the services of a competent professional person
should be sought.

Library of Congress Cataloging-in-Publication Data

Peck, Mark A.
    Integrated account management : how business-to-business marketers
maximize customer loyalty and profitability / Mark A. Peck.
        p.   cm.
    Includes bibliographical references and index.
    ISBN 0-8144-0333-6
    1. Industrial marketing.   I. Title.
HF5415.1263.P43   1997
658.8'4—dc21   96-40049
                                                               CIP

Printing number

10   9   8   7   6   5   4   3   2

Contents

v

List of Figures

Acknowledgments

Although I have been working on this book for only ten months (it seems much longer), the concepts, content, and examples come from fifteen years of consulting with clients in virtually all aspects of business-to-business marketing and sales. I have been fortunate in that time to have been part of Hunter Business Direct and to have had the opportunity to work with, and learn from, many valued associates at Hunter Business Direct and many highly regarded clients. As much as I am the author of this book, it is in reality the sum of all the extraordinary minds of the people that I have worked with over these fifteen years. I am deeply indebted to all of these people. This may be an anonymous acknowledgment. Nonetheless, it is a sincere statement of appreciation for both their direct and indirect support of this work and the concepts herein.

Additionally, there is a group of associates and clients that have had a more specific and direct impact on this book—by sharing their ideas and experiences, by reviewing sections and providing feedback, by questioning me in particular topic areas, and by providing encouragement. My thanks go out to the following for the roles they have played and the support they have provided.

Joe Balthazor
David Cobb
Vic Hunter
Ciarin McCabe
Mike McIntyre
Valerie O'Connor
Nick Poulos
Neil Rongstad
Ed Ryan
Jim Schoemer
Juli Vinik
Carolyn Washburne
Bill Younger

The staff at AMACOM has been extremely helpful in the writing and development of this book. I am especially grateful to Jacqueline Flynn for her thorough review of manuscripts, her insightful questions, and her incisive feedback and suggestions.

A special note of thanks goes to my assistant, Nancy Vogt, for all of her enthusiastic and uncomplaining efforts that helped make this book a reality. She edited, typed, reviewed, managed, kept me organized, and so on. Without her help I would probably still be writing.

And, last but not least, a special thanks to my family for their patience and love, and for making everything worthwhile. Thank you Kim, Ashley, and Stephen.

Preface

I had just finished a meeting with a new client and was relaxing in the back seat of a cab on my way back to the airport. As I reflected on the day, I couldn't help but be struck by a couple of things that had occurred. We had been discussing the company's business—who its customers are, what its customers' needs are, what its products are, what its sales channels are, who its competitors are, and so forth. After an hour or two of this line of questioning, the chairman of the company stopped me in mid-question and asked, "What would you do? If this were your company, what would you do?"

Now you need to understand here that I've been a consultant for fifteen years. In that time, I've been conditioned to thoroughly diagnose before I prescribe, and our less-than-two-hour discussion could hardly be described as a thorough diagnosis. It wasn't unusual for me to be asked this question; what was unusual was that I felt compelled to respond. My response was that the company should set up and run an integrated account management (IAM) program. This wasn't the first time I had given this response, and it wasn't the last. In so many cases, I find myself recommending IAM.

The Value of Integrated Account Management

What is it about IAM? It seems to be right for so many different companies—companies with different customers, different products, and even different selling channels. Although it is not a universal solution for all business-to-business marketing problems, it is an ideal tool to deal with the increasingly challenging business-to-business marketplace.

If you are involved in business-to-business marketing or sales, you are probably already feeling the pain associated with this increasingly complex and chaotic marketplace. The combination of factors in the marketplace—increased competition, customers' growing demands and higher expectations for more and better service, and the rising costs of marketing and selling to customers—is forcing companies to search for new and better ways of doing business with their customers.

Some are embracing an integrated account management approach with remarkable results.

- An automotive aftermarket business turned an $8 million loss into a $400,000 profit in one year while simultaneously increasing revenue and increasing customer satisfaction.
- A technology products and services company created a new sales channel that, in a pilot environment, ran at a four-to-one return on operating expenses.
- A high-tech equipment company used integrated account management to manage its dealer channel, generating a 400 percent increase in a six-month pilot program and supporting a sales environment that allowed it to double revenue in one year with no increase in the size of the field sales force.

In each of these situations, it was essential for the companies to effectively manage their relationships with customers. Your relationship with your customers is what drives both your growth and your profitability. It is why customers buy from you, what differentiates you from your competition, and, most important, why customers remain loyal to you. An account management system geared to effectively handle a relationship marketing strategy is critical in today's marketplace. It is an important—maybe the most important—marketing approach being applied to business-to-business markets today.

How This Book Can Help You

This book is intended to help you understand the IAM approach to marketing, the key principles and concepts that make the approach as successful as it is, and how an approach like this can be built in a relatively short time frame.

Integrated Account Management provides a map that allows you to arrive at an account management system for mutually beneficial individual customer relationships. Like most maps, it will help orient you to the reality of a situation, allow you to compare one route to your destination with another, spot patterns along the way, and, ultimately, guide you to your destination.

It is intended to be used as both a strategic and a tactical tool to allow you to make strategic decisions on using IAM, to understand how to use it when you have it in place, and to understand how to incrementally or significantly augment an existing account management system. It is also intended to be used as a how-to manual to allow a company to actually go through the steps of building an IAM system.

Integrated Account Management is written and designed to be used in a number of ways and can be approached as five books in one.

1. It is an account management guide, emphasizing the importance of the customer relationship and how IAM is an application that supports building customer relationships.
2. It is a sourcebook that you can use as a reference document as you build an IAM capability or augment an existing capability, offering specific how-to's.
3. It is a step-by-step blueprint, providing the charts and graphs you need to either build an IAM system or improve an existing system.
4. It is a case study, providing examples that allow you to see the tangible application of the concepts and to see the evidence and impact of the concepts when they are applied.
5. And, finally, it is a combination of these, a methodology for building a profitable IAM program.

How the Book Is Organized

Integrated Account Management begins by helping you determine where you are. Chapter 1 sets the stage, discussing the conditions in the marketplace that are making account management a necessary competitive tool for business today.

In Chapter 2 key components of IAM are described, along with an operating definition and operating principles for effective integrated account management. Fifteen operating principles are set out for you to apply to building an IAM program or to use as a measure against your existing program.

Chapter 3 is intended to help you with your overall strategy, deciding how IAM is a fit for your company's environment. It tackles this using a couple of case histories and a set of questions and conditions that allow you to look at the external factors and decide if IAM is a good fit for them.

From the more strategic intent of the first three chapters, Chapter 4 moves to a specific work plan to build an IAM system. It is a road map that takes you through a detailed process with tasks and subtasks to help you define and execute the steps you need to take in building an integrated account management system.

Chapters 5 through 15 discuss significant steps in building an IAM program. Used together, they provide a systematic work plan to build such a system. Because they each address particular pieces in the development of an IAM program, the chapters can also be used independently to improve your existing account management program. Charts and worksheets provide a step-by-step approach that allows you to very logically build an integrated account management system.

Chapter 16, "A Day in the Life," demonstrates how your system can work, both from an account management perspective and from a customer perspective.

The approach laid out in *Integrated Account Management*, when competently applied, will allow you to add more value in the marketplace, generating a simultaneous increase in revenue, profitability, and customer satisfaction and loyalty.

It is my hope that this book launches you on this value-creating, profitable journey.

INTEGRATED
ACCOUNT
MANAGEMENT

1

The Changing Business-to-Business Marketing Landscape

The business-to-business marketplace is demanding a new way of doing business. The combination of customers' growing demand for more, better, and faster service, the increasing volume of hungry competitors, and the rising costs of selling and marketing are forcing companies to change their approach. The key to good market strategy is achieving a balanced response to these marketplace factors.

Integrated account management (IAM) is the marketing and sales process born out of this environment. Like the best marketing strategies, it is based upon needs in the marketplace, it is driven by the positioning and capabilities available to (or that can be developed by) the selling company, and it results in a high return on the marketing and sales investment. Integrated account management is a customer retention and cultivation strategy that, as is inherent in its definition, supports a balanced response to the marketplace.

In the book *The One to One Future* (1993), Don Peppers and Martha Rogers discuss the concept of customer share as opposed to market share. "Trying to increase your market share means selling as much of your product as you can to as many customers as you can. Driving for share of customer, on the other hand, means ensuring that each individual customer who buys your product buys more product, buys only your brand of product, and is happy using your product instead of some other type of product as the solution to his problem."[1]

IAM embodies this customer share approach and takes it one step further. The intent and corresponding opportunity in IAM is to manage not only share but also profitability at the customer level.

1

Ultimately, the overall company profit is the sum of the profits of each individual customer.

Effectiveness and efficiency in managing customer relationships is the key to driving this profitability. IAM makes it possible for you to proactively manage a whole continuum of customers, from very large to very small. It allows you to sustain customer relationships by managing the overall customer contact mix; it allows you to carefully manage the quality, frequency, type, and mix of contacts with customers through integrating mail, phone, and field contacts. In its measurability, it provides the tools to optimize individual customer profitability, which ultimately leads to company profitability.

Whether your primary sales channel is a field sales force, a dealer/distributor organization, or direct mail/catalog, IAM can probably be applied in a way that gives you a significant competitive edge.

Even with all these benefits, IAM is an underused marketing approach. Although there is some universal awareness of account management, there is limited knowledge of *integrated* account management and even less understanding of its potential impact and accessibility. Its newness and the limited number of documented cases of its use are obvious factors contributing to this underuse.

How did we—business-to-business marketers—get here? Let's look at some of the factors that have primed the marketplace for the acceptance of IAM, provided the necessary knowledge and competencies, and proved that IAM is the killer marketing application to build competitive advantage in the business-to-business marketplace.

The Increasing Complexity of Buying Decisions

I remember what it used to be like making a buying decision for a PC for the office back in the mid-1980s. The primary question was "Are we going to get an IBM, an Apple, or a Compaq?" The brand we selected then effectively narrowed the choices of—and in some cases determined—*where* we would buy the PC.

This same decision today is very different. Just start with the applications. Twelve years ago, I was thinking I would use a spreadsheet package, a word processing package, maybe an accounting or graphics package—all running in the relatively simple Disk Operating System, or DOS. Today I still include spreadsheets, word processing, and graphics. In addition, I've got to consider network software, time management, a file manager, electronic mail, a World Wide Web browser, fax software, and so on.

I not only have to deal with more features, options, and add-ons,

I have to deal with the compatibility of these features, options, and add-ons with each other. Today it's not unusual for an off-the-shelf PC to be bundled with 75–100 different software packages. This is just the start. Once I've determined what applications I need and address compatibility, I then need to determine what kind (brand name) of computer I will buy and whom I will buy from. Whereas twelve years ago I had a limited number of suppliers to choose from, today I have literally hundreds to pick from. Deciding where to buy increases my options by an order of magnitude. Do I buy from a retailer (there are 24,000 stores in the U.S. to choose from), from a value-added reseller (now we're up to 58,000 choices), direct from the manufacturer (a paltry 5,000), from a cataloger (can you imagine looking through 600 catalogs?), from an on-line service—the World Wide Web/Internet (this number is anyone's guess; even Dun & Bradstreet has no idea)? The number of alternatives can seem overwhelming, and the volume of information that needs to be assimilated is staggering—I've got to decide on the applications, address compatibility (both software and hardware), determine the brand, determine what channel I will buy from, decide which specific seller I will buy from, determine what kind of service I require, look at financing options, and assess the overall price/performance value ratios. In each of these areas, the number of options available to me has increased at least tenfold in the past twelve years. Has this decision become easier in the last twelve years? Absolutely not—the complexity of the decision has increased and continues to increase exponentially.

Now, PCs are obviously part of the high-tech marketplace. As part of that market, there is some change in the decision-making process that is simply due to the rapid advancement of high-tech products. However, a quick look at a mature marketplace, business forms, indicates a similar situation.

Even though the number of suppliers of business forms hasn't changed much in recent years, the complexity of the decision-making process has still increased. This complexity mainly comes from two areas: the number of local printers providing forms and the number of software packages available for companies to make their own forms in-house.

It seems like there are "instant" print shops springing up on almost every street corner, places like Minuteman Press, Kopy-Print, Kinko's, Econoprint. They promise fast service and low cost, not to mention convenient locations.

Then there is the in-house option. Not only do you have to decide among many different software packages, there is also the option of having your form layout hardwired right into the hardware. (This option is available on Lexmark printers, where the form is resident in the printer and printed simultaneously with the text.) You run into the same complexities buying forms software as you do buying any software. Is it easy to understand? Is it easy to use? Is service available? Is it compatible with software already in use? Can current personnel be trained or does someone new need to be hired? The forms catalogs have anticipated this option and have expanded their formats to include not only the forms themselves but also software to create them. The value provided has changed from ink on paper to expertise in design and expertise in understanding how forms support business processes.

Once the software and hardware are working properly, the design process begins. The customization/personalization options can be overwhelming: layout, color, type of paper, and so forth. Some would say that even with the positive cost-effectiveness of doing forms in-house, the value received compared to the hassle may not be worth it. So, do you pay a little more and go to an "instant" print shop that doesn't specialize in forms but can get the job done, or do you pay a little more and have the experts do a really first-class job? Decisions, decisions, decisions . . .

Across the board, as the number of options has continued to increase, buying decisions have become much more complex, and they continue to increase in complexity. This, combined with the fact that business customers usually have less time to make a buying decision, is significantly changing the expectations that customers have of suppliers. In a recent buying decision process study, two types of business-to-business relationships were identified: a "partner" supplier relationship and a "commodity" supplier relationship. The expectations that customers had in a partner supplier relationship were as follows:

- Partner suppliers would maintain a detailed understanding of their business
  —Industry trends and business issues
  —Company business strategy (business strategy has a direct impact on buying behavior)
  —Development of business planning
  —Insight into the company's customers to fully understand the business situation
- Partner suppliers would be integrated into the decision and buying process
  —Proactive participation in the qualification process, including handling on-site audits and thoroughly educating the companies on product and service capabilities

—Product and applications expertise for determining purchasing criteria
—Documentation of the costs and benefits in order to support the project definition and approval process
• Partner suppliers would be proactive
—Unsolicited, independent solutions and recommendations to add value

A company's ability to differentiate itself and to build a competitive advantage with its customers is driven by the degree to which it can fulfill these expectations. Buying decisions have always contained a degree of uncertainty. As these decisions become more complex (and in some cases become more important), it becomes more difficult for the customer to process all of the necessary information, increasing uncertainty in the buying decision. Partner suppliers are best positioned when they are able to reduce the uncertainty inherent in the buying decision. Implicit requirements to reduce this uncertainty are a degree of trust and a degree of mutual commitment—characteristics of sound business relationships.

The focus on customer-perceived value and individual customer relationships within IAM programs builds this trust and provides a demonstration of the seller's commitment to the customer.

Age of the Relationship

In his book *Liberation Management,* Tom Peters aptly describes the marketplace as "a commercial world where everything's gone soft, gone fickle, gone fashion."[2] How do you manage, and compete, in a world like this, a world gone "bonkers"? In this world, having superior products is simply not enough. As Peters wrote (and others have), you survive in this world by providing superior products, providing world-class service, hiring and empowering great people, driving innovation and flexibility and the ability to change into your organization, and focusing on the customer. The question here is, "Can you build an organization with all of these characteristics and not blow away the competition?" The challenging answer to that question is, "Yes!" Although all of these characteristics are valuable components of a competitive business system, they may simply not be enough. You can have a business with all of these components and still not have relationships with your customers and still not have a competitive barrier—one that prevents competitors from taking your customers.

You can have superior products and not have strength in the marketplace. Sometimes the market simply doesn't care. Consider Apple Computers. How many times have you heard the comment, "Windows '95 is a good product, but most of the features are features that have been available in the Macintosh operating system for years." Yet, Microsoft sold a huge number of copies of Windows '95 on the first day that the product was available. Additionally, product superiority is usually short-lived—any advantage gained is not sustainable. One only need look at companies' dependence on new products to realize the volume of new products and the speed at which they are being brought to market. Robert Cooper illustrates this dependence in his book *Winning at New Products* (1986): "[T]he contribution made by new products to sales growth over the next five years is expected to increase by one-third, while the portion of total company profits generated by new products will increase by 40 percent."[3]

In some respects, service is changing a lot like product. How long did it take for all the auto rental companies to follow Hertz's lead and develop an enhanced service program? Hertz has Hertz Gold, Avis has Wizard, and National has Emerald Club.

The other limitation (when attempting to create competitive advantage with service) is that in many companies customer service is interpreted and implemented as a reactive function. When a customer encounters a problem and the company becomes aware of it, it needs empowered people and an excellent recovery system to fix the problem rapidly and to the satisfaction of the customer. However, some customers (in some industries, a lot of customers) have low expectations or simply don't complain.

The combination of the speed and the reactive nature of service in many companies limits its use as a sustainable competitive advantage. Empowering talented people and building innovation and flexibility into the company are essential foundational elements of the business. They do not, however, turn into competitive advantage unless they are consistently applied in a way that adds value—more value than your competitors add—to customers.

Many companies are using relationships with their customers to build share, sustain customers, and build competitive advantage. Consider a distributor for Du Pont, Hallmark Building Supplies. Hallmark Building Supplies is a regional distributor of building supplies products, including some well-known branded products. One of the primary products is Du Pont Corian, a solid-surface countertop material sold to a residential and commercial market segments. In late 1995, Hallmark conducted a customer loyalty study. In the study, 377 customers were surveyed. Loyalty levels were defined by a combination of the customer's overall satisfaction level, intent to continue purchasing from Hallmark, and anticipated increase (or decrease) in purchase levels. Most-loyal customers were defined as those that had a high satisfaction measure, intended to continue purchasing from Hallmark, and were very likely to increase or sustain their purchase levels. Least-loyal customers were defined as those that had a somewhat dissatisfied or very dissatisfied satisfaction measure, probably did not intend to continue purchasing from Hallmark, and anticipated a significant decrease in purchase levels.

In another part of that study, Hallmark asked customers what the most significant factor was that affected the likelihood of their purchasing from Hallmark Building Supplies the next time they had a need. In effect, the question gets at why customers buy from Hallmark. As the company looked at its most loyal customers, the most frequent response was exactly what one would expect: "The reason I buy from Hallmark Building Supplies is because of the strength of the Corian brand name and because they are the sole distributor of Corian in my area." Just over 28 percent of customers gave this response. The second most frequent response was a bit surprising: "The reason I buy from Hallmark Building Supplies is the relationships that I have with my rep and other people at Hallmark." Over 26 percent of customers responded this way.

In fact, a closer look at the data illustrates some very interesting correlations (see Figure 1-1). There appears to be a negative correlation between a "brand reason for buying" and loyalty of customers. Additionally, there appears to be a positive correlation between a "re-

Figure 1-1. Reasons for buying.

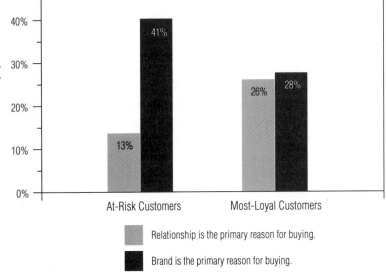

Relationship is the primary reason for buying.

Brand is the primary reason for buying.

lationship reason for buying" and loyalty of customers. So, as reliance on brand as the primary reason for buying decreases (from 41 percent to 28 percent in Figure 1-1), the loyalty of customers increases. And as relationship as the primary reason for buying increases (from 13 percent to 26 percent in Figure 1-1), the loyalty of customers increases.

DuPont Corian isn't a "soft" product. And it doesn't compete in a "soft" market. DuPont Corian is about as "hard" as a product can get. In addition, it's a product with strong brand-name recognition. The market consists of businesses that support residential and commercial construction: cabinetmakers, Corian dealers, countertop fabricators, home building centers, residential builders, and so on. So in this "hard" business, customer loyalty is increased in a very "soft" way—by strengthening the individual relationships with customers.

Let's look to another industry for another example. Bankers Systems, Inc. (BSI) is a company in St. Cloud, Minnesota, that provides products that support regulatory, operational, and marketing needs of the financial services industry—banks, savings institutions, and credit institutions. It provides products to serve these needs, including printed forms, electronic forms, software, retirement plan products, marketing products, newsletters, and educational services. In this industry, and for this product line, it is absolutely essential that products comply with both federal and state regulations. Providing this compliance to its customer base of more than 12,000 financial institutions is a core competence that BSI has built its business on.

In 1996, BSI conducted a customer loyalty study. Compliance expertise, a BSI core competency and a primary value provided to customers, was the third most frequently mentioned "differentiating satisfier" (the differentiating factors that determine why people buy from BSI). The number one factor, again, was the relationship customers have with BSI (see Figure 1-2).

Customers were asked, "Why do you buy from BSI?" "What are the unique factors that cause you to buy from BSI?" and "What advantages does BSI have over the competition?" More often than any other factor, the response was "the relationship."

In today's "bonkers" marketplace, the most impervious competitive barrier and the only truly sustainable differentiation is the relationship that you have with your customers. Account management programs that do not build on these relationships may provide short-term revenue and profitability; however, they do not create a differentiated position with the customer, do not create a competitive edge, and do not build a foundation for long-term customer retention and profitability. IAM explicitly focuses on these relationships.

Figure 1-2. Differentiating satisfiers customer loyalty survey.

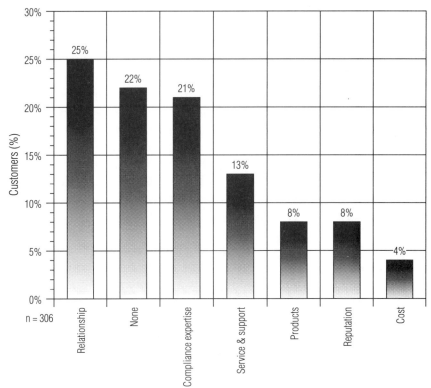

National Account Programs Exemplify Relationship Strategy

The prominence and increasing volume of national account programs is both evidence of a corporate response to this relationship need and an excellent example of how a company can deliver against these expectations.

NAMA (National Account Management Association) defines national account management as "a special strategy used by a selling organization to serve high-potential, multi-location accounts with complex needs requiring individual attention through a carefully established relationship." NAMA goes on to define national accounts as those accounts that have the following characteristics:

- Represent large sales potential
- Have an interest in centralizing their purchasing
- Have an interest in limiting the number of their suppliers
- Display a complex buying behavior (varying operating units, widespread geographic locations)
- Have specialized needs (engineering, inventory, distribution)
- Willing to enter into a long-term alliance or partnership

This strategy plays out in most companies to be very few accounts and a very small percentage of the customer base. It becomes an exercise that invests significantly (does whatever is necessary) in each of these accounts and that is justified because one "simply cannot invest too much in these key accounts." In many industries, companies have their account reps "live" with their national account customers. (In some industries these are large account teams.) This strategy has allowed many companies to build a competitive barrier with relatively few national accounts.

National account management is an excellent strategy to protect a key, albeit limited, part of the business. The only problem is that it doesn't address the vast majority of customers, as illustrated in Figure 1-3. In many companies, national accounts are less than 5 percent of the account base. Additionally, the remaining 95+ percent of accounts (or at least some percentage of these) often represent at least significant sales potential, have multiple locations, have complex buying behaviors and complex needs, are interested in limiting their number of suppliers, and are interested in entering into a partnership. Unfortunately, these other accounts usually become just that—the other accounts, the rest. Determining how to manage these "other" accounts would be an easy exercise if you simply could not invest too much in these customers. The reality is that it is very easy to overinvest in these accounts. Companies should approach with caution their investments in these next levels of accounts.

National account programs are revenue-driven businesses. Profit is a foregone conclusion. With a broader base of customers (those

Figure 1-3. Relationship/customer fit analysis.

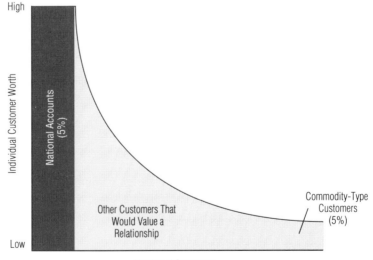

that are not typically part of a national account program), however, the sales and marketing system needs to support a delicate, closely managed balance between revenue and selling cost. Many existing selling systems make less and less economic sense as they move down the continuum of customers to smaller and smaller customers (as defined by sales dollar volume). National account programs are not necessarily flawed in their design. They are, because of their design and the economics inherent in their design, limited in their application. In some cases, national account programs are already causing companies to spend too much on too few customers. In almost all cases, a national account approach simply cannot be expanded to a large base of customers, because the economics don't work. Increasing sales and servicing customers well at a loss is not a long-term business proposition. A well-managed balance between customer investments and customer revenue is an essential part of the sales and marketing strategy and an inherent characteristic of IAM.

Integrated Direct Marketing Spawns Economic Possibilities

Bob Stone has described the expanding application of direct marketing: "The scope of direct marketing has continued to expand for decades, and new applications have been numerous. Long trumpeted as a stand-alone discipline, direct marketing has matured and is rapidly taking its place as a key component in the total marketing mix."[4]

Direct marketing has legitimized a whole set of customer contact tools and provided gobs of evidence that these tools can play a significant role in developing relationships with customers. Both the telephone and direct mail have evolved to become powerful relationship tools. They've also proved to be viable tools to generate large sales, at a fraction of the selling cost. At TeamTBA (short for "tires, batteries, and accessories"), Shell Oil Company's aftermarket sales organization selling branded tires, batteries, and accessories to Shell Service Stations, it's not unusual for the inside sales account managers (telemarketers—a term I would use if it wasn't filled with such baggage) to develop personal relationships with their accounts, even though they may never have met in person. If you walked into one of their offices, you'd see pictures of their customers, their customers' children, occasionally a picture of a customer's new grandchild.

In fact, in the late 1980s, in Amoco's TBA business unit, Amoco dealers were asked why they bought Atlas products (which were being sold and distributed to dealers through Amoco corporate). One in four stated that the relationship with their telesales rep was the reason that they bought Atlas products over the competition. Dell

Computer changed the value delivery equation in the personal computer marketplace with an effective blend of mail and phone contact. These contact tools were certainly enough to propel Dell's growth to a multibillion dollar company in less than ten years.

This is a high volume of direct mail and telephone contact with business customers that is intended to generate (sometimes manipulate) a one-time response. That is not what I am discussing here. I am talking about the application of phone and mail to add relevant customer value and to build relationships.

Thomas Moore in the book *SoulMates* (1994) effectively paints a vision for mail: "One of the most potentially soulful aspects of modern life is mail and all that attends it: letters, envelopes, mailboxes, postage stamps, and of course the man or woman who delivers the mail. . . . The examples of speaking and writing I've given are all from the realm of the personal, but there is no reason why we can't bring some of the same attention to style, careful use of words, and poignant expression of feeling to our business letters and to all our forms of communication."[5]

The effectiveness of these tools and their relatively low cost (compared to face-to-face visits) counter the economic obstacles that prevent key account programs from including a broader set of accounts. Figure 1-4 illustrates the order-of-magnitude differences that

Figure 1-4. Marketing integration cost per contact.

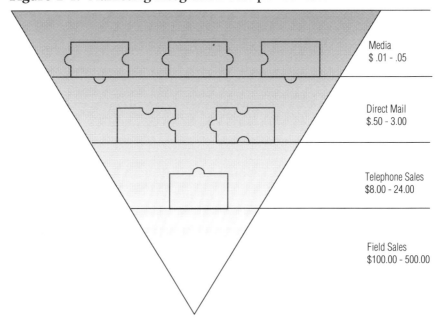

There is an order-of-magnitude increase in per-contact cost from one type of contact medium to the next.

exist in the cost per contact for these different media. It is not unusual for telephone contacts to be one-tenth or even one-twentieth the cost of a field sales contact. And it is not unusual for a mail contact to be one-tenth the cost of a phone contact. The most effective integrated account management contact plans use all these tools blended together to provide value to customers and develop strong relationships, and do so in a way that makes economic sense.

Why Invest in Relationships?

There are a lot of reasons to make this investment in customers; it just seems like the right thing to do, they deserve it, you owe it to your customers, your competitors do it, it feels good, or it's consistent with your corporate mission. As good as these reasons sound, you can't take any of them to the bank. However, there are some reasons that you *can* take to the bank.

Investing in these customer relationships has a significant financial impact on the business—on both the top line (overall sales) and the bottom line (profitability).

This financial impact is the result of two things that happen to relationships with customers: (1) the customers stay customers longer, and (2) they buy more during the period of time that they are customers.

Keeping customers longer—customer retention—has been documented in the business press as an important way to increase profitability. The data provided by Bain & Company (in Figures 1-5 and 1-6) highlight two important effects:

• Increasing customer retention by as little as five percentage points effects a 35 to 95 percent increase in profitability. This result occurs because you keep a higher volume of customers (newly acquired customers incrementally add to the total volume of customers, rather than serve to replace lost customers) and because doing business with mature customers is more profitable (see next point).

• Profitability increases in each subsequent year that you retain a customer. A look at Figure 1-5 shows that increased profitability beyond base profits occurs as a result of four other factors:

1. *Revenue growth.* Mature customers simply buy more from you, more of the same products (products they have purchased in the past) and additional product lines.
2. *Cost savings.* As customers learn how to do business with you, and you learn how to do business with them, you both be-

Figure 1-5. Customer profitability as a function of number of years retained.

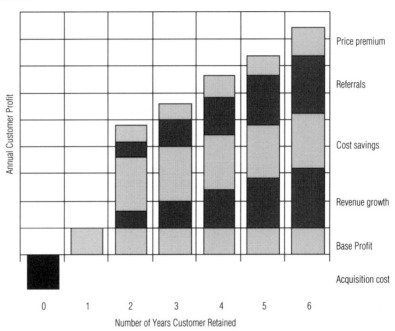

Figure 1-6. Impact of a five-percentage-point increase in retention rate on customer net present value (over a one-year period).

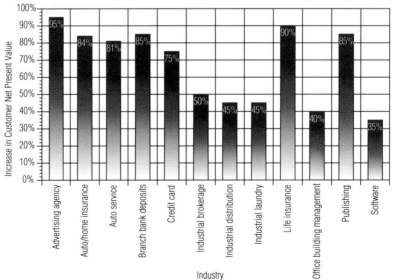

come more efficient, resulting in operating efficiencies and reduced operating costs (e.g., lower customer service expense, lower order processing costs).

3. *Referrals.* Mature customers recommend your business, and your products and services, to others.

4. *Price premium.* Customers who have done business with you for a long time perceive value in the relationship and are less price-sensitive than new customers.

The premises here are (1) through regular contact (with a focus on value) you can add more value; (2) the regular, value-added contacts increase trust and commitment; (3) increased trust and commitment strengthen the relationship; (4) stronger relationships lead to higher customer retention; and (5) higher customer retention leads to growth and profitability.

The second financial impact of a proactive investment in a customer, increased purchases from the customer, isn't as obvious in some companies and industries. A recent conversation I had with a client demonstrates this: "Why would we invest in proactively managing and selling to our customers? They know we're here, they know our phone number, and we already invest in sending them product information and a price guide every year. They will call us when they have a need." Let's look at two examples.

Sometimes the best way to see the impact of something is to take it away for a period of time. That's exactly what happened at Shell's TeamTBA. In the first three months of 1993, proactive contact with Shell Service Stations was put on hold while Shell was in transition, moving account responsibilities from the gasoline reps to dedicated TBA (tires, batteries, and accessories) sales teams. During these three months, customers had the same 800 number to call—to place orders—that they always had. Inbound lines were staffed to provide excellent service. Customers had the same product information that they always had; in fact, they had product on their shelves to sell to their customers and to use in customer repair work. The only difference was the proactive sales/relationship contact—it was nonexistent during this time. Total sales during this transition phase were considerably lower than sales during the account management phase (see Figure 1-7).

Monthly sales, starting in January, were $1 million, and for the next three months went on a steady decline to under $800,000 in March. In the first month that full account management began (April), monthly sales shot up to $1.7 million and stayed at a monthly level above $1.5 million for the remainder of the year.

In the second example, we look again at Hallmark Building Sup-

Figure 1-7. Correlation between account management and sales volume at TeamTBA.

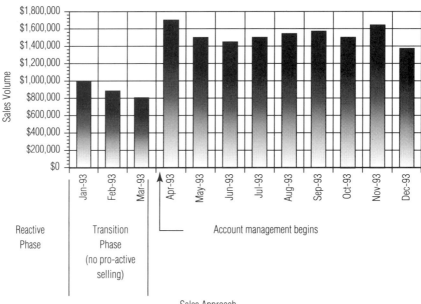

plies. Hallmark Building Supplies sells to the construction industry. This is a project-driven industry—one where the customers' needs are driven by the projects they have at any point in time. In this industry, it is easy to think, "The projects that customers have define what they need. If our products are required or specified, they will call us. If not, they won't. There is little that we can do to influence this." In Hallmark's customer loyalty study, customers were asked how they anticipated their business with Hallmark would change. A look at customers who stated that their business with Hallmark would significantly increase was enlightening. This set of customers was then asked, "Which factor will most impact the amount of business that you do with Hallmark next year?" Twenty-five percent stated the nature of the projects, no one stated the price, and 75 percent stated that "proactive Hallmark contact" would be the factor having the most impact on the amount of business they would do with Hallmark.

Again, customers at all levels are indicating that they need a relationship that more closely resembles a partner supplier relationship. The path that we're on here, and the destination for winning companies, seems inevitable.

Summary

Business buying decisions are becoming more complex; there is more and more information to be dealt with in buying decisions. There are more options (i.e., competitors) to select from. There is increasing uncertainty inherent in buying decisions. Customer/supplier relationships reduce that uncertainty with knowledge, trust, and commitment. The economics coming out of direct marketing, with an acceptance of new and alternative customer contact media, increase companies' ability to cost-effectively develop customer relationships. Corporations are beginning to realize the importance of the profit impact of customer retention, and concurrently the undeveloped potential in a large part of their customer base. Companies that win in this environment will be companies that can successfully and profitably build strong relationships with a large part of their customer base. Relationships will be the primary reason that customers buy from you. They will be the factor that differentiates you from your competition, and that will be the factor that sustains customer relationships, driving both growth and profitability.

IAM is a relationship marketing strategy that works. It focuses on customer relationships, personalizes the relationship and each of the contacts in the relationship, explicitly manages the economics in each individual relationship and overall, and is measurable in its impact on revenue, profitability, and customer loyalty.

Read on as we explore specifically what IAM is, where and when it should be applied, how to build it, and what to expect from it.

Notes

1. Don Peppers and Martha Rogers, *The One To One Future* (New York: Doubleday, 1993), p. 18.
2. Tom Peters, *Liberation Management* (New York: Alfred A. Knopf, 1992), p. 8.
3. Robert G. Cooper, *Winning at New Products* (Reading, Mass.: Addison-Wesley, 1986), p. 10.
4. Bob Stone, *Successful Direct Marketing Methods* (Chicago: NTC Business Books, 1994), p. 1.
5. Thomas Moore, *SoulMates* (New York: HarperCollins Publishers, 1994), pp. 124, 234.

2

IAM: A New Way of Doing Business With Your Customers

In today's "bonkers" marketplace with all of its intense pressures, direct marketing has grown and evolved. It is used to help companies take product to the marketplace faster. It is used to help manufacturers sell more product created by excess production capacity. It is used to grow businesses through increased geographic coverage. It is used to target customers with great accuracy. And it is used to drive more efficiency into the marketing and sales process.

In this environment, business-to-business direct marketing has grown to be big business. In a study conducted by the WEFA (Wharton Economic Forecasting Associates) Group, "Economic Impact: U.S. Direct Marketing Today," 1995 business-to-business direct marketing sales were estimated at almost one-half trillion dollars. The study goes on to forecast growth to $810 billion by the year 2000.

As business-to-business direct marketing continues to grow, it is also becoming more complex. Campaigns that used to entail one contact using one medium (primarily direct mail) now often involve multiple customer contacts through multiple media over longer periods of time. These practices have led to the concept of *integrated direct marketing*, which focuses on the interrelationships between multiple marketing contacts to drive higher marketing productivity through increased response rates. In his book *Integrated Direct Marketing* (1988), Ernan Roman explains the concept this way: "Integrated direct marketing is the art and science of managing diverse marketing media as a cohesive whole. These interrelationships are catalysts for response. The resulting media synergy generates response rates higher than could be achieved by individual media efforts."[1] This concept of integrated direct marketing has moved marketers to a new level of performance. The favorable results generated and the measurability of those results have made integrated direct marketing an attractive approach used by traditional direct marketers and non-direct marketers alike.

Three defining factors of integrated direct marketing account for much of the improved performance: (1) the economic advantages in both the contact costs and in the response rates, (2) the use of multiple media, and (3) the enabling technology. These factors form the foundation for all integrated direct marketing; in addition, they form the foundation for integrated account management.

1. *Economic advantages.* The economic advantages of integrated direct marketing in customer contact costs (as discussed in Chapter 1) have long been compelling. Using direct mail, a marketer can get a message to a targeted customer for less than $1, whereas getting that same message to the same customer using the field sales organization would cost over $400. The concept of integrated direct marketing moved marketers beyond this contact cost-focused, one-dimensional approach to defining campaigns and measuring their success. An integrated direct marketing campaign includes many contacts to customers, combines different forms of media in those contacts (advertising, direct mail, inbound telemarketing, outbound telemarketing, fax, e-mail), and measures success by the campaign response relative to the marketing cost of the campaign.

2. *Multiple media.* The use of multiple media has an impact on results because of the varying costs, the availability, the access to customers and potential customers, the speed of different media, the preferences of customers, and the interactivity of available media. In an IAM program, account managers have the capability to use the medium of choice—the one that is most cost-effective, the one that gets to the customer in a timely fashion, and the one that the customer prefers for the specific type of contact. In an account manager's hands, this choice can have a significant impact on sales and profitability.

3. *Enabling technology.* The enabling technology, the marketing database, allows companies to do what they would naturally do to manage customer relationships in a way that provides them economies of scale. This technology allows marketers to track individual customers within companies, to track characteristics of both the individuals and companies, to track buying behavior, to estimate what customers are worth, to anticipate what they'll value, to predict how they'll respond, and to measure how they actually respond. This closed-loop process delivers a framework for continuous improve-

ment of marketing campaigns. Actual responses can be tracked back to individual customers and companies, their characteristics, their historical buying behavior, their estimated worth, and their anticipated response.

Although these factors have improved marketing performance, for the most part they are still focused on the transaction (or the response). While the view has become a little longer-term—the campaign instead of the mail drop—the desired result is often still a campaign response. To move to the next level of marketing performance requires a focus on customer relationships. This realization of the importance of relationships, combined with the economics of integrated direct marketing, the use of multiple media, and the marketing database technology, is leading many companies to IAM.

IAM Defined

Let's clearly define our playing field. When I hear someone use the term *account management,* I am not always sure what to expect. I hear the words used much more frequently than I see the principles applied. Maybe that is because the term, in its more literal sense, is so vapid. Literally, *account management* could be interpreted as taking charge of and controlling your customers or clients. Companies use the term to describe a number of functions that they perform. I've heard it used to describe order takers, "cold-calling" sales reps, and customer service reps. That is not what we are discussing here. What we are discussing is how a company takes ownership of the relationships with its customers and proactively manages those relationships so that the company, employees, and customers all win through increased customer loyalty, increased sales, higher job security, higher job satisfaction, higher levels of service, ultimately better products, and superior application of products to achieve business results.

Let's begin with a formal definition: Integrated account management is "a system of marketing and selling that is driven out of a proactive, planful, and personal approach to managing mutually beneficial individual customer relationships. In IAM, the account manager uses a variety of contact media to manage customer relationships in an economically prudent manner to drive sustainable, long-term, profitable customer relationships."

There are six key words or phrases in this definition.

1. *Key phrase: "marketing and selling."* Both of these terms, *marketing* and *sales,* have come to mean very different things to different

people. Although in some organizations *marketing* has become a euphemism for the sales function, in most companies the terms in fact refer to two different disciplines and two different functions. One of the best definitions, and the one that clearly delineates these two disciplines, is the definition provided by the old adage: "Selling is getting the customer to want what the company sells, and marketing is getting the company to sell what the customer wants."

Selling tends to focus on the opportunity, the sales transaction. By its very nature sales is a production activity that tends to focus on the short-term closing—the opportunity at hand. It is a tactical activity that is relatively easy to measure.

Marketing, on the other hand, represents the customers' interests inside the organization, using the knowledge gained to create a marketplace. Marketing is a strategic activity, and the long-term impact of marketing actions must be weighed. Because of the ambiguities in every marketplace, marketing efforts can be very difficult to measure in the short term.

These two disciplines should be blended to allow each account manager to effectively manage relationships with customers that are cost-effective in both the short term and the long term. The implicit assumption here is that the market is the sum of the individual customers. The sum of individual customer revenue is equal to total revenue. The sum of each individual customer's profitability is equal to total profitability, and the sum of value received by each individual customer is equal to the total value delivered in the marketplace.

2. *Key word: "proactive."* IAM is not a system that waits for your customers to call you. In other selling models it's okay to let the customer know you are available and let the customer know that you can provide value and just wait for the customer to request that value. IAM takes that approach and turns it around. It proactively takes responsibility for working the needs, for positioning the value against the needs, and for delivering that value. It also takes responsibility for managing the relationship.

3. *Key phrase: "planful."* IAM delivers profitability in an environment that has a delicate balance between the sales volume and profits, and between revenue and the cost of selling. The only way to achieve and manage this balance is through high levels of productivity. The only way to achieve high levels of productivity is through careful planning. Account planning, contact planning, module planning— these are requisite parts of effectively and profitably managing relationships with your customers.

4. *Key word: "personal."* Over the past three years, my firm has conducted or seen other companies conduct more than a hundred

workshops with customers that were intended to help the companies understand how communications with customers add value. (See Chapter 9.) These workshops have covered literally dozens of industries, from telecommunications to health insurance to building supplies to agricultural equipment. In these workshops, one of the most frequently recurring themes has been personalization. Customers state over and over that communications with them must be personal for the communications to be of value. Form letters don't work. Product brochures by themselves are not enough. Letters signed by a faceless company or an executive they don't know or never heard of are unlikely to be of value.

5. *Key phrase: "mutually beneficial."* We are a culture of extremes. When midwesterners escape from winter, they don't go to a moderate climate, they go to a hot climate. When health care specialists or the press announce test results showing that a certain vitamin improves overall health, we quickly get *mega*doses. It is an almost visceral reaction. Consistent with this culture, we get a similar reaction in the business world. Quality problems lead to instituting a *"zero defect"* policy; need to change a process—use reengineering, *radical* redesign. "Top-down" planning not effective—use "bottom-up" planning. Too much of an internal focus—change to a customer focus; not enough—make it customer-driven.

Sometimes the "get on the other side of the continuum" attitude is helpful, not because it takes you to the opposite extreme but because it serves as a balance to the starting point. Sometimes it simply takes a more extreme position to give you and your organization the impetus to move beyond the current state. In the definition of IAM, "mutually beneficial" refers to this balance.

At times, some organizations still make decisions that are too internally focused, defining how they service customers exclusively on the basis of how they create internal efficiencies and defining their customer communications according to what they want to tell customers. At other times, organizations make decisions that make no economic sense but are based upon what they think they should do for their customers. Neither of these perspectives is appropriate in IAM. Integrated account management relationships are best characterized by Stephen Covey, the author of the best-selling *The 7 Habits of Highly Successful People:* "win-win or no deal."

6. *Key phrase: "individual customer relationships."* Sirius Systems Inc. (a software publisher that has developed a sales and relationship management system) concisely states in its product literature: "People buy from people." A customer stated it succinctly in a workshop comment: "I will not open mail from Company A if I cannot tell, by looking at the envelope, that it is a letter from my rep."

When I think of this particular topic, I am always reminded of a discussion a few years back with a high-tech client that was developing a marketing database. We spent some time defining what a customer is. When the conversation had started, "Ford is a customer," I couldn't help but think, Do they mean Henry Ford? A short time later, the discussion and definition focused on 44 individuals (buyers and influencers) at multiple locations within multiple divisions that were part of Ford Motor Company.

People do buy from people. Account managers do not have relationships with accounts. They have relationships with individuals within accounts who use their company's products, influence their purchase decisions, and buy products and services.

IAM Operating Principles

The foregoing definition of IAM gives us a framework to build upon and provides an understanding of what integrated account management is, and what it is not. In its best applications, you see policies, systems, and behavior that provide a more tangible understanding of this definition. This understanding is illustrated in a set of 15 operating principles that come out of my experience and observations in working with many organizations developing world-class account management. While at times these principles are not explicit, they are consistently part of successful IAM programs.

1. Account managers act as small business owners.
2. Account managers own the relationships with their customers.
3. Account managers have a degree of control over all contact with their customers.
4. Account managers have access to corporate systems—all information about their customers.
5. Account managers take accountability for a balance of results, productivity, and quality in the contact.
6. Value for the customer is built on an in-depth understanding of the customer's needs.
7. Development of customer expertise leads to personalized delivery of value.
8. The customer database is the primary customer knowledge tool.
9. Investments are made in customers according to their worth.
10. Building customer loyalty is an economic necessity.
11. All contact with customers is intended to add value.

12. Each contact with a customer is part of a larger system of contacts. Excellence is achieved through integration of these contacts.
13. Account managers sell by not selling.
14. The choice of contact medium is based on individual customer economics and the customer's preference.
15. Account management success comes from attitudes, behaviors, and skills.

The discussion that follows provides a closer look at each of these operating principles.

1. *Account managers act as small business owners.* Companies win by allocating their resources to provide value to customers in an economically prudent manner. Who knows better how to do this than the customer's account manager? Who knows better what the account is worth? Who knows better how much to invest in that account to create a win-win situation? Traditionally, sales organizations have made sales reps accountable for sales dollars and for creating a certain amount of revenue from their customer base. This has created in some organizations a "maximize sales at any cost" mentality. In that kind of environment, salespeople have done just what you'd expect—maximize sales at any cost—which causes a number of problems. Inordinate attention on the transaction puts the focus on sales, rather than on the relationship. It creates insensitivity to the cost of making the sale. Whatever resources you have to throw at a customer to close the sale get thrown. It creates internal price pressure from a sales and transaction perspective in that there is pressure to keep the price down to maximize the volume of sales. TeamTBA has dealt with this last issue by actually making the account managers accountable for contribution dollars, as opposed to sales dollars. This forces the account managers to have a broader perspective and balance their investments, and to be sensitive to price in a way that optimizes margin and profitability as it works the price issues with customers. It also gives the organization more comfort with price flexibility at the account manager level and at the customer level. The ultimate responsibility of a small business owner is to remain profitable.

This profit and loss accountability is also the ultimate responsibility of an account manager. There is absolutely no substitute for P&L accountability. This is where the rubber meets the road. This is where an account manager realizes the full impact of decisions made. You live with the fact that the price discounting for special accounts did not result in increased volume. You live with the fact that the front-end investment in a set of accounts did not generate a corresponding amount of new business. You live with the fact that because of a reduction in customer contacts, two of your best accounts have defected to the competition. This type of accountability forces account managers to productively question their decisions.

2. *Account managers own the relationship with their customers.* Too many companies still allow a degree of ambiguity in the ownership of their customer relationships. This ambiguity results in diminished value to customers and in weaker customer relationships. In world-class account management, account managers own the customer relationships. This doesn't mean that account managers are the only contact with the customer inside the organization. What it means is that (1) they represent the organization to the customer and take responsibility for how the organization provides value to the customer, and (2) they represent the customer to the organization. So, in that dual role account managers facilitate the delivery of value to customers and take responsibility for that delivery of value.

3. *Account managers have a degree of control over all contact with their customers.* In today's typical large organization, there are a number of different departments that contact customers. Obviously, account managers do, and sales reps do. Additionally, channel management groups may, marketing communications or advertising groups may, and product divisions and different product management groups may. The benefit to the company in these contacts comes from the leverage inherent in the contacts. A marketing communications or product management group can generate a direct mail campaign at significantly less cost per contact when it is contacting a large base of customers. The negative in this proposition is that delivery of value in the contact becomes a hit-and-miss proposition.

The only person who can effectively manage the delivery of value in this communication is the account manager. Some world-class companies have addressed this issue by providing account managers with control over how their customers get contacted. Product management and marketing communications groups still define marketing campaigns and direct mail campaigns, but account managers have the option to determine when and how and who to include in these campaigns. So there is leverage in the communication and leverage in the development of the communication. And there is specific delivery value in the communication because account managers have made the decision to use this contact with their particular customers.

4. *Account managers have access to corporate systems—all information about their customers.* The typical organization has a fair amount of data about most of its customers. The market research group has

survey data; the product management group has product reference information; the marketing group has some secondary information, which may include demographics; the order processing group has order transactions; the customer service group has information on returns, credits, and service issues and problems; the accounting group has D&B ratings, credit information, and information about collections and invoicing. Unfortunately, in too many organizations this information lies in disparate, unconnected systems. In addition, in too many of these organizations the person responsible for managing the relationship with customers, delivering value, determining how the company invests in those relationships, and deciding how it allocates customer resources does not have access to this information.

5. *Account managers take accountability for a balance of results, productivity, and quality in the contact.* It is important for account managers in the process of running their "business" to have the ability to incrementally improve the business. This requires them not only to know whether it is working or not but also to understand some of the dynamics of why it's working or why it's not, what things are working and what things are not. As we look at these three balancing categories, we start with the results. The results—the evidence that mutually beneficial relationships are being developed—are twofold. The first, sales volume, is shorter-term in nature. Although short-term sales are not necessarily proof that customer relationships are being developed, lack of sales is evidence that they may not be. Additionally, sales are needed to fund future contacts and to support a mutually beneficial relationship. The second result, customer loyalty, entails a much-longer-term perspective. The economic benefit of customer loyalty comes from keeping customers longer and getting them to buy more of the products they already buy from you. Obviously, having accountability for these results is critical.

The second area of this balance, productivity, tends to be a short-term measure. In effect, productivity provides a measure of the activities that are leading to the sale and to customer loyalty. The measures of productivity are calls, contacts, proposals and presentations to customers, the close ratios, and the average order size. These measures provide a way to assess what steps and activities in the IAM process are leading to results, a way to set and manage activity expectations in the process, and a way to establish authority and accountability for the activities that lead to results.

The third area, quality in the contact, is a short-term measure of each separate additional contact. This is simply the measurement and aspects of the measurement of the "moment of truth," the actual contact with the customer. This tends to be a qualitative look at one of the elements that leads to the long-term results.

6. *Value for the customer is built on an in-depth understanding of customers' needs.* This account management concept is based on a principle of adding value, both through the products and services and through the relationship. Real value is delivered to business-to-business customers when the products and/or services they buy achieve business results for them. The only way that you can ensure that the products achieve the expected business results is through a thorough understanding and diagnosis of the needs and a matching of the needs to the recommended products and services.

7. *Development of customer expertise leads to personalized delivery of value.* There are two levels of expertise that are important here. The first is an understanding of the industry and the business that the customer is in. At that level you need to understand how the product or service helps customers achieve their business results. The second level is individual customer needs. Even though you may call on one hundred tax accountants, no two of those customers are exactly the same. So this second level of customer expertise is targeted to the individual customer level. Then, with these two levels of understanding, personalized delivery of value conveys both an awareness and a sensitivity that is derived from this customer expertise, and it provides value consistent with that awareness and sensitivity.

8. *The customer database is the primary customer knowledge tool.* The customer database is the only way to deliver the kind of in-depth understanding and personalized value that are necessary in IAM in a manner that is cost-effective and delivers high levels of productivity. All world-class IAM programs have, at the heart of them, a robust customer database.

9. *Investments are made in customers according to their worth.* Account managers are accountable for the profit and loss of the "business." One way to think of that profit and loss is to consider the sum of the profit and loss of each individual customer. A significant part of that profit and loss—at least the cost side of the equation—is the marketing and sales investment that the account manager drives into the account. Obviously, it is the one the account manager has the most control over. The principle that drives this is use of those marketing and sales investments in the most appropriate way—spending on individual customers that provide the highest return will sum to the highest rate of return at the account manager level.

10. *Building customer loyalty is an economic necessity.* Customers receive value through the relationship and through the products and services. Value drives repurchase, customer retention, and referrals. Referrals, retention, and repurchase drive growth and profitability. Account management as it is defined here is dependent wholly on

customer loyalty. It is based on the premise that you maximize the business by maximizing each individual customer relationship in the business. That equation, customer loyalty, is much more than a feel-good exercise or a relationship for the sake of relationship exercise. It becomes a core measurement and a core foundation block for the business.

11. *All contact with customers is intended to add value.* When you begin to look at customer contacts as investments, you also look at how you can apply that investment to get the most value out of the contacts. Contacts that don't add value to customers subsequently don't add value to you. Good contacts should provide a balanced return of stronger relationship and some revenue. Contacts that don't provide that kind of return are a waste of money; or worse, they are actually negative impacts on your individual customer relationships.

12. *Each contact with a customer is part of a larger system of contacts. Excellence is achieved through integration of these contacts.* In the catalog business, each mailing is treated as an event; response is measured on that mailing and return on investment is calculated on that mailing. That event kind of thinking doesn't work well in IAM. When you have frequent value-added contact with the customer, it's difficult to determine exactly which contact was the one that provided the impetus for the order. The sales volume you do with the customer is really the net effect of all the contacts that are part of the relationship with that customer. IAM suggests that there is an effective blend of these contacts that provides value and also provides some continuity and reliability in the relationship.

13. *Account managers sell by not selling.* In IAM a sale is not the result of a great sales pitch. The best sales are sales that strengthen the relationship, and the best sales in world-class account management come as a result of the account manager's detailed understanding of the customer's needs and ability to recommend solutions that fulfill the customer's needs.

14. *The choice of contact medium is based on individual customer economics and the customer's preference.* A customer contact plan needs to make economic sense. It needs to provide a win from the seller's perspective, a win in the economics, and it needs to provide, from the customer's perspective, a win in the value provided. That is the only way you can get a mutually beneficial relationship. For a number of reasons, in many marketplaces there is a phenomenon that occurs where smaller customers actually request more contact and a greater investment than larger customers. Larger customers are sometimes more self-sufficient and don't desire or question the value of greater contact levels. It is up to the account manager to balance those issues

and to ensure that every customer relationship provides an economic balance, and not use the larger customer relationships as a cash cow to finance the smaller relationships. The concept of mutually beneficial relationships has to be applied to each individual customer relationship.

15. *Account management success comes from attitudes, behaviors, and skills.* In this context account management success is synonymous with account manager success. While planning, management, and infrastructure are critical, account management is not successful unless it succeeds in the many moments of truth that account managers have with customers on a daily basis. Those moments of truth are optimized by account managers' skills (questioning, listening, understanding business needs, applying products to solve business needs), their behaviors (response to objections, response to complaints), and their attitudes (customer empathy, focus on customer value, enthusiasm, openness).

These principles provide a framework for building IAM and define a way of working with customers that ultimately results in win-win relationships.

Note

1. Ernan Roman, *Integrated Direct Marketing* (New York: McGraw-Hill, 1988), p. 5.

3

Is IAM Right for Your Company?

"The essence of formulating competitive strategy is relating a company to its environment."

Michael E. Porter

There are a lot of reasons why a particular way of doing business works well for one company and not for another. Obviously, different companies serve different markets and customers, have different products and services, have different service delivery systems, utilize different sales channels, employ different strategies, and even possess different competencies. Not so obviously, different companies have different leaderships styles, different cultures, different values, different levels of flexibility and acceptance of change, and even different levels of success.

As a business consultant, I'm occasionally reminded of this by clients and prospective clients who say things like "My company is different," "Our business is unique," or "We're nothing like that other company." And, if you look closely enough, and it doesn't even have to be too closely, no two companies are alike. Each individual company presents its own unique set of factors that determines whether and to what degree a strategy will be successful. These factors can be categorized as either external (those factors that can be observed in the marketplace) or internal (the more subtle factors that even when they are observed in the marketplace seem to be a matter of interpretation). External factors include products, service, sales channels, and even market strategies. Internal factors include leadership, culture, and values.

Integrated account management is targeted at the relationship you have with your customers. An analysis of the external factors allows you to estimate the value and potential response in the marketplace. In effect, this analysis validates the assumptions that drive an account management decision: Will customers value it? Will they buy more? Will they stay customers longer? If your marketplace and the external factors don't support a positive response to these questions, IAM may not be an appropriate strategy.

The conclusion one might draw from this is that IAM is a solution that fits one homogeneous type of marketplace situation or business problem. The marketplace is much more complex than that, and IAM is a much more complex tool than that. Different companies with very different external factors have successfully implemented IAM. In fact, if you looked at these companies on a continuum, you would see that they moved to account management from two very different starting points—you might say opposite ends of the continuum. Let's use the terms *upstream* and *downstream* to characterize these two different investments and two different journeys to the same destination—IAM.

An upstream investment is one that comes out of a marketplace situation where the seller has, at best, an arms-length relationship with customers. The investment in any one individual customer is usually relatively small, communications with customers are typically not personal, and it is not unusual for the seller to wait for the customer to place the order. An example of this might be a business-to-business cataloger where the customer is a name in the database and gets a catalog that is probably targeted at the recipient's needs, but is not personal, and where customer service reps take inbound calls from customers, provide excellent service, and take customers' orders. The question here isn't whether this is a good marketing model—it's an excellent model that has been very effective. The question is, Would an incremental investment to develop a higher-level relationship with some of these customers provide a corresponding incremental return?

A downstream journey originates in a marketplace situation that is very different from that upstream. It typically is a situation where the seller is investing too much in customers or is investing in the wrong way. This translates to a selling model that shows a negative return on investment. Examples of this include some industrial sales and larger-ticket technology sales, where the selling model has been "feet on the street" and growth means *more* feet on the street. In contrast to an upstream journey, a downstream change is frequently a necessity because the current selling model no longer generates a positive return on investment.

The case examples in this chapter should help explain these different situations and the respective journeys.

The decision to build and apply IAM is based on its potential effectiveness with your customer base and is best arrived at through an analysis of factors in the marketplace. Often, internal and external factors reflect conflicting indicators about integrated account management. The external/marketplace factors seem to suggest IAM. The internal facts seem to be either obstacles or reasons to substantiate not using IAM. The obstacles sound like "our sales force wouldn't accept it," "we have a history of being successful with our current sales model," "it wouldn't fit culturally," "we tried proactive selling and it didn't work."

When faced with a situation where the external factors suggest integrated account management and the internal factors don't, our recommendation is usually to focus on the external factors. Companies don't become world-class marketers with an internal focus. They become world class by focusing on and winning in the marketplace. The issues raised by the internal factors are not issues regarding whether IAM is the right thing to do. They are issues that help a company assess its ability to implement integrated account management and anticipate the cost of building an IAM business system.

Using IAM Strategically

In addition to being a meaningful reaction to marketplace conditions, IAM can be used as a proactive strategic tool. As such, it can be used to implement a market strategy or to achieve strategic objectives. Let's look at some strategies that are particularly meaningful and that could be achieved through IAM.

Creating a Competitive Barrier

Competitive barriers are particularly relevant in industries where competition is increasing or in industries that are going through deregulation. The concern is that this new level of competition will cause customer disloyalty and result in a number of lost customers. In fact, it does not even take superior competitors to effect this kind of behavior. Unless it is clear that their current supplier is superior, some customers will switch simply to try a new supplier. In this situation, the only time to strengthen customer relationships is when you still own the relationship. When IAM is implemented in these situations, account managers assess the worth and importance of each individual customer relationship. They manage the marketing and sales investments in those customers to a level that ensures a positive return on investment in individual customers and a positive overall return on investment.

Reducing the Cost of Selling

Reducing the cost of selling is probably the most appropriate strategy in a mature industry, one where there is a traditional selling model, probably some pressure on product margins, a fairly high degree of competitiveness, and often increasing difficulty in differentiating the product. In this kind of industry, what companies need to do is focus on building productivity (more ''bang for the buck'') into the sales model, and IAM provides a good tool for doing so, resulting in a decreased cost of selling and an improved cost of sales to revenue ratio. Use of the marketing database and multiple contact media allows companies to contact more customers more frequently at an incremental cost that is usually an order of magnitude less than the cost of additional field sales contacts. In industries with declining markets, realizing an improvement in the cost of sales to revenue ratio may require a reduction in sales resources. In markets that are still growing, existing sales resources can usually be maintained and the incremental cost of other contacts can be funded by sales growth. In these situations, growth is accelerated through better use of existing field sales resources.

Growth Through Account Penetration

Growth through account penetration is the most appropriate strategy in a marketplace where the buying decisions for the product are made at multiple levels or across multiple divisions. Typically, this situation occurs when companies are selling in a marketplace that consists of medium to large companies. From a marketer's perspective, the structure of customer accounts within the marketplace can be thought of as three-dimensional (see Figure 3-1). As illustrated, these customer accounts have individual buyers and decision makers within buying groups (which are typically functionally defined). These buying groups reside in a particular location, and multiple locations frequently have a different role in or influence on decision-making processes. It is helpful to think of these customer accounts as analogous to markets. The question then becomes, once you have a position in a market (customer account), how can you capitalize on that position. Growth comes through expansion within each of the existing customer accounts. Figure 3-2 illustrates this pattern of growth. The center of this graph represents the ''active buyer,'' or the individual customer within an account. When growing the business through account penetration in an IAM program, an account manager would work from the center of the circle outward to find and

Figure 3-1. The marketing perspective of the structure of customer accounts.

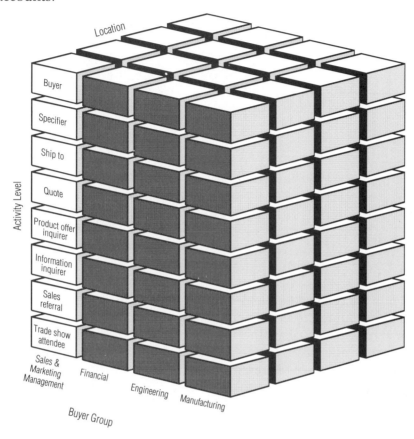

develop additional relationships within an account that either influence buying decisions or make independent buying decisions.

Growth Through Product Penetration

Growth through product penetration is most appropriate for organizations that provide a broad set of product lines to the marketplace. This strategy has a dual impact when it is implemented: it creates incremental sales while at the same time strengthening customer relationships.

Growth through product penetration is based on the premise that existing customers are more likely to buy new product than are new customers. This premise is supported by research done at the Strategic Planning Institute and at GE in the PIMS database. (PIMS stands for "profit impact of market strategy" and is a database of more than 2,000 business units that tracks the strategies used by these

Figure 3-2. Leveraging customer equity.

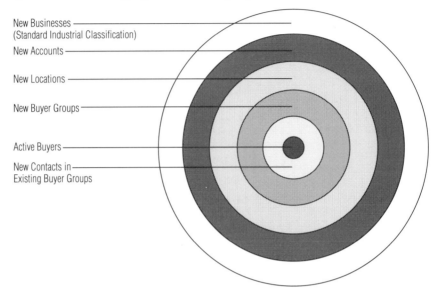

New Businesses
(Standard Industrial Classification)
New Accounts
New Locations
New Buyer Groups
Active Buyers
New Contacts in
Existing Buyer Groups

units and the corresponding results.) Figure 3-3 highlights an important PIMS finding: the customer factor has more effect on the success of business growth than the product factor. The most successful growth strategies take existing product to existing customers (with a success probability of 95 percent). The next most successful growth initiatives take new product to existing customers (with a probability of 50 percent). The next take existing product to new customers (with a probability of 25 percent). The least successful strategy is taking new product to new customers (at 5 percent).

Product-penetration strategy supports the upper left-hand quadrant in Figure 3-3 (existing product to existing customers) and also focuses on marketing new product to existing customers—the two most likely to succeed growth strategies.

Let's look at the logic here. You have an existing customer. He has already purchased from you and it has been a positive experience. The product provides some value to the customer. You have a

Figure 3-3. Probability of successful growth: the customer factor vs. the product factor.

	Old products	*New products/services*
Established customers	95%	50%
New customers	25%	5%

Source: Data from PIMS.

new or related product or service from which the customer would receive additional value. The customer knows how to do business with you and you know how to do business with him (this creates efficiency in the transaction and in the relationship). Account management provides the kind of customer relationship that allows you to meaningfully explore the customer's needs and make the appropriate new product and product expansion decisions. Direct marketers have for years tested and seen results that indicate that two-product purchasers are more likely to purchase an additional product than one-product purchasers.

This results in product recommendations to the customer (and ultimately purchases) that add value. In this way, product penetration grows the business through these incremental sales and actually strengthens the relationship, improving the loyalty of customers.

Harvest Strategy

Frequently in declining markets or declining industries companies are faced with making a decision regarding one of three difficult options. The first is to maintain their sales system as it is, which in a declining industry is usually too expensive. In many of these industries, the sales system provides some degree of service to customers but ultimately loses money. The second option is to simply downsize the sales component and reduce the sales cost. In most traditional selling systems, this option typically reduces the service level. You get a reduction in sales costs that obviously falls to the bottom line if it doesn't cause more rapidly declining sales. You end up with a reduction in the sales cost and a reduction in the service level. Integrated account management—the third option—is particularly intriguing in the harvest strategy because of its flexibility in incrementally adjusting and controlling the cost of selling and in managing sales and productivity. It increases productivity to reduce the cost of selling and allows marketing to adjust the cost of selling downward to support the rate of decline in the market. It is not unusual in these situations where IAM is applied to see a simultaneous decrease in sales costs, increase in productivity, and increase in customer satisfaction. With IAM it is possible to improve the ratio of sales cost to revenue while the market and overall sales are declining.

External Factors Indicating Integrated Account Management

A move to IAM demands that value beyond the product is provided to customers, and that the economic benefit of an improved ratio of sales cost to revenue is realized by the seller.

An assessment of conditions in the market is required to determine the appropriateness of IAM. This assessment considers these demands in addition to the operational and tactical feasibility of IAM. Specific questions to address in this assessment are as follows (see also Figure 3-4):

1. *Do your products or services have an impact on the customer's business?* IAM requires a mutual commitment of time from the seller and the customer to build trust and work the relationship. Customers are more likely to make that commitment if it results in business value for them.

2. *Is your product a complete business solution or a significant part of a business solution?* By their very nature, complete business solutions have more of an impact on the customer's business. A company that sells only computer hardware is an example of a company that does

Figure 3-4. External factors indicating appropriateness of IAM.

Core Factors	Unique Upstream Factors	Unique Downstream Factors
• Products/services have an impact on customers' business • Products are a business solution or significant part of a business solution • The applications of products are important to realize value • Products need support • Ongoing change in the value equation • There is complexity in the buying decision • Customers buy frequently or in high volume • Customer decision makers are accessible	• Incremental potential • Underserviced sets of customers	• The product line is mature • There is margin pressure • Traditional, unchanged selling model

not offer a complete business solution. One that sells hardware, software, training, installation services, and maintenance services is an example of a company providing a more complete business solution.

3. *Is there information of value that can be exchanged in customer contacts?* IAM assumes that all customer contacts provide value to customers. This value is arrived at through a secondary set of questions, each of which indicates a different type of value that could be provided through customer contacts.

- Are the applications of your product variable and important enough for customers to realize value?
- Do your products need support, either pre- or postsale?
- Is there more change in your industry than customers can track and understand the implications of?

4. *Is there complexity in the buying decision for your products?* Complexity in the buying decision usually means a greater investment on the part of the supplier—in relationships with additional buyers and influencers and in more contacts with each individual buyer and influencer. This complexity can be managed quite effectively within IAM, which provides an effective framework for managing a cost-effective contact plan for multiple individuals within an account.

5. *Do your customers buy frequently or in high volume?* Frequent purchasing and high-volume purchasing provide reasons for contacting customers on a regular basis. In both cases, IAM can provide leverage through customer contacts. With high-volume purchasers, it can work to eliminate competitive vulnerability through strengthened relationships and increased contact levels.

6. *Are your customer decision makers accessible?* Can you make contact with decision makers and influencers in your accounts? For example, it can be extremely difficult to contact CEOs in large companies. Mail is reviewed and screened by a secretary, along with faxes and phone calls. So, even though some of the concepts and tools defined in this book could apply to all account relationship management, the application of a full IAM system may just not be feasible in some market segments.

7. *Is there incremental potential in your existing customers?* This factor, more likely in an upstream scenario, suggests that an investment in existing customers will generate incremental revenue through higher volume of products already purchased and through additional product purchases.

8. *Are there sets of your customers that are underserviced in your current marketing and sales process?* Most businesses have a set of cus-

tomers that are not being serviced in a way that is consistent with their needs and their worth. Some whole industries have this situation. In the banking industry, for example, bankers have developed methods of working with large corporate customers and consumer customers, but are still trying to determine how best to work with middle market (small businesses) customers.

9. *Is your product line mature?* A mature product line suggests that there is little or no growth available in the market. Any growth in number of customers would have to come from customers switching from one supplier to another. With this maturing, there is usually intense competition for customers, increasing the need to sustain relationships. Additionally, this maturing frequently creates price competition and, in turn, pressure on margins. This margin pressure reduces profitability unless other expense improvements are identified and realized. IAM positions the marketing and sales process as an area where significant expense improvements can be had. However, the most important advantage IAM provides for a mature product line is its capability of allowing incremental change in service levels and marketing and sales expenses, fitting these as closely as possible to revenue and adjusting them as revenue declines or increases.

10. *Are you employing a traditional sales model that has not been assessed or changed in decades?* It is only in the past two decades that the marketing and sales process has begun to be subjected to the rigorous analysis and creative thinking that other business processes (accounting, manufacturing, etc.) have gone through. If your sales model has not been thoroughly analyzed, there are probably significant opportunities to drive efficiencies into the process.

Determining the IAM Economics Case

In all cases, IAM works the delicate balance between optimal investments in customers and the revenue realized from those investments. In an upstream situation, you are assessing this balance to determine the economic viability of the incremental customer contact investment and, ultimately, the viability of IAM. In a downstream situation, you are assessing the opportunity for improvement and validating the potential profitability of IAM.

These economics can be modeled by calculating the minimum average contribution from an "average" customer to determine whether IAM will work in a particular market segment. This calculation helps you build the front-end economics case. (More detailed work regarding contact costs and contact levels is done during development of the customer contact plan; see Chapter 11.) The model involves five steps.

1. Run a quintile analysis of your annual customer revenue. The analysis shown in Figure 3.5 shows a wide range of per-customer annual revenue and an average per-customer annual revenue of $5,918.
2. Estimate contact costs by medium. Field and inside account manager contact costs are determined by estimating a fully burdened cost for an account manager and then dividing by the anticipated number of annual customer contacts. This fully burdened cost includes all the expenses (both direct and indirect) associated with employing an account manager.
3. Determine the minimal annual contact level by medium (see Figure 3-6). This contact level needs to include enough interactive contact (face-to-face or phone) to develop a meaningful, substantive, value-adding relationship with customers. A contact level of three interactive contacts per year per customer is probably the bare minimum required to develop and sustain a relationship.
4. Calculate potential customer contribution dollars (see Figure 3-7).
5. Match customer contribution dollars to total contact cost to determine return on investment. According to Figure 3-7, an "average" customer generates a contribution margin of $2,040 to offset selling expenses and provide profit. Adjusting the contact level and potential revenue allows you to determine the performance levels that you need in IAM to make it work.

Figure 3-7 demonstrates a sales team environment that can be modeled at a 10 percent profit margin level. If that is not an acceptable profit level, can you reduce the contact levels without sacrificing

Figure 3-5. Annual customer revenue quintile analysis.

Quintile	Number of Customers	Total Annual Revenue	Per-Customer Annual Revenue
1	8,110	$168,500,000	$20,777
2	8,110	$35,011,000	$4,317
3	8,110	$18,200,000	$2,244
4	8,110	$10,255,000	$1,264
5	8,110	$4,990,000	$615
	40,550	$239,956,000	$5,918

Figure 3-6. Minimum annual customer contact levels.

Example A
A Sales Team (Field and Phone) Environment

Contact medium	Number of Contacts	Individual Contact Cost	Total Contact Cost
Field	3	$400	$1,200
Phone	6	$20	$120
Mail and electronic	6	$3	$18
Total			$1,338

Example B
A Phone Account Management Environment

Contact medium	Number of Contacts	Individual Contact Cost	Total Contact Cost
Phone	12	$20	$240
Mail and electronic	6	$3	$18
Total			$258

the individual customer relationships? Or can you realistically anticipate more revenue from accounts?

This economic model is used as part of the business case to justify an investment in IAM.

Upstream Investment Management

The Scenario

Let's take a look at how one company, a technology products company, made the decision to develop and implement an integrated

Figure 3-7. Potential average annual customer contribution dollars.

Average Potential Customer Revenue*	Cost of Goods Sold	Gross Margin	Allocated Costs	Contribution Before Selling Expense	Minimum Estimated Selling Expense	Potential Net Profit Per Customer	% of Sales
Example A: Sales Team Environment							
$6,800	50%	$3,400	20%	$2,040	$1,338	$702	10%
Example B: Phone Account Management							
$6,800	50%	$3,400	20%	$2,040	$258	$1,782	26%

* Potential revenue includes current customer spending levels plus incremental revenue gained from managing the relationship and based on additional products and services sold that fit customers' needs.

account management program. (The company will be referred to here as The Technology Company.)

The Technology Company provides a broad set of technical products directly to the business marketplace with a focus on small to medium-sized businesses. Company products include office PCs, notebook computers, power protection, peripherals, modems, and monitors.

The Technology Company contacted its customers in a number of ways. These methods included their customer service center (where customer service reps took orders, answered questions, and solved problems but did little or no proactive selling), direct mail, and print advertising. Periodically, limited outbound telemarketing campaigns were run. Typically, these campaigns consisted of handing the telemarketers a list of potential customers with the description of a product or products and having them call the list and offer the product. These campaigns were usually based upon specific promotions: special sales, product introductions, product closeouts, and so on.

This approach is what I call "provisional selling." Provisional selling involves selecting a product, identifying a number of potential customers for that product, and trying to sell the product to those customers. The customer contact is focused on closing a sale for a particular product, there is little or no relationship between seller and customer, and there is no in-depth understanding of customer needs.

Customers generally felt good about The Technology Company. This feeling was based on the products they purchased, the competitive prices, and the service they received.

While The Technology Company was able to maintain a good level of profitability in an extremely competitive industry, there was increasing evidence that its strength in the market was declining. An analysis of the customer database highlighted three areas of concern:

- Customer retention was declining—only 65 percent of the customers that purchased in 1994 continued to purchase in 1995.
- The average order size was flat at just under $900. In the previous five years, average order size had increased by four to eight percentage points per year.
- Average annual revenue per customer decreased from the previous year. While this decrease was small, less than one percentage point, in each of the previous five years annual customer revenue had increased.

To begin to deal with the above concerns, The Technology Company decided to develop an IAM capability. It hoped to achieve the following:

- Strengthen long-term relationships with customers
- Protect its current customer base—or at least a significant percentage of it—against the competition by building a competitive barrier
- Create a profitable new sales channel
- Turn the management of customer relationships into a proactive activity.

Most important, the company wanted its customers to see it as a broad solution to many of their technology needs, including hardware and new technology products.

The Key Factors

It was clear that The Technology Company could benefit greatly from an IAM approach because of several factors:

• *The right economics.* In making this kind of investment in IAM, The Technology Company would have to manage the delicate balance between the revenue realized from customers and the incremental cost associated with building and maintaining a new kind of relationship with customers.

At The Technology Company this was relatively easy. There was a set of customers that not only had high ''current'' value in the business they did, but also had high potential to buy more product (based on their needs, their historical performance, and performance of other similar customers).

For IAM to work, you need a total customer value that exceeds the marketing and sales investment required to build a customer relationship.

• *The potential to develop complex customer relationships.* The Technology Company's desire to have its customers perceive it as the broad solution to their technology needs meant that it was necessary to develop complex customer relationships over time. This in-depth relationship is necessary because of both the complexity and the importance of technology to business customers.

• *The opportunity to add value.* Implicit in its decision was the assumption that this service would be of value to its customers. Because the technology products industry is continually changing, customers need continual updating about products, services, applications, and so forth. The Technology Company could support this need by helping customers understand how they could more effectively achieve their objectives through a combination of better use of what they already had (hardware and software) and new products and services. There was clearly enough complexity and uncertainty in buying decisions to infer that customers would value a relationship.

• *Untapped potential.* Untapped potential became evident in three ways. Campaign selling efforts generated a positive, but limited, return on investment. A limited number of most valuable customers demonstrated what a good customer relationship could result in. These most valuable customers were the highest-performing customers (in terms of sales dollars) within an industry (SIC—standard industrial classification—code) and within a company size category. The needs of customers suggested potential for significantly more products and services at an individual customer level. This type of analysis indicated that the incremental untapped potential was quite high. In fact, incremental sales alone were enough to justify IAM.

• *Access to decision makers.* From a pragmatic standpoint, it is necessary to be able to get to your customer using the contact medium that drives your economic model. For The Technology Company that meant having to identify and then contact key customer decision makers by phone.

The Diagnosis

It was clear that the situation at The Technology Company called for IAM and that an upstream investment was necessary. An increased investment in customers would result in higher customer loyalty, and The Technology Company would retain more of these customers when the competition tried to take them away. And this approach would result in both higher customer satisfaction and incremental sales, sales that would not have been made without this investment.

Downstream Investment Management

The Scenario

The following example, that of Shell TBA, presents a situation that was, in many ways, just the opposite of that faced by The Technology Company. Shell TBA, a division of Shell Oil Co., was an aftermarket business that sold branded tires, batteries, and accessories (thus "TBA") to some 2,000 Shell service station dealers throughout the United States through eighty-five reps.

In the oil industry, the spiraling cost of keeping field sales reps on the road and collapsing margins from mature products have been a major contributor to entire business segments' either disappearing altogether or having to radically change how they go about their business. The branded parts and supplies are increasingly vulnerable to competition from local discount houses, and yet the TBA business is critical to the profitability of the full-service gas station. Healthy service station businesses are necessary for maintaining Shell's market share for parts and supplies, its gasoline sales, and its assets built up over time.

But Shell was losing $8 million a year on its TBA program. Something had to be done. The company wanted to remain in the TBA business to support its dealers, but only if it could do so profitably. It did not, however, believe that sales and sufficiently high customer satisfaction levels could be maintained if face-to-face contact with customers was reduced. By the summer of 1992 the situation had reached a critical point and needed to be resolved.

The Key Factors

It was clear that Shell TBA could also benefit from an IAM approach, but for different reasons from those for The Technology Company:

• *Ongoing customer relationships were required or were supported by frequent contact.* Shell TBA already had a relationship with its customers that was based on frequent contact. Most customers ordered frequently, and the best customers ordered as often as three or four times a month.

• *Customers with high worth.* A significant percentage of Shell TBA customers had high worth. The best customers were buying upward of $50,000 worth of product per year.

• *The opportunity to add value.* The contacts Shell TBA had with its customers were more than selling product. The sales reps helped customers with managing inventory, merchandising, product application, and product and sales support. All of these offered avenues to add value to the relationship beyond just selling the hard goods.

• *The need to revamp.* Shell TBA fit the profile of a company whose sales and marketing approach had developed over time without much attention being paid to reviewing and revamping the process as needed. This was a traditional sales model that depended, almost exclusively, on face-to-face selling—and it was no longer profitable. It simply cost too much: product margins were declining, the cost of selling was increasing, competitors were chipping away at the customer base, and it was getting increasingly difficult to determine how to generate a positive return on the marketing and sales investment.

The Diagnosis

The time was right for Shell TBA to step back and figure out how to build efficiency into the selling process by using different sales and marketing tools to work the customer relationships. It needed to incorporate focused, value-added contacts; account planning; account investments based on worth; and leveraging of a customer and transaction database. This situation, in contrast to that at The Technology Company, required Shell to manage its investment in customers differently, in effect moving the investment downstream by using a customer contact mix that included the expensive face-to-face contacts but, in addition, leveraged those with a blend of substantially lower-cost contacts. This contact mix would be positioned to sustain customer relationships and to maintain profitability in these relationships.

When Not to Use IAM

Integrated account management can obviously have a positive impact on how you do business with your customers and the results that you achieve. Like any good tool, there are some environments where it is not of value. Don't use IAM in these scenarios:

- You can't make a difference in what and how much customers buy
- There isn't a way to define and provide value in contacts to customers
- The cost of selling is not an issue—the selling investment expense in customers has little impact on profitability
- It makes sense to treat all customers the same—there is little or no variability in needs and preferences
- There is only one acceptable and appropriate medium to talk to customers
- Competitive vulnerability is not an issue

4

Building an IAM Program

Well begun is half done.

—Horace

On Tuesday, July 19, 1994, I received a call from one of my clients. She was calling to ask me to attend a meeting two days later, July 21, to discuss the new marketing initiative that was being kicked off. At this meeting, project teams were designated for each of the major projects in the initiative, one of which was an integrated account management pilot program.

On the following Monday, July 25, a team meeting was held to set up the work plan for this account management pilot. The initial target date for this effort, set in the July 21 kick-off meeting, was early September, which gave the team eight weeks to define, develop, and implement the account management pilot. I couldn't help but think back to reactions in other companies to condensed time frames for an initiative like this: "It will take at least six months." "This is a significant change, and we can't change the organization that quickly." "Do you want it done fast or done well?" "Are you insane?" The reaction of this project team was, "Give us one more week." Nine weeks later, account managers were calling on customers. In that time frame, the following tasks were accomplished:

- Customers were segmented into account management modules.
- A customer grading model was developed and applied.
- The account manager position was defined.
- Account manager candidates were selected and hired.
- The account management process was defined.
- Management and coaching responsibilities were aligned.
- Customer communications were defined, designed, and developed.
- Software was evaluated, selected, modified, and installed.

- Hardware was selected and installed.
- A customer loyalty study was designed and conducted.
- Program measures and economic models were defined.
- Training was designed, developed, and conducted, including product training, customer training, account management training, and systems training.

This was a significant achievement, accomplished in a remarkably short period of time. I have seen other companies spend four, five, even six months putting integrated account management programs in place. It would be nice to say that there is a direct correlation between the length of time spent developing an integrated account management program and the quality of the program, that is, its results. But it simply does not work that way. There is a point of diminishing returns—a point where the best way to further develop the program is to put it in place and improve it "in the field." The importance of account management in the customer relationships, the changing nature of the marketplace, the significance of the change in the business culture, and the immediate potential economic value are all important justification points for a "slam-dunk" project development and implementation approach to account management.

Even more astonishing than the speed with which the program was installed is that it was done so in a situation filled with obstacles. Like many companies, my client had a number of obstacles to overcome in its development of an IAM program. It is a large company with a bureaucratic history. Its culture did not support rapid change. And, even though it is a large company, it runs lean from a marketing and sales management perspective.

Nonetheless, it managed to launch a quality IAM program in a very brief period. How? What was different about this case? Four key factors were involved:

- *Sense of urgency.* Urgency begets action. Action begets results. At my client, there was a certain degree of analysis and rigor in the process of developing account management. This rigor, blended with a high degree of urgency, drove the quick, positive results achieved. An aggressive target completion date was determined at the outset, and team members were encouraged to do whatever it took to meet the target completion date.

- *Clear vision and strategy.* There was no confusion about what this account management capability was. It was clearly defined as a strategy to provide value to strengthen customer relationships, increase customer loyalty, and drive incremental sales to existing customers. This clarity of vision provided the focus needed to pull this off in an extremely short time frame.

• *Committed management and project team.* Obviously, this is not a one-person task, either in volume of work or in the broad set of skills required. You need analytical skills to do the segmentation and grading, creative skills to develop communications, systems skills to handle the software components, training skills to develop and deliver training, and project management skills to keep this effort focused, coordinate quality completion of tasks, and ensure effective integration of components. At my client, this was not viewed as one of a number of current projects on the lists of team members. Most team members were totally dedicated to this effort.

• *Tightly defined work plan.* What we had here was a complex project critical to the organization. The project had a number of disparate tasks, various dependencies among the tasks, tight (in some cases, extremely tight) completion dates, and simply a large volume of work to be done in a short period of time. My client did it with classic project management principles wrapped in an ambiance of urgency to "get it done" irrespective of the barriers. This approach included the following:

- Clearly defined tasks and subtasks
- Individual task ownership and accountability
- Authority consistent with task ownership
- Task activities and completion dates defined by week
- Regular, quick project team updates

Building an IAM Program

Building an IAM capability consists of six major tasks:

1.0	Developing the project work plan
2.0	Creating a strategic foundation
3.0	Developing an in-depth understanding of customers
4.0	Building internal service value
5.0	Acquiring account management resources
6.0	Developing marketing and sales campaigns

Each of these major tasks, illustrated in Figure 4-1, is not only essential but quite large and complex.

Given that I recommend that companies develop their IAM program in a relatively short time frame (I usually recommend a nine- to

Figure 4-1. Building an IAM program.

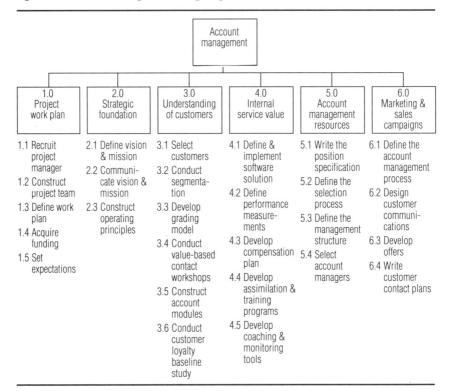

Account management

1.0 Project work plan	2.0 Strategic foundation	3.0 Understanding of customers	4.0 Internal service value	5.0 Account management resources	6.0 Marketing & sales campaigns
1.1 Recruit project manager 1.2 Construct project team 1.3 Define work plan 1.4 Acquire funding 1.5 Set expectations	2.1 Define vision & mission 2.2 Communicate vision & mission 2.3 Construct operating principles	3.1 Select customers 3.2 Conduct segmentation 3.3 Develop grading model 3.4 Conduct value-based contact workshops 3.5 Construct account modules 3.6 Conduct customer loyalty baseline study	4.1 Define & implement software solution 4.2 Define performance measurements 4.3 Develop compensation plan 4.4 Develop assimilation & training programs 4.5 Develop coaching & monitoring tools	5.1 Write the position specification 5.2 Define the selection process 5.3 Define the management structure 5.4 Select account managers	6.1 Define the account management process 6.2 Design customer communications 6.3 Develop offers 6.4 Write customer contact plans

twelve-week time frame), it might be tempting to take a more loosely defined project management approach—an approach that seems like "let's fly the plane while we're reading the instruction manual." Such a loosely defined approach is not likely to be successful. In this time frame, it is essential to move forward quickly, to not agonize over what to do, to have a tactical focus on the tasks to be completed, and to work with confidence. The following represents the kind of detailed work plan needed to direct this intense effort. Although every organization will most likely have some unique elements in its work plan, the following plan lists the majority of tasks required in almost any account management installation. In most cases it will constitute up to 80 to 90 percent of a given IAM work plan.

Developing the Project Work Plan

The importance of the project work plan is self-evident. It is the foundation upon which the rest of the project is built. In apparent contradiction of this importance is the urgency to complete this step—it needs to be completed in the first week.

Developing a solid work plan to implement IAM in a relatively short period of time is essential. It just can't be accomplished without a well-defined and thoroughly documented work plan that clearly identifies what the tasks are, when they should be started and when they should be completed, and who is responsible for completing them. Getting that work plan developed and building that foundation for moving forward consists of five steps or subtasks:

1. Recruiting the project manager
2. Constructing the project team
3. Defining the work plan
4. Acquiring project funding
5. Setting organizational expectations

Recruiting the Project Manager

Every project must start somewhere in an organization. Here the assumption is that there is a corporate champion or sponsor for account management. One of the first, and most important, responsibilities of that corporate sponsor is to identify and recruit a project manager to build IAM. In some organizations the assignment of the project manager happens by default because it automatically goes to the national sales manager or to a channel manager. In these cases the assignment functionally defaults to an individual who already has responsibilities for customer relationships (e.g., the director or manager of sales). In others the organization selects someone to manage the project. In any case, you need a strong project manager. An ideal project manager is a strong communicator, has a high degree of drive and energy, has an appropriate level of authority in the organization, is able to hold other people accountable for task completion, has a balanced perspective between sales and marketing and ideally experience in both, has experience managing large projects, and is disciplined in managing against the task plan.

Ideally the project manager selected will be committed to this project full-time over the course of development and at least part-time for some period after implementation. At the end of this step you need a project manager in place who is committed to the project, is willing to take ownership of it, and has a mutual understanding with the corporate sponsor of the objectives and scope. In an ideal situation, it is best to involve the project manager in definition of objectives and scope. This is possible in environments where the project manager selection defaults to a specific person or position, or where you have identified a specific person as project manager and can get an allocation of that person's time before the project is tightly defined and scoped.

Constructing the Project Team

The project manager's first task is to put together a project team. Obviously, team members need a fairly broad set of skills to provide a balanced perspective and to accomplish the tasks in the work plan. Typically the team consists of anywhere from five to eight people working primarily on the work plan tasks. Those five to eight people typically bring a range of perspectives to the project: a sales management perspective (someone who manages account managers), a marketing communications orientation, a marketing analysis and segmentation background, a channel management perspective, one or two systems people, somebody from the human resources and development area, and somebody from a training area. It is the project manager's job to identify and recruit these people and get their commitment to the project.

Defining the Work Plan

Defining the work plan entails the following steps:

• *Reviewing background.* Summarize the current business situation and the marketplace and internal needs to be addressed in the program.

• *Reviewing and changing objectives and scope.* Clearly define the primary objectives of the program as well as any supporting or secondary objectives. Define scope to communicate the limits of the project and to define parameters within which to operate. At this point, there are usually some expectations set in the organization. Changes to objectives and scope at this point are usually intended to clarify or fine-tune. Any changes beyond clarifying and fine-tuning need to be made with caution and should be communicated to all involved.

• *Defining quantitative and qualitative measurements of success.* These are measurements to help gauge the effectiveness of the project team in building an IAM capability and the impact of integrated account management in the marketplace. Measurements to gauge the effectiveness of the project team include actual versus planned completion dates, internal communication effectiveness and completeness, and the internal perception of the quality of the analysis and the outputs produced by the team. Measurements of the impact of IAM in the marketplace include financial results, account manager productivity, and customer loyalty measures.

• *Defining deliverables.* Identify the important tangible outputs from this program (e.g., reports, economic models, work plans, performance requirements customer definition, documented approaches to market, systems definitions, process diagrams). In this context, important outputs are defined as those that

- Provide tangible evidence of completion of a project task
- Provide rationale for and drive critical project decisions (e.g., selection of customers to participate in IAM program, economic models to determine IAM success and rollout)
- Are used to communicate with customers
- Are used to communicate with the rest of the organization

• *Defining milestones.* Define specific critical steps that clearly lead to project completion and are evidence that the project is on track.

• *Defining timing.* Identify major-task time frames.

• *Developing task-level work plan.* Figure 4-1 provides a graphic illustration of the tasks required to build IAM. Although in some organizations the tasks are different, in all organizations the task categories (1.0, "Project work plan," through 6.0, "Marketing and sales campaign") are all critical and need to be addressed. In all cases, IAM projects need to be planned (1.0), be based on a strategy (2.0), be based on a thorough and multidimensional understanding of customers (3.0), be supported by internal tools and infrastructure (4.0), be implemented and managed by predetermined people (5.0), and be effectively communicated to the marketplace (6.0).

• *Assigning work plan responsibilities.*

Acquiring Project Funding

The first step in acquiring funding is to determine the amount needed. To do that, it is necessary to estimate the development and implementation costs. In effect, there are two budgets necessary here. The first, the development budget, addresses all the costs associated with defining, designing, and setting up IAM. The second, the implementation budget, includes all the costs associated with running the IAM program. It is important to separate these two budgets because one, the first, is a one-time start-up expense and the other is an ongoing operating expense. The IAM pilot profitability is calculated by subtracting the pilot implementation costs from the estimated revenue. Any estimation of pilot profitability must include an estimate of pilot implementation costs. Even a pilot project of reasonable size, say, ten people for six months, using a combination of phone and field, could cost as much as a half a million dollars.

The ability to leverage existing corporate resources, such as existing computer hardware, existing phone systems, and existing staff/personnel, obviously could have a significant impact on the amount of funding required. Another area to consider is total labor costs for design, development, and implementation. This includes the actual outside and inside account management people who will staff the pilot, the development and implementation team, the project manager, and the sales managers who will manage the account managers during the pilot. An area frequently missed in the planning, but essential, is the time and expense required to measure and assess the pilot and develop the rollout plan.

Another expense category is outside services. Most organizations implementing a pilot of this size, scope, and complexity must get some outside support, which may include general consulting support or research support (e.g., qualitative research to facilitate customer focus groups and customer loyalty research or research to aid in developing some of the economic models). The outside services may also include some support with the systems design and development or implementation. Another category of development cost is equipment and capital expenses. These include hardware, software, fax machine, phones (both inside and cellular for the field), facilities, and automobiles (for outside account managers during the pilot).

The last expense category is miscellaneous costs. (It seems inevitable that there are always miscellaneous costs.) These include general supplies and travel expenses. Even in a regionally run pilot, it is not unusual to incur some travel expenses during the implementation phase. These may be for trips to visit other account management sites to observe or to check out software and different operations.

Setting Organizational Expectations

The relatively short time frame that I recommend doesn't allow for a lot of internal communication. However, there are a few internal communication steps that can make both the development and implementation run smoother.

• Conducting the project kick-off. In this short time frame, there will be only a small number of progress update meetings. It is important to build momentum early in the project. The kick-off consists of a written document and a launch meeting including all members of the project team. The following topics are usually included in this kick-off communication:

- The current business situation. The current situation (and espe-cially the external factors discussed in Chapter 3) was most likely the reason for the decision to use integrated account management. Detailing this background, in particular the ele-ments in the current situation that create a compelling need to do something different, provides an overall context within which to assess IAM and its potential impact.
- A definition of IAM.
- The vision for IAM.
- The objectives of IAM and of the pilot program.
- Rationale. This should result in a succinct overview of why the program is important, why this definition and vision for IAM provide a meaningful way to deal with the business situation as defined, and why and how the objectives will be achieved through this strategy.
- Milestones and timing. In this brief time frame, it is probably helpful to communicate only a few milestones. In fact, you could make a case for there being only one milestone—the pilot start-up date.

- Publishing and tracking against the milestones. The milestones become a point of discussion during the project kick-off and in all subsequent follow-up communication. They should communicate progress and indicate any resulting timing changes.

- Conducting informal meetings with affected managers. Be-cause this vision of account management ultimately encompasses a company's relationship with its customers, it can have an impact throughout the organization. Meeting with managers whose areas could be affected (e.g., customer service, technical support, customer accounting, sales support) to discuss the potential impact, get their input, understand and deal with their concerns, and get their support is a valuable activity. It can facilitate a smooth implementation.

For any project, a well thought through and well-communicated plan and a capable project team are critical for success. This work plan provides the road map to develop IAM. Subsequent chapters (Chapters 5 through 15) address key tasks in the workplan. Please refer to Figure 4-1 to understand how these tasks and corresponding chapters fit into the overall work plan.

Chapter 5 addresses the development of a vision statement for account management.

Chapter 6 outlines and discusses approaches to and applications of customer segmentation and customer grading.

Chapter 7 deals with design and construction of account management modules.

Chapter 8 provides the rationale and discusses the approach for defining, assessing, and selecting account managers.

Chapter 9 provides a method for defining value-based contacts.

Chapter 10 describes the introduction process for IAM.

Chapter 11 defines the processes to create customer contact plans.

Chapter 12 provides a training and development framework.

Chapter 13 addresses the measurement systems for account management.

Chapter 14 illustrates the importance of customer loyalty, describes the important account manager applications of customer loyalty, and discusses the core components of a customer loyalty study.

Chapter 15 describes a process for selecting and implementing an account management system.

If you are building a new account management capability, use the work plan in this chapter as a road map and use each of the relevant subsequent chapters to provide detailed support, to explain the core concepts and rationale, to understand qualitative aspects of the task, to identify potential pitfalls and roadblocks, and to understand the value inherent in IAM and in each of the tasks outlined.

1.0 Develop project work plan (Timing is illustrated in Figure 4-2. Note that the time lines included in this work plan assumes a nine-week schedule for the planning and implementation of the IAM program.)

Figure 4-2. Building an IAM project work plan.

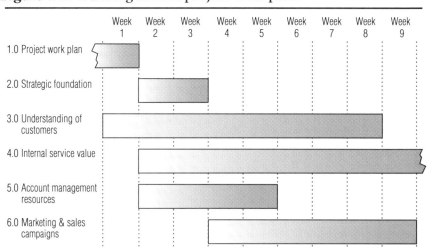

1.1 Recruit project manager
    1.1.1 Define objectives and scope
    1.1.2 Get commitment from project manager
1.2 Construct project team
    1.2.1 Recruit project team members
       • Sales management
       • Marketing communications
       • Segmentation and analysis
       • Economic modeling
       • Channel management
       • Systems
       • Development and training
    1.2.2 Get commitment from project team
    1.2.3 Conduct team orientation
    1.2.4 Schedule kick-off/work plan meeting
1.3 Define work plan (in team kick-off meeting)
    1.3.1 Review background
    1.3.2 Review objectives and scope
    1.3.3 Define measurements
    1.3.4 Define deliverables, milestones, and timing
    1.3.5 Develop task-level work plan
    1.3.6 Assign work plan responsibilities
1.4 Acquire funding
    1.4.1 Estimate development cost
       • Time cost
       • Capital expense
       • Miscellaneous expense
    1.4.2 Calculate pro forma operating profit and loss
    1.4.3 Calculate return on investment
    1.4.4 Document and present budget estimates for funding approval
1.5 Set organizational expectations
    1.5.1 Develop internal communications plan
    1.5.2 Identify related/affected functional areas
    1.5.3 Schedule and conduct review meetings

2.0 Develop strategic foundation (Timing is illustrated in Figure 4-3.)
    2.1 Develop vision and mission statements
       2.1.1 Get input from project team members
       2.1.2 Draft vision and mission statements
    2.2 Communicate vision and mission
       2.2.1 Identify key stakeholders

Figure 4-3. Building IAM task 2.0—develop strategic foundation.

	Week 1	Week 2	Week 3	Week 4	Week 5	Week 6	Week 7	Week 8	Week 9
2.1 Develop vision & mission statements		▨							
2.2 Communicate vision & mission			▨						
2.3 Construct operating principles			▨						

      2.2.2 Identify key influencers
      2.2.3 Present vision and mission to stakeholders and influencers
      2.2.4 Gain commitment from key stakeholders

   2.3 Construct operating principles
      2.3.1 Define specific behavior and attitudes that support vision and mission
      2.3.2 Define and document set of operating principles
      2.3.3 Review with team
      2.3.4 Revise as indicated

3.0 Develop understanding of customers and supporting tools (Timing is illustrated in Figure 4-4.)
   3.1 Select customers to include in IAM

Figure 4-4. Building IAM task 3.0—develop understanding of customers.

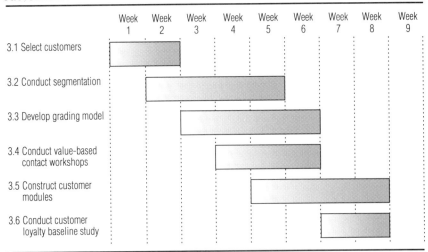

	Week 1	Week 2	Week 3	Week 4	Week 5	Week 6	Week 7	Week 8	Week 9
3.1 Select customers	▨	▨							
3.2 Conduct segmentation		▨	▨	▨	▨				
3.3 Develop grading model			▨	▨	▨	▨			
3.4 Conduct value-based contact workshops				▨	▨	▨			
3.5 Construct customer modules					▨	▨	▨	▨	
3.6 Conduct customer loyalty baseline study							▨	▨	

3.1.1 Construct overall economic model based on market assumptions

3.1.2 Determine customer economic/revenue requirements

3.1.3 Determine related customer defining characteristics
- Types of customers
- Counts of customers

3.1.4 Reconcile customer counts with economic model

3.2 Conduct customer segmentation

3.2.1 Develop data-gathering framework
- Customer needs categories
- Domains of influence
- Product/service/relationship needs

3.2.2 Develop the target list for data gathering
- Sampling plan

3.2.3 Develop the interview guide

3.2.4 Train/educate interviewers
- Customer overview
- Interview guide
- Questions and relevant responses
- Interview role plays
- Diagnoses

3.2.5 Conduct data gathering

3.2.6 Conduct segmentation analysis and synthesis
- Consolidate needs
- Group needs
- Define work segments
- Test for commonality of needs
- Consolidate to define segments
- Document segments

3.3 Build grading model

3.3.1 Develop first-level account-grading segments

3.3.2 Identify revenue-defining attributes

3.3.3 Define best-in-class performance

3.3.4 Develop incremental revenue calculation

3.3.5 Apply incremental revenue calculation

3.3.6 Run customer worth deciles

3.3.7 Build total worth matrix

3.3.8 Define grade parameters

3.4 Conduct value-based contact workshops

3.4.1 Recruit and invite customers to participate

3.4.2 Coordinate facility

3.4.3 Send confirmation

3.4.4 Call to confirm

3.4.5 Determine incentive
3.4.6 Conduct workshop
3.4.7 Document results
  • Communications performance standards
  • Value-based contacts

3.5 Build customer modules
  3.5.1 Estimate average customer contact levels
  3.5.2 Calculate account manager capacity
  3.5.3 Determine module size
  3.5.4 Determine account mix (customer types and grade mix)
  3.5.5 Construct customer modules
  3.5.6 Test module construction
    • Size
    • Worth
    • Account mix
  3.5.7 Revise, if indicated

3.6 Conduct customer loyalty baseline study
  3.6.1 Define loyalty metrics
  3.6.2 Measure available historical performance
  3.6.3 Interview a limited number of customers
    • Qualitative interviews
    • Gather information to build survey instruments
  3.6.4 Develop survey instrument
  3.6.5 Develop the list for loyalty survey
    • Sampling plan
  3.6.6 Conduct the survey
  3.6.7 Document results
  3.6.8 Run economic models
    • Customer-at-risk
  3.6.9 Define and document account management implications

4.0 Build internal service value (Timing is illustrated in Figure 4-5.)

4.1 Define and implement software solution
  4.1.1 Define business processes
    • Account management
    • Support processes
  4.1.2 Determine optimization model
    • Depth of relationship
    • Contact productivity
    • Home run productivity
    • Contact integration

Figure 4-5. Building IAM task 4.0—build internal service value.

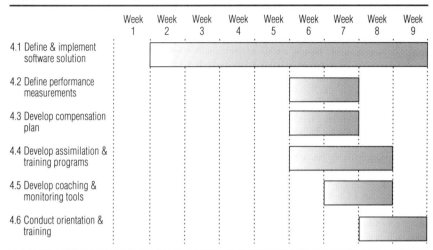

- Proposal generation
- Campaign management
4.1.3 Define requirements
- Reporting requirements
- Functional requirements
- Data requirements
4.1.4 Conduct software fit analysis
4.1.5 Assess software packages
4.1.6 Select package
4.1.7 Design modifications
4.1.8 Implement
- Install
- Test
- Train
4.2 Define performance measurements
4.2.1 Define financial results
- Sales
- Contribution
4.2.2 Define customer loyalty results
- Satisfaction levels
- Intent to repurchase
- Willingness to refer
- Customer purchase behavior
4.2.3 Define productivity measures
- Customer contact time
- Customer calls and contacts
- Proposals

- Close ratios
- Average order size

4.3 Develop compensation plan
    4.3.1 Draft compensation plan objectives
    4.3.2 Gather and review industry salary data
    4.3.3 Develop compensation plan
    4.3.4 Reconcile with performance measurements
    4.3.5 Test plan with representative performance
    4.3.6 Document and present compensation plan

4.4 Develop assimilation and training programs
    4.4.1 Determine account manager development needs in key
           areas
- Customer knowledge
- Product knowledge and application
- Account management skills
- Account planning
- Module planning

    4.4.2 Define learning objectives
    4.4.3 Determine training format(s)
    4.4.4 Develop training and assimilation components
    4.4.5 Conduct training and assimilation

4.5 Develop coaching and monitoring tools
    4.5.1 Set coaching performance expectations
    4.5.2 Develop monitoring tools
    4.5.3 Test monitoring tools

4.6 Conduct orientation and training

5.0 Acquire account management resources (Timing is illustrated in Figure 4-6.)

Figure 4-6. Building IAM task 5.0—acquire account management resources.

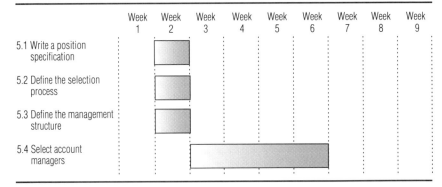

5.1 Write the position specification
    5.1.1 Define position responsibilities and accountabilities
    5.1.2 Determine behavioral requirements
    5.1.3 Determine chemistry requirements
    5.1.4 Define minimum experience and education levels

5.2 Define the selection process
    5.2.1 Define and document selection process steps
      • Generate candidates
      • Résumé screen
      • Knockout interview
      • Behavioral interview
      • Role play (skills)
      • Sales manager interview
    5.2.2 Define selection process responsibilities
    5.2.3 Define timing requirements

5.3 Define the management structure
    5.3.1 Define organizational objectives
      • Include account management and support organizations
    5.3.2 Construct alternative structure models
    5.3.3 Assess alternative structures against objectives
    5.3.4 Select and document organizational structure

5.4 Select account managers
    5.4.1 Execute the selection process
    5.4.2 Hire account managers

6.0 Develop marketing and sales campaigns (Timing is illustrated in Figure 4-7.)

    6.1 Define the account management process

Figure 4-7. Building IAM task 6.0—develop marketing & sales campaigns.

      6.1.1 Define and document the customer enrollment process

      6.1.2 Define and document the ongoing account management process

  6.2 Design customer communications

      6.2.1 Review performance requirements, value-based contacts, and segmentation results

      6.2.2 Define communications structure
- Standard campaigns
- Standard pieces (letters, brochures, etc.)
- Semicustom pieces

      6.2.3 Define communications relationships and continuity

      6.2.4 Develop communications library

  6.3 Develop offers

      6.3.1 Review segmentation to assess customer needs

      6.3.2 Review competitive offerings

      6.3.3 Define and document offerings

  6.4 Write customer contact plans

      6.4.1 Develop overall contact plan

      6.4.2 Develop module contact plans

      6.4.3 Develop individual customer contact plans

5

Managing to the Vision

In most companies and industries, moving to an IAM environment requires nothing less than a transformation, both operationally and culturally. Several conditions make this transformation difficult. For one, you are asking account managers to focus on the relationship with customers, provide value, and invest in accounts in a way consistent with the long-term value of those accounts. At the same time, you are holding account managers responsible for achieving sales objectives and performing at a certain degree of productivity. This broad set of demands can at times help an account manager achieve exceptional performance. At other times, these demands can create a degree of dissonance.

An important element as you move your organization and your customers through this change is an integrated account management vision statement that clearly defines the purpose and direction for IAM within your organization. The vision statement is a compelling description of what IAM is in your organization and in your marketplace. During the transformation, it helps you focus on how you intend to do business with customers.

Developing and institutionalizing a vision for integrated account management early in the building process is critical. An effective vision statement for IAM should address the following:

- Who the customer is
- How you intend to do business with the customer
- What value is provided to customers
- How the value is provided to customers
- What benefit is provided to the organization and to account managers

The vision statement provides numerous positive results:

- *It focuses on and continually reinforces the value.* In many cases, account managers have been exposed to the value of relationships with customers (the value to the customer) and to some degree understand and believe that value. Often, however, they haven't yet internalized it; it is in the head but not the heart. If account managers do not fully embrace the concept of providing value, customers may become skeptical and impatient. When the vision is strong, when specific behaviors are addressed in operating principles, and when they are continually reinforced through the vision statement, account managers have the belief system and the confidence to live the vision and focus on the value in their role.

• *It drives ownership to the front line.* The definition of IAM in Chapter 2 states that the account managers operate like small business owners. The vision should support this principle and provide the authority to account managers to act in accordance with this principle. There is no way to anticipate all of the issues that account managers will have to address in their planning and in their contacts with customers. A vision and supporting operating principles give them guidance and ground them in their day-to-day business ownership decisions.

• *It creates energy and resilience.* It's relatively easy to start an IAM program with a lot of energy. But lack of short-term results, customers that expect you to act like a peddler and treat you like one, product and service glitches—all these day-to-day problems of the business world can quickly sap an account manager's energy. A vision serves to make account managers more resilient by focusing them on the positive long-term results and the worth of what they are doing.

• *It allows account managers to see "the big picture,"* to understand the interdependence and complexity of an organizational system. To be successful, account managers need to understand and believe in the long-term results of their work. They need to understand how their company's support systems work to support both them and their customers, and they need to develop a high level of trust in those support systems. I've seen too many account managers not meet their productivity goals because they felt that they had to personally address and resolve every customer issue, complaint, or concern that they received from their customers.

• *It provides consistency and continuity in the organization.* A vision provides a foundation to drive organizational behavior. It drives better decisions, not because all decisions are exactly the same but because decisions are based on a similar set of values. This, in its ideal state, creates an environment where tactically different decisions are strategically aligned.

Although most people would admit that a clear, documented vision is a positive thing, many are doubtful that such statements have much impact on an organization. And often they're right. Vision statements, during their development, are exciting, energy-creating entities. Over time, the reality of day-to-day work steals the focus and saps the initial energy out of the vision, and it ends up as an attractive plaque in the front hallway or gathering dust in someone's files.

Actions companies can take to keep the vision alive in an IAM environment include the following:

- Build constant reminders in the organization. This can include the plaque in the hallway; but to be effective, it needs to be much more. For example, include the vision statement on the top of call-monitoring forms. Find and document examples of behavior that are consistent with the vision. Include the vision in and explicitly link it to customer communications and company and product literature.
- Create operating principles. Operating principles help account managers interpret the vision because they identify the specific, expected behaviors that are consistent with the vision. Examples of operating principles as support for IAM are discussed in Chapter 2.
- Recognize and reward behavior that exemplifies the vision. While the reward systems that support sales results and productivity are positives, they can create an imbalance in attitudes and in account manager behavior. There are healthy ways to achieve sales and productivity results and there are unhealthy ways. The vision can provide the balance to ensure that all results (sales, productivity, and quality) are achieved in a healthy manner.

Find examples of behavior that demonstrate the vision. Make these examples visible in the organization. Call out these examples in group meetings. Illustrate how these behaviors link to sales results. Include these actions in account manager performance evaluations. Create financial and nonfinancial rewards that encourage and support actions that are strongly supportive of the vision. Build an explicit link to the vision in training programs. The vision should permeate training programs designed for account managers. In this sense, the vision becomes the foundation upon which account managers are trained and developed.

Let's use an example to illustrate how things can go awry. My firm was working with a company that had an IAM program that was in the middle of a significant rollout/expansion. Not only was this company adding a significant number of account managers, it was also adding a number of sales managers, whose primary responsibility was to monitor, coach, and develop the account managers.

In developing its IAM capability, the company had worked to develop a vision statement, build clarity in the process (which was a well-documented process), develop call guides to drive an appropriate degree of consistency in the message, and tightly define performance measures, which included both sales results measurements and calling productivity measures.

We were in a training session with sales managers to work on monitoring and coaching processes and skills. As part of this training session, we listened to taped phone calls with customers. One of these calls was to introduce this new account management program, explain the value to the customer, determine the customer's level of interest, and make a decision to include or not include the customer in the program. (Note: Although IAM is designed to be a fit for a large set of customers of any particular organization, it may not fit all customers. Some customers may not perceive value in the contacts in an IAM program or may not want the relationship with their supplier that is suggested by IAM.) As we listened to one caller introducing the IAM program, we became increasingly uncomfortable.

We were aghast at what we heard in this call. The caller was apologetic, there was no explanation of the program's value, and there were no questions to allow us to ascertain the customer's level of interest. It was almost as if the account manager was in a hurry to get it over with because he was embarrassed. This account manager had gone through approximately one month of training and had since then been on the job about six to eight weeks. In fact, this account manager was generally thought of as a reasonably capable performer who was well intended.

We had to step back and as ourselves what had happened here. Where had we gone awry? How did the vision get lost in the shuffle?

Somehow the balanced perspective that we attempted to build into the IAM program didn't happen. Somehow in the account manager's drive to do a good job, he focused on meeting the productivity goals at the expense of not conveying the value of the program and not developing the kind of relationship with customers that the program was intended to develop. In his drive to achieve daily and weekly sales goals, he was jeopardizing future customer relationships to cream sales today.

As we looked back at this situation and the environment, we determined that the following factors all had an impact on this issue:

• Stronger emphasis on measurable sales and productivity goals. Daily sales goals were tracked. Daily customer contact goals and performance were tracked. If account manager performance fell below these goals, it was very visible and encouraged the account manager to get his or her performance in these specific quantitative areas back up. The vision and the qualitative side of the work the account managers were doing, however, was more "background music." Only periodically did that come up in conversations; and it came up much, much less frequently than the quantitative sales and productivity goals. It wasn't that the measurable goals were wrong. In fact, they were, and are, exactly right. There simply was not a balancing factor focusing on *how* to do business with customers.

• Immediacy of feedback regarding productivity and sales results. Both the sales results and contact productivity provided immediate positive feedback to account managers. When they achieved the contact goals, they automatically felt good about achieving that goal. When a customer contact actually resulted in a sale, there was immediate positive feedback both from the customers and from management. So, these more quantitative short-term goals provided immediate positive feedback and encouraged account managers to achieve these goals, sometimes at the expense of the goals supplied by the vision.

• Implicit nature of the link between the focus specified in the vision and the sales results. Management and many of the account managers knew that IAM is driven by providing value in customer relationships. They also knew that over the longer term the relationships would provide the kind of sales results and productivity that they were looking for from an IAM program. That outcome wasn't made explicit, and for some account managers it wasn't clear how the behaviors that supported the vision also supported sales results.

• Results and productivity explicitly linked to compensation. In addition to a social reward system that encouraged a focus on sales and productivity, sometimes at the expense of the quality of the contact, the compensation scheme did the same. It actually provided a variable component that provided additional compensation for meeting or exceeding sales goals and additional compensation for meeting or exceeding productivity goals.

• No operating principles to help account managers achieve an understanding of management expectations. Although most of the account managers understood and felt good about the vision, their approach to implementing it varied quite a bit. In some cases their interpretation or implementation of the vision was not accurate.

• Unarticulated benefits to account managers. The vision statement was written in a way that, as least implicitly, provided significant benefit to account managers. However, their benefit was conveyed at a conceptual level, and many account managers did not make the link to tangible benefits.

• An implicit link between the vision and account manager training. Although there was a small section of training where the vision was actually presented, it wasn't explicitly linked to any other components of the training. So, account managers went through product training, customer training, training on listening and questioning the customer, and account management training, but these components of training did not have an explicit link to the vision.

There's an interesting paradox in account management that needs to be conveyed by management and internalized by account managers. Account managers need to understand and believe that they don't make sales by focusing on selling throughout every contact with a customer. A sales manager put this succinctly when explaining why one of the account managers that worked for him was having a difficult time: "He's got his pocketbook on his mind while he's talking to customers." Generating sales is not the result of "selling." Sales don't come because an account manager is thinking about his compensation, thinking about how the next sale will affect his compensation, or thinking about how the next question or comment in a customer contact will result in a sale. Sales come because the account manager invests time in the customer, understands the customer's needs, provides value by helping the customer determine how to address immediate needs and achieve long-term objectives, builds trust with the customer, and ultimately sells a product or service to the customer that meets the customer's needs.

This paradox is part of the vision that needs to be internalized by account managers and conveyed, not explicitly but through demonstration and behavior, to customers. Customers may not consciously resist this perspective, but they will be skeptical. Their expectations may be that "this is another one of those calls where they're just trying to sell me something." It takes continual reinforcement to overcome this skepticism and avoid falling into the trap of behaving the way the customer is expecting you to behave.

The IAM program just described featured a solid training program built on the company's vision for account management. As such, it was solidly linked to the vision. The only problem was that the linkage was implicit. Many account managers went through the training and never made this implicit connection. They accepted the tactics and tools of IAM as the way of doing business, and in the complexity of a customer relationship, they weren't able to adapt their behavior appropriately.

Summary

In implementing IAM, companies frequently go through a transformation, because this new way of doing business doesn't have a historical precedent and goes beyond customers' historical expectations. The barriers it presents require a certain amount of time and a certain degree of conviction to overcome, and it attracts its share of internal resisters and marketplace doubters.

A vision that's understood and believed helps overcome these obstacles. A vision provides a framework upon which to define value, define processes, and design training for the development of IAM. It also provides perspective, energy, and guidance throughout the implementation of IAM.

The first operating principle of integrated account management (see Chapter 2) is, account managers act as small business owners. Like the business, in world-class account management the account managers own the vision. The only way the vision can become a reality is through the behavior of the account managers.

6

Segmenting and Grading Customers

"All customers are not created equal."
Bob Stone

Segmentation is a commonly misunderstood concept in business today. In many companies "segmentation" has become a euphemism to describe the customer grading model. There is value, however, in thinking of segmentation and grading as two separate disciplines.

According to John Berrigan and Carl Finkbeiner, in their book *Segmentation Marketing* (1992), segmentation answers four questions:[1]

- What? What products and services to offer.
- Who? To whom to aim products and services.
- Where? Where to advertise and market.
- Why? Why customers do what they do.

In segmentation these questions are typically answered through a detailed analysis and understanding of customers' needs. Grading, on the other hand, is designed to answer the question, How much? How much should you invest in a customer to retain existing business and to secure incremental business? It is true that in a grading model some understanding of customer needs, attributes, and buying processes is necessary. However, assuming that segmentation and grading are the same is a little like assuming that baseball and cricket are the same because they both use a ball and a bat.

In the context of integrated account management, *segmentation* is defined as "the process of identifying, analyzing, and categorizing customer needs to define how homogeneous sets of customers will be communicated with, serviced, and managed." The delivery of value (in the relationship between account managers and customers, in the products and services offered, in the communications with customers, etc.) that is relevant to customers' needs is fundamental to the concept of IAM. As such, segmentation provides information that can be used throughout the process of building IAM.

Grading is defined as "the process of evaluating and defining a customer's (or set of customers') worth and assigning a grade or score to individual customers to reflect that worth. In the process of building IAM, customer grades are used when assigning accounts to account managers and are used in the customer contact plan to determine a marketing and sales investment in customers that is commensurate with the revenue expected to be realized from those customers.

Developing a Segmentation Framework

In IAM, segmentation is focused on building a framework of understanding of customer needs and identifying customers that have common sets of needs. Specifically, this step drives toward a rich understanding of needs—what functional requirements exist for your products, what business results customers expect to achieve through your products, what service/delivery expectations exist, and what customers need and would value from the relationship—an understanding of the relative importance of those needs, and an ability to associate those needs with the characteristics of individual customers.

The following six steps are involved in segmentation. These steps are shown graphically in Figure 6-1.

1. Develop a framework to gather data.
2. Develop the target list of customers for data gathering.
3. Develop the interview guide.
4. Train/educate interviewers.
5. Conduct the data gathering.
6. Conduct the segmentation analysis and synthesis.

Segmentation is primarily a process of interviewing customers to get a detailed definition of their needs from their perspective. In simple terms, it consists of a number of preparation steps (steps 1 through 4), an interviewing step (step 5), and an analysis step (step 6). The quality and accuracy of the results depend largely on the quality achieved in each step.

Figure 6-1. Developing a segmentation framework.

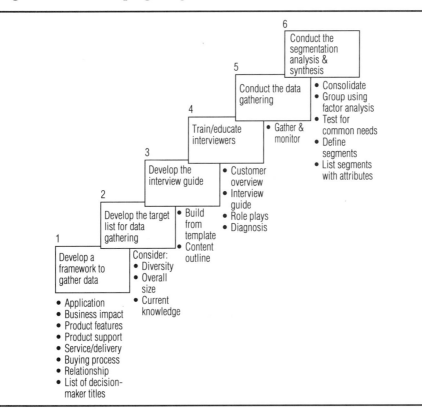

Step 1: Develop a Framework to Gather Data

In the first step of the segmentation process you review your existing information and knowledge to plan the subsequent data-gathering steps. First, you select the categories of customer needs questions that you want asked in the interviews. Then, you assess the purchasing responsibilities and corresponding titles of decision makers and influencers in customer companies in order to define the profile of people you will interview at customer companies.

It is important that you invest the time to be thorough in this step because it provides direction for the rest of the segmentation process. There are typically two considerations that are addressed here.

First, you need to assess how your product or service affects the customer's business. Can it help to increase the customer's market share, help grow the business, help provide superior service, build a competitive advantage, significantly improve internal productivity, or simply perform a specific, necessary function? The answer to this question will affect the needs questions that you ask and the people that you target for interviews.

Then assess the complexity and cost of your product. As the cost and complexity of products increase, typically the decision-making process increases in complexity and the number of decision makers and influencers increases. Additionally, there is more strategic involvement on the customer's part in the decision-making process (i.e., the titles of decision makers in customer companies will reflect a more strategic role). This could affect which people and how many people you target for interviews.

Using your knowledge of your products and markets, work through the template shown in Figure 6-2 to select relevant needs questions and categories that you want included in the interview guide.

- *Introduction.* The introduction sets the tone for the call. An explanation of the purpose of the call and a request for the customer's time (with a realistic estimate of how much time the call will take) help set an appropriate tone.
- *Application understanding.* How is your product used in the customer's business? Who are the primary users? What other products is it used with? For example, if your product is a laser printer, it might be used to print letters, proposals, and other communications with clients, be used by sales staff, and be used with word processing software in a network environment.
- *Business impact.* What business results are likely or desirable from use of the product? Consider results achieved in the customer's markets (better service to customers, a competitive advantage, increased access to markets) and internal business results (e.g., reduced operating costs, increased productivity, increased security).
- *Product features.* What products are currently used (consider both your products and competitive products)? What are expected product features and expected product functionality? How do the product features help the customer achieve business results?
- *Product support.* What support is required to help the customer achieve the highest level of business results through optimal use of the products (consider manuals, training, technical support, other products)? How does the customer receive this support and how would the customer like to get it (phone, manuals, on-site, etc.)?

Figure 6-2. IAM customer segmentation interview guide template.

1.0 Introduction	• Introduce self & company • Get to decision maker(s) and/or key influencers & specifiers • Explain purpose of call (research, not sales) • Ask permission for time • Confirm company data
2.0 Application understanding	• Develop an understanding of overall business solutions products are used in (an understanding of the use of your products in an overall business solution context) • Identify any unfulfilled needs in these business solutions
3.0 Business impact	• Develop an understanding of what important business results are likely to be achieved from the product application
4.0 Product features	• Identify or confirm current products used (or needed) • Identify value-adding features and benefits of products used — how they support business results • Determine new features that would add value
5.0 Product support	• Determine specific support requirements that enhance the use of the product (e.g., product training, technical support, start-up manuals) • Determine customer-preferred method of receiving support (phone, manual(s), on-site training, etc.)

6.0 Service/delivery needs	• Determine customer preferences and needs in the transaction process (ordering, delivery, payment)
	  - Frequency of purchase
	  - Frequency drivers (e.g., inventory levels, requests)
	  - Preferred ordering method (phone, fax, electronic, etc.)
	  - Preferred delivery method(s)
	  - Preferred payment method(s)

7.0 Buying process	• Determine supplier selection process
	  - Criteria for selection
	  - Individuals, titles, and roles
	  - Type of process (bid, preferred supplier list, informal)
	• Determine purchasing process
	  - Budgeting process
	  - Budget owners
	  - Approval process and specifications
	  - Specifiers

8.0 Relationship needs & expectations	• Supplier integration into buying process • Proactive support • Integration or input into business planning

- *Service/delivery needs.* What types and levels of service facilitate the transaction process—give the customer convenience and comfort once having made a buying decision? Include ordering methods, delivery and payment methods, and communication throughout this process.
- *Buying process.* What specific information and support is needed by the customer to help make and justify a buying decision? What is the current, and the desired, level of supplier involvement in the supplier selection and purchasing process?
- *Relationship needs and expectations.* How much and what kind

of personal contact does the customer expect or desire from a supplier? How proactive are current suppliers? How proactive should a supplier be?

After you have selected needs questions and categories, you then define positions you will target for your interviews. This results in a list of responsibilities and titles of the decision makers and influencers in customer companies. Because of the variable use and definition of titles in different companies, it is important to also consider the employees' functional responsibilities. For instance, the title of the individual responsible for computer hardware purchases might be information technology manager, management information system (MIS) manager, technical services manager, data processing manager, or, in some cases, office manager. Figure 6-3 provides an example of an interview target position list.

Step 2: Develop the Target List of Customers for Data Gathering

This step results in the names of individuals at customer accounts that you will call to conduct the data-gathering interviews. This step consists of determining your sampling method, identifying the companies you will call, and then identifying the individuals who have the appropriate responsibilities and titles (targeted in step 1) within the selected companies.

The sample size that you define depends on the diversity of your

Figure 6-3. Sample IAM customer-segmentation interview target position list.

Functional Responsibilities	Titles
1. Purchaser or influencer of computer hardware products	• IT Manager • Director of Information Technology • MIS Manager • Technical Services Manager • Office Manager
2. Purchaser or influencer of computer software products	• MIS Manager • Office Manager • Systems Analyst • Systems Manager • Programmer/Analyst
3. Purchaser or influencer of computer and peripheral supplies	• Office Manager • Purchasing Agent

customer base. A more diverse customer base requires a larger sample size because there will probably be more "segments" and a more diverse set of needs. A good rule of thumb for sampling is a minimum of fifty interviews for each identifiable discrete segment. You must then consider the level of your current knowledge concerning your customer base. The less you know about your customers, the more you want to offset that lack of knowledge with a larger sample size. The rule of thumb here is to double the sample size (to one hundred interviews for each identifiable discrete segment) if you feel you have limited knowledge and information regarding the needs of your customers. It is important to remember that these sample sizes represent completed interviews; it is best to make the total target list three times the required sample size of completed interviews to ensure obtaining the required number of interviews. The target list sample size needed to obtain your sample may vary for different industries and different audiences depending on the ease of contacting individuals and their willingness to complete interviews.

Once the sample size is determined, you then select the customer companies that will be contacted and obtain the names of decision makers and influencers at the companies. The best sources for identifying customer companies are your own internal systems (accounting, order processing, marketing). However, in many organizations these internal systems are not a good source for names of individual decision makers and influencers. Frequently, these systems contain the names of accounts payable staff, individuals in shipping and receiving, and, at times, no individual names at all. In most organizations a methodical review and assessment of multiple sources of individual names is required, such as the following:

- Internal systems (accounting, order processing, customer service, etc.)
- The sales force
- Customer service personnel and/or manual files
- External lists (subscription lists from trade publications, associations lists, and other compiled lists)

In this review and assessment, you are looking for the names, phone numbers, and titles of individuals who appear to have the responsibilities that were identified in step 1 in the interview target position list (see also Figure 6-3).

Step 3: Develop the Interview Guide

We use "interview guide" here to differentiate this document from a survey or a script. Because you are going for depth, this is not going to be a "check this box" approach to data gathering. The interview guide is a content outline for the interview that defines the categories of needs that are to be addressed in the interviews and provides specific explanations, ideas, and triggers. It also provides reminders for standard types of information (e.g., level of importance of stated needs). An interview guide template is shown in Figure 6.2. Use this template along with the needs questions selected in step 1 as references to construct the interview guide.

Additionally, you need descriptive information about each of the interviewed individuals and companies, including company demographics (SIC code, size of company, etc.) and characteristics of the individuals (title, department, budget responsibility, etc.). If there is no other source for this information (frequently, it is available in internal databases; if not, there are a number of list compilers that can provide it in "enhancement files"), or if you have concerns about its completeness or accuracy, you need to add to this data in the data-gathering step (in addition to the customer needs data gathered). Your interview guide will then include demographics queries. A sample interview guide is provided in Figure 6-4.

Step 4: Train/Educate Interviewers

The most important training component for the interviewers is their understanding of the various customer needs and what constitutes a relevant response from a customer. Because the interview guide for the most part asks open-ended questions, the questions are open to interpretation by the customer. Interviewers must be able to discern between a superficial and a substantive response, to recognize a relevant response, to explain the intent of the question and provide examples of appropriate responses, to probe for depth, and to relate to the interviewee. Interviewers need a detailed understanding of the intent of the question in order to know whether the respondent understood it and answered appropriately. Understanding the intent also allows interviewers to probe for depth of information.

This understanding of intent of questions should be validated and honed during "mock" calls or role plays. It should become clear during this stage who "gets it" and who doesn't. Simply being able to explain what a question means is not enough to verify that an interviewer really understands its purpose and intent. Interviewers demonstrate their level of understanding through their performance in simulated interviews. How do they react to an answer that indicates the customer did not understand the question? How do they respond to questions from the customer? Do they recognize misunderstanding or confusion on the part of the customer?

(text continued on p. 85)

Figure 6-4. IAM customer segmentation sample interview guide.

Company Information

Company name   _____

Address   _____

City, state, zip   _____

Phone number   _____

Company size   _____

SIC code   _____

Contact name(s)   _____

Title(s)   _____

Interviewer name   _____

Date   _____

Attempts   _____

Introduction

Hello. This is _____ from _____Company. I am calling to conduct research and at no time will I attempt to sell you anything.

Are you the person responsible (key decision maker) for purchasing products such as (specify target products here)?

If yes, continue. If no, ask for the name and title of the appropriate individual and repeat the introduction. Identify the key decision maker for every product category as appropriate.

The purpose of my call is to better understand how our company can provide you with products that are designed to meet your unique needs.

Would you have ten minutes to complete a short survey. *If yes, continue. If no, schedule and document a call back.*

(continues)

Figure 6-4. *Continued.*

Application Understanding

1. Specifically, which business functions do our products impact or support?
2. Are there any business functions which our products could support but do not currently support? Why?

Business Impact

3. What are the key business results this product application impacts?

Product Features

4. Which of our products do you currently have a need for?
5. For each product you just listed, what are the specific features or benefits that add value to your business?
6. Are there any features or benefits that you would like to see added to our products?

Product Support

7. For the products you mentioned, is there any additional support needed for you to effectively use the product? If yes: Specifically, what type of support is needed? (product training, customer support)

Service/Delivery

8. How do you prefer to order these products?
   a. Phone
   b. Fax
   c. In person (sales rep)
   d. Mail
   e. By computer
   f. Other _____
9. What delivery method do you prefer?
   a. Federal Express
   b. UPS
   c. US Mail
   d. Delivery by salesperson
   e. Other _____
10. What payment method do you prefer?
   a. Billed
   b. Have an established account
   c. Credit card
   d. Invoiced
   e. Other _____

Buying Process

11. How do you select vendors for these products?
    a. Preferred vendor
    b. Bid process
    c. An informal process with one decision maker
    d. An informal process with a group decision
    e. Other _____

12. Is there anything our company could do differently to make it easier for you to purchase our products?

Relationship Needs and Expectations

13. What are your expectations of your relationship with a supplier?

14. *Interviewer summarizes needs that have been identified throughout the interview and asks respondent to identify the three most important needs.*

Thank you for your time.

The training agenda for interviewers is relatively simple:

- Present customer overview
  —Types of customers/companies
  —Demographics
  —Target individuals (titles, department, responsibilities)
  —Typical customer relationship with your company
- Present interview guide
  —Hand out interview guide
- Discuss each question and relevant response(s)
  —Review typical anticipated responses
  —Discuss the rationale and intent for each question
  —Provide examples of a good response, a superficial response, and a response that indicates the customer did not understand the question
- Conduct interview role play
  —Simulate actual customer calls using a trainer or marketer to play the role of the customer
- Diagnose role plays
  —Seed the simulated interviews with questions from the customers and with responses that would require interviewers to respond and react—to explain questions, to provide examples to customers, and to rephrase questions
  —Did interviewers respond well to customer questions?
  —When interviewers asked one question, and customers an-

swered another, did the interviewers recognize and capture the data and reword the original question?

Step 5: Gather the Data

These interviews can be conducted face-to-face or over the telephone. Although in some cases you can get more information from customers in a face-to-face interview, I recommend using the telephone. It is usually far less expensive, it takes less of your time and the customer's time, and it allows closer management of interviews for consistency and depth. If you have effectively prepared during steps 1 through 4, actually gathering the data becomes a relatively easy exercise. Because this is a qualitative exercise, it is also to some degree a subjective one. As such, it is important to manage this data-gathering step closely.

First, you need to test the interview guide. Conduct this test with five to ten actual customer calls, assessing the customers' responses to the questions and determining whether you are getting the type of, and quantity of, information that you need. Depending on the results, you may need to adjust some questions in your interview guide before conducting the remaining interviews.

You ensure quality in the remaining data-gathering interviews by monitoring calls (either sitting next to the caller or monitoring silently using a different phone set) and reviewing interview documentation (the capture of customers' answers and verbatim comments by the interviewers).

Are you getting enough information from the questioning and the answers? Are you noticing trends? Are some lines of questioning more productive than others (for example, are there some questions that are consistently misunderstood by customers)? Are some not productive at all (not getting answered by customers)? Are there any serious gaps in the information? If you are using multiple interviewers, are there inconsistencies in the level of detail or type of information gathered?

Step 6: Conduct the Segmentation Analysis and Synthesis

After you have gone through the data-gathering step, you are typically inundated with massive volumes of data. It is now your job to sort through this information in order to consolidate, group, and synthesize it; determine its relevance and importance; and ultimately determine how it can be applied. Your objective here is to identify sets of customers who have similar sets of needs. To do this, you need to identify the needs that tend to occur together. These sets of needs that occur together are the basis upon which segments are defined. Once these sets of needs are identified, the customers that have them are determined and their demographics identified. Knowing these demographics allows you to apply these segment definitions back to the universe of customers.

To conduct this step, you need to take in a substantial amount of information and distill it into similar groups based on customer needs that occur together. Although there are other statistical techniques to do this, factor analysis is a technique that works well and one that I recommend for this analysis. Factor analysis is a statistical technique that examines the relationships of each variable in a series with every other variable to determine which variables are correlated. In this segmentation process, factor analysis is used to examine each need and to identify its relationship to every other need so that you can determine which needs occur together. Most statistics or market research textbooks provide a detailed explanation of factor analysis. Most marketers will want to get some research or statistical help with this analysis.

To conduct factor analysis, execute the following steps:

1. Code and input data into a statistical software package (the most frequently used packages are SPSS, SAS, and Minitab). Coding can be a difficult task because customers can state the same need many different ways. The need for a twenty-four-hour technical support 800 number may be stated by customers variously as, "I need the answer to a technical question when I have the question"; "I need an immediate response when I have technical problems"; "I need availability of technical staff"; or "I need technical support in the evening when I have equipment problems." In this step you need to interpret and consolidate the needs that have been stated by customers.

2. Conduct the factor analysis using the most important needs identified by customers. The computer will test each need against each other need to identify all the correlations and to determine which needs occur together. A sample factor analysis output is provided in Figure 6-5. In this output, 1.0 represents a perfect positive correlation, 0 represents no correlation, and −1.0 represents a perfect negative correlation. This sample indicates that the first six needs indicated in the left-hand column tend to occur together (there is a high correlation) in a set of customers ranking high in factor 1 and that the next four needs tend to occur together in a set of customers ranking high in factor 2. This allows you to identify customers whose needs correlate highly with certain factors, which subsequently can be defined as needs-based segments.

Figure 6-5. Sample factor analysis.

Needs	Factor 1	Factor 2	Factor 3
24-hour delivery	.85	.02	.56
Inventory management	.75	−.09	.23
Product customization	.76	.13	.01
Volume pricing	.51	.19	.32
Postpurchase support	.58	.23	−.12
Product training	.62	.11	−.23
Credit card acceptance	.11	.65	.18
Product literature	.21	.56	.29
Product catalog	−.17	.78	.30
24-hour technical 800 number	.33	.66	.40

Needs listed in bold correlated highly with factor 1.

3. Once you've identified the customers whose needs correlate to each factor, you can run frequency distributions to identify the characteristics/demographics of customers for each factor. Factor frequency distributions should be run for each relevant customer characteristic or demographic. Figure 6-6 illustrates the frequency distribution of customers for factor 1 using the characteristics of type of health care business, number of beds, rural or metropolitan location, and revenue size. Frequency distributions provide a profile of the different types and numbers of customers in certain factors.

For example, the frequency distribution in Figure 6.6 shows you that of the customers that have the set of needs identified with factor 1, 42 percent are hospitals, 18 percent are group practices, and 40 percent are nursing homes. This will allow you to determine the demographics of needs-based segments.

Figure 6-6. Frequency distribution for factor 1.

Type		Hospitals 42%	Group Practices 18%	Nursing Homes 40%
No. of Beds	< 100 0%	101–250 1%	251–400 9%	>400 90%
Rural/metro		Rural 6%	Metro 94%	
Size <$100MM 0%	$101–200MM 5%	$201–300MM 8%	$301–400MM 10%	>$400MM 77%

Figure 6-7. Needs-based segmentation documentation.

Segment	Number of Customers	Needs	Characteristics
Large hospitals and nursing homes	175	• 24-hour delivery • Inventory management • Product customization • Volume pricing • Postpurchase support • Product training	• Hospitals and nursing homes • More than 400 beds • Located in metro areas • More than $400MM in annual revenue

4. Use the frequency distributions to define segments and determine the identifying characteristics for each segment. As Figure 6-7 illustrates, these decisions are based on the customer characteristics reflected in the factor frequency distributions (Figure 6.6).

5. List segments and their important needs and the defining characteristics that allow a customer to be identified with a particular segment. Each segment should be explicitly and discretely defined by needs and characteristics. Segments should not be determined exclusively by a formula; the segments defined should make intuitive sense. Those closest to the customers should validate the segmentation model. Over the long term, account managers become the best sources of validation for the segment definitions.

Customer Segmentation Summary

The foregoing segmentation framework provides a list of customer needs and demographically identifiable needs-based customer segments (i.e., you can segment customers by their demographics). These segments are used to help define the customer modules presented in Chapter 7.

An in-depth understanding of customer needs is a vital part of account management. I recall a discussion some years ago with the management team of a Fortune 1000 company. We were discussing the launch of a new product. One of the executives stated, "Some of the people that buy this product will buy it in spite of the fact that they don't have a need for it. That's fine—it's good for business." This short-sighted perspective—it's good for business if people that don't have a need buy our product—is the antithesis of world-class account management. IAM is built on a foundation of satisfying real needs.

This foundation becomes apparent from a review of three of the IAM operating principles outlined in Chapter 2.

- Value for the customer is built on an in-depth understanding of the customer's needs (principle 6).
- Development of customer expertise leads to personalized delivery of value (principle 7).
- Building customer loyalty is an economic necessity (principle 10).

These principles tell us that long-term profitability with existing customers is driven by the relationship. Customer relationships depend on the delivery of value to customers. And the delivery of value is determined by an understanding of needs. Customer segmentation is intended to provide that rich understanding of customer needs that ultimately leads to a highly profitable business.

Customer Grading

Throughout this book you will find discussions and comments that deal with the inherent value of IAM. It provides business results like providing value to customers, building stronger relationships, providing higher employee satisfaction, and so forth. For many of these results there is empirical industry evidence, anecdotal evidence, and intuition to tell us that these are good investments. The business result that tends to overshadow the rest, however, is profitability. You can provide value, satisfy customers, and have happy employees, but if you do not do so profitably, you do not have a viable long-term business.

A unique aspect of IAM is the built-in ability to plan and manage profitability—at a total level, at an account manager/module level, and even at an individual customer level. This ability is provided by a principle that says investments are made in customers according to their worth. The investments are primarily customer contacts: face-to-face contacts, phone contacts, mail contacts.

Optimization in IAM is synonymous with the most effective distribution of resources. In this case, the most important and limited resource is the account manager and the customer contacts that he or she is able to make. If an account management team (one field account manager and one phone account manager) has a module of 500 accounts and can make 1,000 face-to-face and 5,000 phone contacts per year, what is the most effective use/distribution of those contacts to the 500 customers? The traditional mass marketing perspective might be to treat them all the same, so in this case they would each get 10 phone contacts and 2 face-to-face contacts annually. Using a retail perspective, we might just let them all know where we are and how they can reach us and take their incoming orders. The IAM perspective says that you proactively manage these relationships and that you distribute your available contacts to customers in a way that generates the best return. The tool used to help plan and manage the distribution of these contacts (i.e., the investment) is the customer grade.

There are two approaches to grading customers. The first is a group grading approach; the second is an individual grading approach.

In the first, group grading, accumulated factual knowledge about customers is used to estimate the likely worth of a customer. This accumulated knowledge consists of buying history, company demographics, and possibly survey responses and psychographics. (Psychographics are variables that measure psychological aspects of customer behavior, for example, opinions or beliefs.) Models of customers at various estimated worth levels are developed. Individual customer data are electronically matched to the various models, and an appropriate grade is assigned to the customer. Typically, in the group grading approach, grades are calculated by a marketing group and given to the account managers.

In the individual grading approach, each customer is "hand graded" by an account manager.

Now you might ask, which of these two approaches is preferable? At the risk of sounding like a consultant, it depends. That is one answer. The other answer is that using both approaches concurrently, sort of a hybrid approach, is best.

The individual grading approach works best in an environment where the module size is small (fewer than twenty-five accounts per account manager), where buying and investment decisions are based more on intangibles, or where account manager success is driven by hitting home runs. In this type of environment, the product is usually less tangible (e.g., professional services, consulting, outsourced services). When an account manager secures a commitment from a customer, it is typically a very strong commitment, it is typically a very large (in terms of revenue) commitment, it usually extends over a long period of time (greater than one year), and it is one where the buying decision is almost exclusively driven by the buyer's attitudes and the relationship between the account manager and the buyer. In these situations, the account manager's judgment is the only viable predictor of account worth—account characteristics are not usable as determinants of account worth.

The group grading approach works best in an environment where the module size is large (500-plus accounts per account manager), where buying and investment decisions are based on tangibles, and where account manager success is driven by hitting base hits and requires the account manager to close a large number of sales with a large number of customers throughout the course of a year.

A hybrid system of grading combining the individual and group grading approaches is the only effective grading system for moderate-size modules (26–499 accounts). Frequently, it is also the most effective grading system for large and small modules. In this hybrid system, a preliminary grade is calculated by marketing management using a group grading approach. The preliminary grade, with supporting information, is provided to account managers. Account managers then take ownership of the grade and, using corporate guidelines, modify the grades as they see fit according to their individual estimation of the worth of the customer. In all IAM environments, I recommend starting with a hybrid approach, changing to a different approach only if there are obstacles to using the hybrid approach or if it does not work effectively.

There are three factors to be considered in these types of grading systems: actual worth, potential incremental worth, and probability. You need to estimate each factor for each customer company.

• *Actual worth.* This is either a current revenue stream or a historical revenue stream. In the telecommunications industry, for example, this is the revenue stream from currently installed products. In other industries, such as business forms or automotive accessories, this is simply the annual revenue stream from purchases that the company has come to depend on.

• *Potential incremental worth.* This is the potential revenue stream from products that a customer has not purchased in the past but either has a need for or already purchases from another supplier. Potential incremental worth is usually represented by a specific dollar value. It tells us how much additional business we have some chance of doing with a customer.

• *Probability.* Probability indicates the likelihood (reflected as a percentage) of achieving the potential incremental worth of a customer. This factor is estimated by the account manager. The estimate is usually based on the customer's attitudes (for example, the customer may be averse to technology and, regardless of the previous purchase history or business needs, be unlikely to purchase an upgraded technological product), the account manager's and company's relationship with the customer, and the instincts of the account manager. Factors an account manager would evaluate to determine probability include:

- Individual relationships with customer decision makers
- Other supplier relationships with customer decision makers
- Cultural/chemistry fit
- Financial condition of customer
- Buying process of the customer

These three factors are not constants. They change over time. In fact, it is an objective of the account manager to improve these three areas: increase actual revenue, increase revenue potential (identify additional products a customer needs or is already purchasing from another supplier), and increase the probability of getting the incremental revenue. Increasing the probability may include building a good relationship over time, leading to increased likelihood of incremental revenue from an additional product or service that previously was supplied by a different vendor. Although the three areas are tracked separately, they are interrelated. They are also foundational for driving specific customer investment decisions and the behaviors of account managers.

Tracking these three factors separately provides depth of understanding of the grade and additionally provides an audit trail of change in a hybrid grading system. This audit trail can be used to track and evaluate the grade changes made by an account manager. The audit trail shows you specific grade changes made by the account manager and allows you to assess the account manager's judgment in changing the grade, helping you identify training needs of the account manager.

In some hybrid grading environments, the initial grade is set by marketing management and is based on actual worth and calculated potential incremental worth. The factor that is then managed by the account manager is the probability. This maintains the purity (or consistency across multiple accounts and multiple account managers) of the potential incremental worth, which is based on needs, and uses the probability factor to deal with the less tangible considerations that determine worth. In this hybrid grading approach, the account manager can consider any number of issues that might drive purchases without losing the integrity of calculations of the potential incremental worth.

Developing the Grading Model

The process of developing a grading model consists of seven steps, as follows. These steps are depicted graphically in Figure 6-8.

Figure 6-8. Developing the grading model.

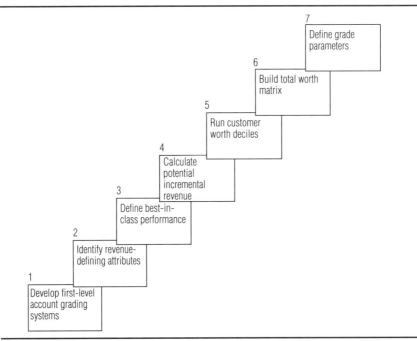

1. Develop first-level account grading segments.
2. Identify revenue-predicting attributes.
3. Define best-in-class performance.
4. Calculate potential incremental revenue.
5. Run customer worth deciles.
6. Build total worth matrix.
7. Define grade parameters.

Step 1: Develop First-Level Account Grading Segments

The best input to develop these grading segments is the customer segmentation just completed in the last section. (These grading segments are based on needs, and the customer segmentation provided a thorough listing of needs by segment.) The assumption is that customer needs are the best indicators of the types of products and the volume of products that customers purchase (and thus the amount that they spend). Define these segments so that the attributes that determine revenue volume are discrete within a segment.

Let's use an example to illustrate this. The hypothetical company ABC Supplies serves a number of health care markets. Two potential grading segments in this business are group practices, where the attribute that drives revenue volume is the number of doctors in the group, and hospitals, where the attribute that drives revenue volume is the number of beds. Grading segments are frequently industry-defined.

Step 2: *Identify Revenue-Predicting Attributes*

The intent of this step is to determine the strongest predictor variable of sales volume—the customer attribute that appears to be the most related to sales volume. This determination is made by looking at the degree of correlation between the variables and the sales volume. Correlation refers to the extent to which two variables are related to each other. The "coefficient of correlation" is a statistic that measures the degree of linear relationship between two variables. (Note: The scope of this book does not allow a detailed discussion of correlation. This subject is discussed in virtually all statistics books. All statistical packages and most spreadsheet programs also allow you to calculate this statistic.) The coefficient of correlation measures this relationship on a scale from -1.0 to 1.0 (see Figure 6-9), with -1.0 indicating a negative relationship, 1.0 indicating a perfect positive relationship and 0 (zero) indicating no linear relationship. A positive relationship exists between two variables when an increase in one is accompanied by an increase in the other. A negative relationship exists when an increase in one variable is accompanied by a decrease in the other. Figure 6-10 displays this relationship graphically. In the first example, there is a strong positive linear relationship between sales volume and number of beds. This indicates that, as the number of beds in a hospital increases, you can expect a related increase in sales volume. The second analysis indicates no linear relationship—you cannot expect an increase in sales volume as the number of staff cardiologists increases.

   This step allows us to determine which attribute or attributes to use to calculate incremental revenue in subsequent steps.

Step 3: *Define Best-in-Class Performance*

In our hospital example, best-in-class performance is determined by the highest sales dollar per bed. Conduct a decile analysis using the revenue-predicting attribute or attributes identified in the previous

Figure 6-9. Coefficient of correlation linear relationship scale.

Negative Linear Relationship	Positive Linear Relationship
-1.0 — $-.7$ — $-.3$ — 0 —	$.3$ — $.7$ — 1.0

Figure 6-10. Correlation analysis example—hospital segment.

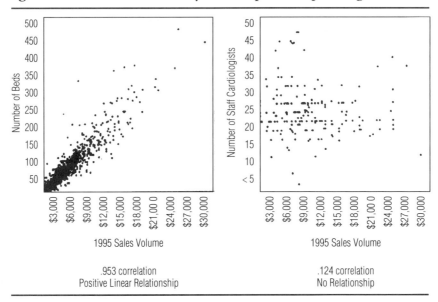

.953 correlation
Positive Linear Relationship

.124 correlation
No Relationship

step. Best-in-class performance is usually defined as the top decile (or top 10 percent) of customers in sales dollars per defining attribute (see Figure 6-11). In this example, with 1,070 customers in the hospital grading segment, the top decile includes the top 107 customers in average sales per bed. The combination of their sales volume and number of beds sets best-in-class performance at $49 per bed for the hospital market.

Step 4: Calculate Potential Incremental Revenue

If best-in-class performance is defined as $49, total potential revenue across all accounts in the hospital segment is $49 per hospital bed.

Figure 6-11. Best-in-class decile analysis—hospital segment.

Decile	Number of Customers/Hospitals	Total Annual Sales	Average Annual Sales	Average Number of Beds	Sales $ per Bed
1	107	$2,282,000	$21,330	433	$49
2	107	$1,852,600	$17,064	412	$41
3	107	$1,460,480	$13,652	391	$34
4	107	$1,168,348	$10,922	370	$29
5	107	$934,708	$8,738	349	$25
6	107	$747,767	$6,991	328	$21
7	107	$598,214	$5,593	307	$18
8	107	$478,572	$4,475	286	$15
9	107	$382,858	$3,580	265	$13
10	107	$306,287	$2,864	244	$11

For a hospital with 400 beds with annual sales of $11,300, incremental worth would be as follows:

400	×	$49	=	$19,600
(total hospital beds)		(best-in-class performance)		(total potential)

$19,600	−	$11,300	=	$8,300
(total potential)		(actual revenue)		(potential incremental revenue)

Steps 2 through 4 are executed at a segment level. For each segment, identify the attributes that are related to sales volume, define best-in-class performance, and calculate potential incremental revenue. These steps need to be completed for each segment before beginning step 5—running customer worth deciles.

Step 5: Run Customer Worth Deciles

Run a decile analysis of all segments based on annual sales to the customers, and then run a separate decile analysis based on potential incremental sales to customers. Let's assume that in our ABC Supplies example there are two additional segments (in addition to the hospital segment) that will be included as you define customer grades—a group medical practices segment and a nursing home segment. First, these three segments are combined in one decile analysis for actual worth (average annual sales), as shown in Figure 6-12. Run a similar decile analysis for potential incremental worth (see Figure 6-13).

Figure 6-12. Actual worth (annual sales) decile analysis.

Decile	Number of Customers	Total Annual Sales	Average Annual Sales
1	322	$8,105,100	$25,171
2	322	$5,989,220	$18,600
3	322	$3,100,500	$9,629
4	322	$1,840,000	$5,714
5	322	$811,120	$2,519
6	322	$490,390	$1,523
7	322	$325,100	$1,009
8	322	$299,440	$930
9	322	$162,180	$504
10	322	$27,060	$84

Figure 6-13. Potential incremental worth (annual sales) decile analysis.

Decile	Number of Customers	Total Annual Sales	Average Annual Sales
1	322	$9,115,550	$28,309
2	322	$7,333,000	$22,773
3	322	$4,545,050	$14,115
4	322	$3,308,250	$10,274
5	322	$2,999,500	$9,315
6	322	$2,304,100	$7,156
7	322	$1,999,310	$6,209
8	322	$1,760,300	$5,467
9	322	$1,332,900	$4,139
10	322	$880,200	$2,734

Step 6: Build Total Worth Matrix

The total worth matrix (see sample in Figure 6-14) provides a profile of the customer base relative to both actual worth and potential incremental worth. Determine the values of the ranges used on both axes from the deciles run in the previous step. You are looking for a reasonable distribution of accounts in the matrix. In the example provided (Figure 6-14), range parameters for actual worth are set so that accounts are distributed across five levels, in the following percentages: 10, 15, 25, 30, and 20. Actual worth (historical sales) typically follows Pareto's principle, with 20 percent of accounts providing 80 percent of the sales. Potential incremental worth is less predictable, and a distribution usually places a large percentage of accounts at the high end and very few at the low end. The objective with potential incremental worth is also to achieve a distribution of accounts across levels. However, because the potential worth is typically higher than actual worth (it is simply easier to identify potential than it is to realize it), the number of accounts will be skewed toward the upper

Figure 6-14. Total worth matrix.

Potential Incremental Worth					
<$3,000	33	15	3	0	0
$3,000-6,999	54	75	114	25	0
$7,000-9,999	69	90	319	376	356
$10,000-22,999	96	123	223	349	280
>$23,000	33	178	126	235	48
	>$25,000	$15,000 -24,999	$3,000 -14,999	$1,000 -2,999	<$1,000
	10%	15%	25%	30%	20%

3,220 customers   Actual Worth — Historical Sales ranges. In the example in Figure 6-14, accounts are distributed in the potential incremental worth ranges, from highest to lowest, in the following percentages: 19, 33, 38, 8, 2. In this matrix, the bottom left-hand corner represents the best customers (highest actual and highest incremental worth), and the upper right-hand corner represents the worst, least-valued customers (lowest actual worth and lowest incremental worth). It is now time to use this matrix to define grades.

Step 7: Define Grade Parameters

In most environments, a five-level grading model is sufficient, providing enough levels to vary the contact plan substantially and to guide the investment levels in customers. To define grade parameters, start with your best customers (the lower left corner of the total worth matrix) and work diagonally upward and to the right, assigning grade levels from AA through D.

Use the following distribution model as a guide, giving more weight to actual sales (than to potential) and using your judgment to assign grade levels:

AA	5% of accounts
A	15% of accounts
B	25% of accounts
C	25% of accounts
D	30% of accounts

The distribution model is offered as a guide. Most actual grading models will not follow this distribution exactly. You don't want to make a different level of investment in two different customers with very similar worth simply because the model indicated that you already had your full quota of AA customers. In the example provided in Figure 6-15, grading parameters are defined as follows:

Figure 6-15. Total worth matrix (with grading parameters).

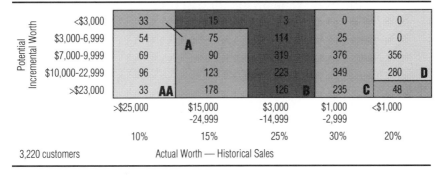

AA Customers	Actual worth > $25,000 and Potential incremental worth $3,000–$23,000+ This grade is assigned to 252 customers, or 7.8%
A Customers	Actual worth > $25,000 and Potential incremental worth < $3,000 or Actual worth $15,000–$24,999 and Potential incremental worth $3,000–$23,000+ This grade is assigned to 499 customers, or 15.5%
B Customers	Actual worth $15,000–$24,999 and Potential incremental worth < $3,000 or Actual worth $3,000–$14,999 This grade is assigned to 800 customers, or 24.8%
C Customers	Actual worth $1,000–$2,999 or Actual worth < $1,000 and Potential incremental worth > $23,000 This grade is assigned to 1,033 customers, or 32%
D Customers	Actual worth < $1,000 and Potential incremental worth $0–$22,999 This grade is assigned to 635 customers, or 19.8%

This grading model provides a sound, logical framework for making customer investment decisions. In a hybrid grading approach, an organization uses this framework to blend a historical and potential sales perspective when evaluating customer worth. Additionally, the account manager's closeness to and knowledge of the customer should play a major role in determining the probability of achieving the potential in that customer.

Summary

Segmentation and grading have created a knowledge base with which to drive customer decisions regarding how to add value, how to invest and how much to invest, and, most important, how to treat each customer uniquely. This knowledge is a foundation element for defining the IAM process (Chapter 10), contact planning (Chapter 11), and account manager development (Chapter 12).

Note

1. John Berrigan and Carl Finkbeiner, *Segmentation Marketing* (New York: Harper Business, 1992).

7

Design and Construction of IAM Modules

The design of customer modules is a critical and complex component in the development of an integrated account management program. In IAM programs, *module* takes on the same significance as *territory* has in field sales programs. A module is the set of customers owned by an account manager or by an account management team. In traditional field sales organizations, territories are generally defined by geography and size. In IAM programs, modules are defined by leverage and capacity.

Although leverage and capacity are two important elements in IAM module design, the limitations inherent in working these two issues have been reduced. From an inside account manager's perspective, the historical limitations of territory design have been diminished, if not eliminated, by the increased level of contact achieved by inside account managers and by the elimination of geographical boundaries. Because of the detailed knowledge inside account managers have of their accounts, they can make customers feel as though they are calling them from across the street, when in reality they may be calling from across the country. From an account management team perspective (teams consist of at least one outside field account manager and at least one inside account manager), the geographical limitations have been reduced, but not completely eliminated. Because of the work continuity between inside and outside account managers in an IAM team, field account managers can support a significantly larger module—both in terms of number of accounts and geographic size—than they could by operating independently.

Leverage

In the traditional field sales model, efficiency is the lever for increasing sales. If accounts are geographically close, a rep can plan his or her calling activity in a way that increases face-to-face time (by reducing travel time) or increases the number of sales calls in a given time period. Although geography is still a meaningful leverage point, IAM uses the more powerful lever of customer business knowledge to drive value to the customer. Customers care more about an account manager's detailed knowledge of their needs and those of similar companies than they do about the account manager's proximity. For the customer, the value comes as much from the account manager's knowledge of similar businesses as it does from knowledge of the customer's own. The information and experience the account manager has gained in other accounts is usually highly transferable to similar businesses.

The opportunity here is to define and build modules that provide enough consistency across account types so that knowledge of customer business needs and product applications can be leveraged to provide significant customer value.

Capacity

As mentioned earlier, the availability and acceptability of alternative media choices has had a significant impact on communications with customers. In effect, when you make valued contacts using media such as mail, fax, or e-mail, you are increasing your capacity to manage accounts and are doing so in an economically effective way. These media will never take the place of face-to-face or telephone contacts because of the lower degree of interaction, but they are tools that augment an account manager's contact plan, and do so in a way that is exponentially less expensive than a field or phone contact.

Obviously, the most limited resource is the account manager (field or inside), so the number of available account manager contacts is the primary input when determining the optimal module size. Using account management capacity as a reality check, from both a numbers perspective and an economic perspective, is an essential step in module design. As Figure 7-1 illustrates, as average contacts per day increase, capacity, represented by total annual contacts, also increases.

Let's look at how capacity and leverage are considered in the design of a module. The two questions being answered in module design are (1) What is the optimal number of accounts that can be supported by the desired level of customer coverage and existing account manager capacity? and (2) Which accounts and types of accounts should be grouped together to allow account managers to leverage knowledge and relationships?

Figure 7-1. Account management capacity.

Number of Days in Year	Average Vacation Days	Holidays	Administrative and Training Days	Planning Time/Days (@ 2 hrs/week)	Total Calling Days	Average Contacts per Day	Total Annual Contacts
260	10	10	15	12	213	18	3,834
						19	4,047
						20	4,260
						21	4,473
						22	4,686
						23	4,899
						24	5,112
						25	5,325
						26	5,538
						27	5,751
						28	5,964
						29	6,177
						30	6,390
						31	6,630
						32	6,816
						33	7,029
						34	7,242
						35	7,455
						36	7,668
						37	7,881
						38	8,094
						39	8,307
						40	8,520

Module Design Objectives

The objectives of module design are as follows:

1. *Develop customer expertise.* In late 1995 a customer loyalty study was conducted for Hallmark Building Supplies, a building supplies distributor in Milwaukee, Wisconsin. Prior to this study there was a general feeling among Hallmark management and marketing staff that customer expertise was of some value, and this study confirmed that feeling and highlighted, in a quantitative manner, the importance and impact of customer expertise.

Customers were grouped into three loyalty segments according to their repurchase intentions (likely to continue buying from Hallmark Building Supplies and likely to increase purchases), willingness to refer (to friends and associates), and overall satisfaction level. The degrees of loyalty were defined and evaluated:

- *Secure:* The best, most loyal customers.
- *Complacent:* Some degree of loyalty, but not secure.
- *At-risk:* Some indication that these customers do not have a strong degree of loyalty; there is some risk that these customers will be successfully targeted by competition.

Figure 7-2 shows a decrease in satisfaction levels for most loyal to least loyal customers (you would expect to see this because loyalty is defined in part by the satisfaction level). It also shows a corresponding decrease in customers' perception of knowledge of their business: At the most loyal level, 74 percent are very satisfied with Hallmark's knowledge of their business; at the least loyal level, only 31 percent are very satisfied with Hallmark's knowledge of their business.

What Hallmark found was a high correlation between the degree of loyalty customers conveyed and demonstrated and the customers'

Figure 7-2. Knowledge and understanding of business and account/customer loyalty analysis.

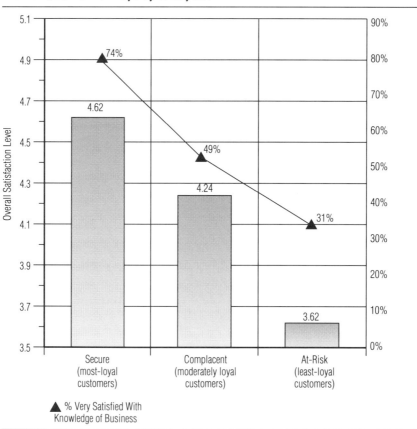

perception of Hallmark Building Supplies' knowledge of their business. (See Figure 7-2). This means that the more you understand a customer's business, the more likely you are to engender loyalty in that customer. The logic here is relatively simple: The more you know about your customer's business, the more likely you are to have a good understanding of the customer's needs. As your understanding of the customer's needs increases, your ability to provide value in contacts increases, and your ability to recommend products and services that provide value increases. As your ability to provide value increases, credibility and trust in the relationship increase. Credibility and trust, combined with an increased ability to recommend the right products, lead to higher close ratios, more sales, increased loyalty, and increased lifetime value of customers.

Grouping accounts with similar needs into modules increases the ability of an account manager to develop specialized expertise at fulfilling the needs within that module.

2. *Support P&L accountability at the account manager module level.* In Chapter 2 we talked about how "account managers act as small business owners." Module design needs to support and drive that accountability. This means that the number of accounts and the sales potential of a module should be enough to support the anticipated sales and marketing expenses incurred by account managers or account management teams.

3. *Drive a high degree of account manager productivity.* If you look at a capacity model (see, for example, Figure 7-1), you will see a wide range of productivity, as reflected in the number of contacts per day. Driving high productivity through module design becomes a matter of working the numbers. Once you determine a desired and reasonable number of contacts per day for both field and inside account managers (the assumption here is that desired and reasonable levels have to coexist), you can calculate the number of contacts per year. The number of available contacts per year divided by the average number of contacts per customer gives a rough approximation of the number of accounts in a module. However, in most environments this rough approximation will be too low. An estimate 10 to 20 percent higher provides room to account for customer "churn" (defection) and account manager efforts to achieve higher-than-expected productivity.

4. *Support the development of customer and industry relationships.* In every industry and in every well-constructed customer module there are influential companies and individuals. When relationships with these companies and individuals are nurtured, there is an opportunity to enhance these relationships, providing additional value and

gaining additional credibility. The additional credibility comes from association with influential organizations; the value comes from applying industry knowledge gained from those relationships.

5. *Provide a foundation for significant leverage by grouping the right accounts.* It is important to look at all of the leverage points within a module. The more you can build leverage into the module design, the more you can increase account management effectiveness and increase the probability of success for individual account managers. Leverage points include industry knowledge, business results in the industry, tangible examples of customer impact through use of your products, industry relationships, product application expertise, competitive (or complementary) product knowledge, specific sales campaigns and offers, and even the aforementioned geographical proximity. The question that needs to be asked here is, How can accounts be grouped in a way that narrows the field to achieve depth within a module—depth of understanding, depth of relationships, and so on?

Designing Modules

The design process for customer modules consist of five steps, as shown in Figure 7-3:

1. Determine module size
2. Determine customer segment mix(es)
3. Define account grade distribution
4. Build and test modules
5. Assign modules to account managers

Figure 7-3. Module design.

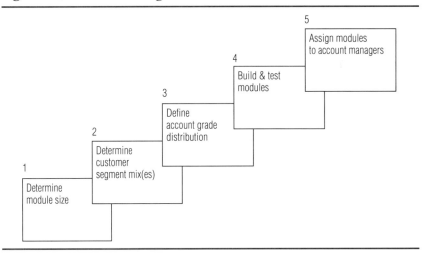

Step 1: Determine Module Size

This is a critical step in building an IAM capability. If you build customer modules too large (that is, with too many accounts assigned to an account manager), your coverage to those customers is reduced, making it difficult for account managers to build relationships with individual customers. Some customers invariably don't get the attention they need and their worth warrants, leaving them vulnerable to competition.

If you build customer modules too small (with not enough accounts assigned to an account manager), you are not effectively using your account manager resources. The account manager expense is usually the largest expense in an IAM program. Considering account manager cost a fixed expense, if you increase the number of accounts that an account manager handles, you will get a corresponding improvement in profitability. An optimal module size balances these issues of profitability and coverage.

Determine the optimal module size as follows:

1. Define the average anticipated capacity of an account manager. Figure 7-1 gives you a good frame of reference for this average anticipated capacity. A reasonably good productivity level for inside account managers is 30 contacts per day, and for outside account managers, 5 contacts per day. Let's use an inside account manager to illustrate. At 30 contacts per day, you have an anticipated capacity of 6,390 contacts per year.

2. Calculate the anticipated average annual customer revenue. After grading customers, you have an annual actual customer worth and a potential incremental customer worth. Using the actual and potential worth and an estimate of the likelihood of achieving the potential worth (15 percent in the calculation below) from the grading exercise in Chapter 6 (Figures 6-12 and 6-13), calculate anticipated average annual customer revenue as follows:

$21,150,110 +	($35,578,160 ×	15%)	=	$26,486,834
(Total	(Total	(Estimated		(Anticipated
Actual	Potential	Probability)		Total
Worth)	Incremental			Annual
	Worth)			Revenue)

$26,486,934	÷	3,220	=	$8,226
(Anticipated		(Total		(Anticipated
Total		Number		Average
Annual		of		Annual
Revenue)		Customers)		Revenue)

3. Determine the average contact cost. At a fully burdened cost of approximately $89,000 for an inside account manager and assuming the 6,390 contacts, the average contact cost is approximately $14 per contact.

4. Use an average customer coverage plan to determine an average contact investment per customer. If the customer coverage estimates a contact level of 24 times per year (twice per month), the average investment per customer is $336.

5. Do a reasonableness check against the average customer revenue. At $336, the average customer contact investment is approximately 4 percent of revenue.

6. Using anticipated total annual revenue as a base, determine the percentage of total actual worth and the percentage of total potential incremental worth. $21,150,110 is approximately 80 percent of $26,486,834, so total actual worth is 80 percent of anticipated annual revenue. Total potential incremental worth, $35,578,160, multiplied by 15 percent (estimated probability) is $5,336,724. $5,336,724 is approximately 20 percent of $26,486,834, so total potential incremental worth is 20 percent of anticipated annual revenue.

7. Calculate average module size by dividing the account manager capacity (6,390 contacts) by the average customer contact level (24 contacts per year). The average module size in this example is 266 accounts. In the design of modules, a module size of plus or minus 10 percent of the average is an acceptable range, and will be used in the example here. At 266 accounts and at an anticipated average revenue of $8,226, the revenue size of a module is $2,188,116, with approximately 20 percent ($437,623) of this coming from potential incremental worth (see step 6) and the remainder, $1,750,493 coming from actual worth.

Step 2: Determine Customer Segment Mix(es)

In an ideal situation, you would want to build a module for an account manager that consists of a set of accounts (in our example, 266 accounts) that have exactly the same needs. The needs-based segmentation that has been completed in Chapter 6 is the primary input here. The size of the segments defined will most likely not fit the module size defined. By assessing the needs, you can determine which segments have at least some match in needs and, as you need to place more than one segment in a module, can put segments together that have some similar needs. A balancing factor that you need to consider in this step if field account managers are part of your IAM program is geography. Even though I recommend treating geography as a subordinate factor to customer needs, it obviously can have a significant impact on field account manager leverage and productivity. Therefore, you want to build modules with accounts that have a common set of needs, and if field contacts are part of your contact mix, build modules with accounts that are geographically close to one another. The needs match will allow account managers to build expertise in supporting a focused set of customer needs that are segmented in their modules; the geographic match will provide leverage and increase productivity of field account managers.

Step 3: Determine Account Grade Distribution

In most organizations, you will want to build modules of equitable size—modules that give each account manager an equal opportunity to achieve revenue goals and usually a corresponding equal compensation opportunity. A reference to grade parameters (as defined in Chapter 6) provides a reasonable starting point for grade distribution within modules. In the example in Chapter 6, the percentage distribution of grades across all customers was AA, 7.8; A, 15.5; B, 24.8; C, 32; D, 19.8. Modules of perfectly equitable size and mix would each have 266 accounts with the same distribution of grades as the overall customer base.

Step 4: Build and Test Modules

Because you are trying to balance an optimal module size with a desired segment mix and with a desired grade mix, there are almost always trade-offs that you need to make. The odds that these three components will fit exactly together is like picking puzzle pieces at random out of a 500-piece puzzle box and finding that they all fit together. The size of modules may not match segment sizes well. In the segment example in Chapter 6, the large hospital and nursing home segment contained 175 accounts. If you were to put these all into one module, you would need another segment of 91 accounts to fill the module. However, it is likely that this segment (large hospitals and nursing homes) consists mostly of AA and A accounts. So, putting all accounts from this segment into one module would create a grading imbalance in that module. In fact, in this example over 66 percent of accounts would be AA and A accounts.

Defining modules requires good judgment and generally some trial and error. Start by breaking up segments that are too large or that inherently have an unbalanced mix of high- or low-graded accounts. The size of these segment pieces as a percentage of a module should not exceed the overall grade mix. For example, if the large hospitals and nursing homes segment has 175 accounts that are all AA or A customers, you would break the segment into at least three pieces. (Because AA and A accounts represent 23.3 percent of the total customer base, they should also constitute approximately 23 percent of the module. That means that each module would have approximately 61 AA and A accounts. So the 175 total segment accounts would be spread over three modules. Assume that you will have at least two segments in each module; however, this may vary significantly depending on the diversity or lack of diversity in your customer base.

After each module-building trial, check for reasonableness:

- Calculate the total actual worth in each module. Is the total actual worth of each module reasonably close (within 10–15 percent) to the average actual worth of a module calculated in the first step, "Determine Module Size" ($1,750,493)?
- Calculate the total potential incremental worth in each module. Is the total potential incremental worth of each module reasonably close (within 15–20 percent) to the average potential incremental worth of an average module calculated in step 1 ($437,623)?
- Calculate the total revenue (both actual and potential incremental) in each module. Is the total revenue in each module reasonably close (within 10 percent) to the average module revenue calculated in step 1 ($2,188,116)?
- Evaluate segment distribution within each module. Do any modules have only one segment? Do any modules have more than four segments? Are there any modules where the mix of segments and corresponding needs doesn't intuitively feel right?
- Evaluate grade distribution within each module. Do any modules have a grade distribution that is significantly different from the overall?
- Evaluate account size of modules. Are there any modules either 20 percent larger or 20 percent smaller than the defined module size? Some variation of module size can be used to offset low or high worth in a module.

Step 5: Assign Modules to Account Managers

After modules are effectively designed and developed, this is a relatively easy step. The primary consideration is an account manager's previous knowledge and/or fit (fit can be determined by the account manager's industry experience or specific skills that might support needs in a particular segment) within the segments that make up each module.

These steps represent an effective model for developing modules in an IAM environment that has solo (inside or field) account managers owning account relationships. In a sales team environment, this module design approach is effective with some minor variation. In a sales team environment with inside and field account managers, one inside account manager is usually teamed with three to five field account managers. In that environment, modules are defined at the field level, and the inside account manager's module is the sum of the modules of the field account managers on his or her team.

Summary

Effective module design has a significant impact on account managers and, consequently, on customers. Coverage, capacity, leverage, value to customers, and account manager productivity are all aspects of IAM that can be affected by the module design. Building solid modules provides a good foundation for the development work that follows.

8

Profiling and Selecting the IAM Team

Q: What do you want, a marketer or a salesperson?
A: Yes.

Mark Peck

Don't try to teach a pig to sing. It's frustrating for the teacher, and it annoys the pig.

Bill Younger

As is the case in many companies, it was easy for the marketers at Company A to get focused on building the technical aspects of their account management system. They invested heavily (in both time and dollars) in defining the process, designing and developing software, building a grading model, creating the communications with customers, and defining the integration between the field account managers and the inside (phone) account managers. Unfortunately, also like many organizations, Company A underinvested in the selection process.

Company A already had a field sales organization, but in addition it needed to hire two inside account managers to work in sales teams with the field people. Following a path that many companies do, Company A decided to hire these inside people based on what the company saw as relevant experience. One of the new inside account manager hires, Fred, was a field sales veteran with more than twenty years' experience; the other, Jane, was a candidate with about three years of telemarketing experience, some consumer and some business-to-business.

On the surface, these both seem like reasonable hiring decisions. Let's look at how they played out.

Fred had what appeared to be wonderfully relevant field experience. In his twenty-odd years in the field, he was always an average performer. You could almost see the gears working the rationale for hiring him: Fred was an average performer in the field. . . . working as a phone rep is a little bit easier; . . . therefore, he should turn out to be a very good inside account manager.

After a couple of weeks on the job, this rationale proved to be flawed. To begin with, Fred's productivity was absolutely horrendous. The initial productivity objective included fifteen to twenty contacts per day with decision makers (which, incidentally, in most industries is quite low). Fred was contacting only three decision makers per day. In addition, an assessment of the data that he captured and put in the database identified another problem: Customer needs were not being entered in the database.

This led Fred's supervisor to monitor his calls. She discovered that customer needs were not being entered in the database because Fred was not asking customers questions about their needs. Not surprisingly, his discussions did not seem consistent with Company A's message, customers did not seem to value his calls, and he was attempting to close business prematurely.

Jane, the other inside account manager, was a very different story, also not a happy one. Her productivity numbers looked okay, and she captured good information in the database about her customers. The concerns developed when her calls were monitored and her sales results reviewed. Jane's calls sounded like she was reading a script even when she wasn't. She gave the impression that she was reading her script, then going for a predefined close—not dealing with any customer objections—and then quickly moving on to the next call.

Not a pretty picture, is it? What went wrong here? To help understand the problem, let's take a look at the "TEC" model developed by MPR, a Chicago-based worldwide consulting firm specializing in productivity improvement through the selection of talented personnel for all positions within an organization. In this model, TEC stands for the three factors/criteria that are used in most selection and hiring situations:

T = Talent:	The critical skills and behaviors necessary for success on the job.
E = Experience and Education:	The minimum acceptable levels necessary to perform the job, and the desired levels.

C = Cultural Requirements: The environment within a given company, including management styles and expectations. The "C" in TEC can also stand for "Chemistry"; that is, is there the right "chemistry" between the potential account manager and your firm? Is there likely to be a good "fit."

The stories of Fred and Jane illustrate what is frequently done in many, if not most, hiring decisions: the only factor used to make the decision is experience. But the TEC model tells us that there are two additional factors that need to be taken into account when making a hiring decision. One only need look at how these factors blend together to see how important they are.

What happens when you hire a "tEc" (low talent, high experience, low chemistry)? This is a candidate who has no talent and does not fit well culturally but has a lot of experience doing what he or she does. These people don't last long, and there is very little, if any, return on hiring investment. Unfortunately, if a résumé is the primary tool used in the selection process, the likelihood of hiring this candidate is high.

What happens to a "tEC" (low talent, high experience, high chemistry)? When I ask this question in seminars, I invariably get at least one person who responds, "They get promoted." Think about that as a business model: these are employees with no talent who have been doing the job for a long time and are a good fit in their respective companies. Figure 8-1 illustrates how permutations of these three factors affect performance.

Experience is easy to specify, to quantify, and to test for. You can see it on a résumé. Identifying chemistry, on the other hand, requires a more intuitive skill and at the very least requires a candidate to meet with members of the sales and marketing teams and with management. Talent is also difficult to identify. Talent is defined as the skills and behaviors that get the job done. You can't see talent on a résumé, and talent is not necessarily easy to assess in an interview. Some people intuitively do well at recognizing talent. But the question is, Do you want to base the success of your program on an intuitive and non-replicatable process?

Another problem is that there is an aversion in some organizations to investing a significant amount of time in the hiring process. Edward R. Ryan, the founder of MPR and an internationally known

Figure 8-1. Impact of talent, experience, and chemistry on performance.

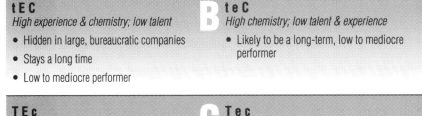

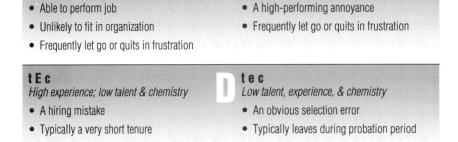

TEC
High talent, experience, & chemistry
• Star performer

TeC
High talent & chemistry; low experience
• Potential to be star performer
• Likely to be a long-term valuable employee

tEC
High experience & chemistry; low talent
• Hidden in large, bureaucratic companies
• Stays a long time
• Low to mediocre performer

teC
High chemistry; low talent & experience
• Likely to be a long-term, low to mediocre performer

TEc
High talent & experience; low chemistry
• Able to perform job
• Unlikely to fit in organization
• Frequently let go or quits in frustration

Tec
High talent; low experience & chemistry
• A high-performing annoyance
• Frequently let go or quits in frustration

tEc
High experience; low talent & chemistry
• A hiring mistake
• Typically a very short tenure

tec
Low talent, experience, & chemistry
• An obvious selection error
• Typically leaves during probation period

expert in the area of recruitment, selection, and management of talented personnel, has found that the root of most turnover problems in companies is taking shortcuts in the hiring process. "Most managers simply don't like hiring, especially the interviewing," he says. "It often interrupts their busy schedule, so they keep it short. And because they're in a hurry to fill a position, they have a tendency not to take a hard look at negative information—especially if they have already spent hours with a potential candidate. They don't want to hear any bad news because that means they have to go back and start the hiring process all over again. So they rationalize and hire someone who isn't going to get the job done." In contrast, Ryan says, the Japanese take their time; they spend an average of 150 hours interviewing a potential manager before they hire.

The four levels of performance indicated in Figure 8.1 can be both enlightening and deceiving. In each of the four levels, A through D, a distinct performance outcome can be anticipated. The A level represents the best candidates and over the long term the highest performers in the position. B-level candidates typically have a long tenure and at best become only mediocre performers. C-level candidates perform well for a period of time, sometimes inconsistently, but are usually not long-term employees. Candidates at the D level who make it through the screening process (if the screening process is effective, they usually don't get through) are usually not around long either.

Surprisingly, the biggest risk in many organizations and in many positions is hiring a large number of B-level candidates. Although their tenure is usually short, C-level candidates are productive in that time frame. D-level candidates usually leave the position after a short time, either not making it through a probationary period or self-qualifying (deciding the position is not a fit for them) once they understand the position in detail. The reason B-level candidates are the biggest risk is that they stay in the position a long time, frequently at a borderline performance level.

Recently I had a conversation with a consultant (who was helping clients set up call centers) that bore out these concerns regarding the level of investment in the selection process. She said she was "appalled" that anyone would consider spending more than a half hour interviewing a candidate for a call center rep position. There are a set of reasons, both rational and irrational, for logic like hers. Here are some common myths and excuses people give for not investing time and resources in the hiring process:

- *Employee turnover is good; it revitalizes the work force.* To some degree, turnover *can* be good. But this is usually the case only under specific circumstances and in isolated cases, such as when an employee is not productive or is ready to move on. Most customers see employee turnover as a negative; they say that one of their most annoying tasks is having to train a new sales rep. So it should not be surprising that there is often a strong correlation between high employee turnover and high customer turnover.

- *High turnover is inevitable.* It doesn't have to be. If you hire the right people, they will have not only the skills but also the motivation and behaviors to enjoy working for your company and performing the tasks required in the position. Additionally, they will be strong producers.

- *Experience is the best indicator of future performance.* Experience is not a negative; it can, however, be deceiving. There are a lot of people in a lot of positions who have many years of experience but who have never done their job particularly well. It is difficult to look at a potential employee's experience and map it to a position. Just look at organizational titles. What means one thing in one organization can mean something totally different in another, depending on the company's industry, marketplace, and set of customer relationships. A given employee may or may not have been doing well, but it is difficult to know what factors will lead to success in a new environment. The key in hiring is getting to a candidate's behaviors; this will enable you to understand the root causes of both problems and successes.

• *I can't afford to invest* that *much time selecting and hiring a candidate.* You can't afford not to. These account managers have the most impact on the customer relationships. The success of account management is built upon these relationships and the resulting customer loyalty. Having the wrong people in the position or accepting high turnover are strategies for both damaging customer relationships and preventing sales.

• *"Hire easily, fire easily" is an acceptable solution.* Obviously not. High turnover in an organization leads to a high degree of employee discomfort. Employees see people coming and going and wonder, "What's wrong?" And worse, "Will I be next?" In the long run your choice comes down to this: you can either invest a little bit of time in a lot of candidates or a lot of time in a few candidates. Most experts estimate that the cost of firing a bad employee and hiring and training a new one can run as high as 200 percent of the fired employee's salary, maybe more. A recruiting process that seems expensive at the front end can in fact be more cost-effective over the long haul.

• *Field sales is good training experience for account managers.* I have rarely seen it work well to take someone from the field and put him or her on the phone. Additionally, I have seen a number of unsuccessful attempts to take successful "salespeople" and turn them into field account managers. Although these people can be successful in an account management role, this experience is not a guarantee. Being a field sales rep means having lots of face-to-face contact with customers. Period. The fact that you are in the face-to-face environment only says that you have experience working face-to-face. Being an account manager is a much different job. It requires selling and servicing accounts in a complex selling environment, working under a tight account management productivity model, and implementing modules that include a large number of accounts.

Everything else in an account management program can be right, but if the appropriate people have not been hired as account managers, the program is doomed to failure. These account managers are the business owners that control the company's contact with its customers. Astute personnel selection and performance appraisal is critical to success, because the successful account manager needs to have a certain combination of behavioral traits and selling skills. What follows are descriptions of the job requirements of the account manager and a set of interviewing tools that allow you to quantify the desired behavioral traits and assess the desired sales skills of potential account managers.

The Account Manager: A Salesperson Who Thinks Like a Marketer

Usually salespeople and marketing people are, as the cliché goes, horses of a different color. The typical salesperson is used to relating to customers. He is most comfortable with transaction-type relationships and is focused on the short term, that is, closing business *today.* If he does look at the relative worth of a customer, he tends to do it intuitively rather than analytically.

The marketer, on the other hand, steps back from day-to-day transactions to take a broader view. In assessing the marketplace, she is used to thinking analytically and holistically. She uses analytical tools to measure the relative worth of customers. Her emphasis is on positioning products and services, not just closing sales.

In the new integrated account management paradigm, someone with a predominantly sales orientation may fail because he has difficulty developing account plan modules and perhaps even planning each day effectively. Similarly, someone with a predominantly marketing orientation may fail because she has difficulty relating to customers. She may not be productive enough on a day-to-day basis and may even be afraid to ask for the order.

In this paradigm, then, the successful account manager needs to be a blend of these two types: a salesperson who thinks like a marketer. This idea of a "person for all seasons" is not a new one, but the IAM environment has brought this need into high relief.

As you look over the following tasks of the account manager, keep in mind the definition of IAM: "a system of marketing and selling that is driven out of a proactive, planful, and personal approach to managing mutually beneficial individual customer relationships." In other words, IAM designates the account manager as the owner of customer relationships, specifies a planned approach, and encompasses all contacts with the customer. The account manager must

- Develop a long-term plan for each module (set of accounts):
  —How to achieve sales goals
  —How to work within a productivity model

—How to add value to customers
—How to achieve sufficient customer coverage within a module
—How to increase the loyalty of customers
• Develop account plans for individual accounts within a module:
—Assess the business situation
—Determine the customer needs
—Apply products and services to address needs
—Determine how to engage with each customer to develop a relationship
• Internalize these plans and apply them to daily activities:
—Plan and monitor weekly and monthly activity
—Leverage different resources in the organization to provide value to accounts (e.g., go to the marketing group to develop a direct mail package)
• Contact customers:
—Be sensitive to each particular customer relationship
—Ask good questions and have good listening skills
—Figure out what is important to and motivates the customer
—Understand the products and services your company provides, not just their features, but also the benefits they have for customers, and understand how the products will be used by the customer
—Match those products and services with customers' needs
• Close business/make sales
• Get resolution of customer service problems
• Develop relationships with customers to whatever degree possible

In short, the account manager needs to be skilled at soft selling in a quantitative productivity model operating in the context of a long-term, strategic plan for working with accounts.

Developing Hiring Criteria

Before attempting to recruit candidates for the account manager position, it is important to develop criteria for selecting from among those candidates, in particular criteria that will work for your company. Although there are common characteristics in most account management environments, there is no completely generic description of the "ideal" account manager; each complete portrait is situation-specific. A common way to determine which behavioral traits (talent) and aptitudes and skills (experience/education) are appropriate for a given company is to review the characteristics of the most successful account managers and then develop a test to compare the candidates' characteristics to those of successful current employees.

Using this process, you can describe three sets of attributes to look for in applicants for account manager positions. These characteristics are typical of those that will emerge on the "must have" list of most organizations. The three sets of attributes are grouped into (1) minimum background requirements, (2) aptitudes and skills, and (3) behavioral traits. Each company must decide for itself the minimum background requirements. What follows are tools for quantifying the desired behavioral traits and assessing the desired sales skills.

Behavioral Traits

The key to getting good account managers is to focus on identifying and hiring talent. Skills can be developed. Behavioral traits are less likely to be developed. They are typically not trainable over the short, or medium, term. A list of the commonly desired account manager behavioral traits follows. The discussion for each trait indicates why and how that trait is important for account management. Figure 8-2 provides a summary of the eight most common critical account manager behavioral traits.

Motivations

• *Achiever.* The achiever is confident, self-assured, and very proud of all his accomplishments. He has a strong desire for independence and an inner need to excel. Someone who scores very high in this trait may have what MPR senior consultant Juli Vinik calls "externalized ego"—the desire for a big house, a fancy car. Applicants who score low in this trait often lack self-confidence, do not strive to achieve goals, and exhibit what Vinik describes as "management dependence." "Someone who scores low in the achiever trait would be one of your 'high maintenance' employees," she says.

This trait is important for an account manager because he needs to set and own his sales goals. If he is not confident and does not possess the drive to achieve those goals, he will simply not be successful. A world-class account manager relishes and is energized by the quest for success. A word of caution, however: someone in whom the achiever trait is too highly developed may have difficulty developing relationships with customers.

• *Competitor.* The competitor loves to win, hates to lose, and is never satisfied with anything but the top spot in every recordbook.

Figure 8-2. Account manager behavioral traits.

Achiever	• Confident and self-assured • Seeks independence and recognition • Driven to high levels of accomplishment	Discerner	• Skilled in self-appraisal • Quickly sorts the critical from the superfluous • Acts appropriately
Persuader	• Skilled listener who identifies motivations • Probes and questions others' agendas • Strives to influence others	Proactivity	• Looks for solutions • Initiates change and improvement • Doesn't blame or shift responsibility
		Competitor	• Energized by competition • Responds to measurable performance goals • Driven to produce
Mission of Service	• Service-oriented • Team player • Committed to family and community	Intensity	• High stamina & endurance • Focus on work activities • Active hobbies
Prospector	• Targets accounts carefully • Continually probes and penetrates accounts • Methodical assessment of "fit" between prospects and his/her company		

Rather than being frightened of or intimidated by competition, she is energized by it. Someone who is weak in this trait is uncomfortable being compared to others and is very intimidated by competition.

The nature of the business world is such that most selling situations are becoming increasingly competitive. The account manager needs to be comfortable with being compared to the competition. In fact, she will thrive on trying to win in competitive situations.

• *Mission of service.* Someone who scores high in this trait is motivated externally and has a strong sense of service to others. A significant part of his life is directed toward other people and the world at large, in particular the mission of his company. This person is also very loyal. The flip side, or low mission of service, according to Vinik, is disloyalty and selfishness. "A low mission-of-service employee might sell a competing product line on the side and not think he was doing anything wrong," Vinik says. A person scoring low in mission of service would not, for example, be a good choice for a customer service position.

Part of the account manager's job is taking care of customers, which often means solving their problems. His customers also need to be able to trust him and rely on him. Someone with a high mission of service is customer-focused. If asked, for example, how he knows he is doing a good job, an account manager with high mission of service would say, "I am keeping my customers happy" rather than "I was the top sales person in my company." The caution: if someone has an overdeveloped mission-of-service trait, he might invest too much in customers without getting the appropriate return. He might be providing service for the sake of service without heeding the economics of the situation.

Modes of Thinking

• *Discerner.* A discerner is a quick study but is also good at in-depth, analytical thinking. In addition, she has a lot of street smarts and is curious to know how things work. She is able to assimilate knowledge, sort out the useful from the superfluous, and then make an appropriate response or chart a successful course of action. Someone who scores low in this trait can spend a lot of time fiddling around with unimportant details; she has difficulty getting the big picture.

The discerner trait is critical because of all the planning that goes into world-class account management. Not only does the account manager have to develop a good strategic plan, but in every customer contact she needs to listen and sort through which requests and problems are important and which are a good match for the products and services her company has to offer. She needs to be able to get quickly to the heart of issues, whether the customer contact is face-to-face or by phone.

Modes of Acting

• *Prospector.* This is an important trait for someone in sales. In a big marketplace, a prospector is able to concentrate his efforts on viable targets. He keeps his ear to the ground for business opportunities—anywhere. "I think of prospectors as a lot like the old miners,"

Vinik says. "They literally had to keep their ear to the ground to find gold." A person who scores low in this trait can be hit in the face with an opportunity and not even recognize it.

In the account management environment someone who scores high in this trait can target accounts carefully and methodically assess whether there is a fit between prospects and what his company has to offer. He will be able to decide decisively whether a prospect warrants additional investment of his time and resources. The down side is that someone who has too much of the prospector trait may wind up selling too much, in particular in situations where selling is not appropriate. Or he may fall into the trap of trying to get the customer to buy what he is selling, not what the customer wants.

• *Proactivity.* The basic nature of someone with the proactivity trait is to act rather than be acted upon. This person takes initiative, can step outside of her "comfort zone," and gets inspired by the possibilities of things to come. A person low in this trait is the classic "the glass is half-empty" type of person. She usually sees the dark side of any situation and is reluctant to take action because . . . what's the point?

The value of this trait is apparent in the definition of an account manager: skilled at soft selling in a quantitative productivity model operating in the context of a long-term, strategic plan for working with accounts. This trait enables the account manager to take ownership of accounts and operate independently with the high degree of accountability that is necessary. Too much of this trait, however, might make it difficult for the account manager to delegate or work as part of a sales team. Some balance is necessary.

• *Intensity.* The person who scores high here is gifted with very high stamina, endurance, and ability to focus on work activities; he works both harder and smarter. However, someone with high intensity can lack balance in his life—the "all work and no play" type of guy. Someone who scores low on this trait may burn out quickly or may insist on having the type of personal lifestyle that is detrimental to the position.

There is no way around it: being an account manager is a tough job. A high energy level is required in order to be successful at it.

Modes of Interacting

• *Persuader.* This is another key trait for someone in an account management position. The persuader uses every means at hand to convince others of the merits of her position. She has well-developed listening skills, in particular the ability to listen for information about another person's needs or agenda and then use that information to bridge to her own position. Someone who scores low in the persuader trait simply does not listen well. In account management, a low persuader would be reluctant to give up the "tell-sell" mode.

This is another especially important trait for an account manager. An account manager must be a "pragmatic listener" because she is called upon to get inside someone else's head on a regular basis. If the customer is objecting to something, for example, she needs to ask questions about what the objection really means. Then, if she has been given enough information to reposition her product *and* the product is a good fit for the customer, she can attempt to address the customer's objection. Her skill is being able to persuade by understanding.

Vinik offers a caveat about doing this type of categorization. "There is a tendency to want to put people into boxes," she says. "But each person has a unique combination of behaviors, and how those behaviors interact is that person's special contribution." She says there should be a good fit between the behaviors and what the company needs and what the position requires. "And just because someone doesn't have certain characteristics doesn't mean he or she isn't a good person," she adds. "It just means the traits don't match up well with the position."

Aptitudes and Skills

In addition to the behavioral traits described, account managers need to have the following aptitudes and skills:

• *Pre-call planning.* The ability to prepare for a customer sales call/presentation by knowing the function of the customer's business, the critical issues the customer faces, and how the customer can benefit from the product offered. The typical customer has a limited amount of time. Anything the account manager can do by way of background work to make the contact more efficient adds value to that contact.

• *Introduction.* The ability to make a good impression within the first few minutes of the sales call. The skilled account manager will, at the outset of the contact, explain the purpose of the call and why it will be of value to the customer.

• *Questioning/discovering needs.* The ability to use probing and listening skills to assess the customer's needs. This is the only way to develop an understanding of what the customer needs, which is at the heart of effective account management.

• *Conveying features and benefits.* The ability to convey the features of the product or service to the customer. To do this, the account manager needs to understand the difference between features and benefits. Features are the physical characteristics of a product; benefits are the advantages the customer receives from using the features.

• *Listening.* The ability to effectively listen to the customer to obtain customer needs and wants. Some people are just behaviorally better at this than others. People we have just described as persuaders intuitively listen well, and listen pragmatically. Other people have worked hard at honing this skill. A good account manager needs to listen, not only for content, but for emotion. He needs to listen for what is explicitly said and what is implied. This core skill is the essence of good account management. It is the primary way account managers develop a foundation of understanding of needs, against which all value they provide to customers is based.

• *Objection handling.* Good objection handling is clearly based on some of the listening skills and some of the questioning skills that were dealt with earlier. A good account manager will, when she hears an objection, make sure she understands the root cause for that objection. In the kind of relationship you are trying to develop in account management, superficial responses to objections are simply not effective in developing long-term relationships. What is effective is getting at the reasons behind the objections, getting clarity around whether the product or application of the product can effectively deal with those objections or whether the selling process can effectively deal with those objections. After determining the reasons for the objections, a good account manager will then either reposition, recommend another product, or walk away from the sale because it simply isn't a good one at this time, or ever.

• *Asking for the order and closing.* The ability to secure customer commitment to "the next step." The key here for account management is the ability to directly and confidently ask for the order. As opposed to other sales environments, you are not looking for "slick" indirect closes here; this is an explicit close.

• *Presentation skills.* The ability to present himself and his product or service in a positive manner, clearly articulating the product, usage of the product, and the benefits that customers would receive from using the product. In that presentation, a good account manager demonstrates interest, enthusiasm, and professionalism.

Selecting Talented Candidates

The key portions of the recruitment and selection process for account managers are a role play and a behavioral interview.

Role Play

In general, a role play is an effective way to test a person's ability to perform on-the-job functions and demonstrate job-related skills in a simulated setting. In this situation, the purpose of the role play is to measure the interpersonal and sales skills of the potential account manager, in particular his or her ability to operate within a sales process. During the role play, the candidate plays a sales representative talking to an existing customer. A well-designed role play will take into account the most common tasks, problems, and situations the account manager will face. It also needs to be self-contained, in that no knowledge outside of the role play is needed to perform well; this puts all candidates on an equal footing. To diminish any bias in the selection process, each candidate's background should be taken into consideration and a role play chosen for the interview that does not mirror the candidate's experience.

The items rated on the role play are the candidate's:

- Ability to make an effective introduction, thus encouraging the customer to want to stay on the line
- Intuitive questioning skills
- Listening skills
- Ability to apply information gathered throughout the call
- Ability to convey benefit to the customer
- Persuasiveness, in particular turning objectives into positive sales opportunities
- Ability to secure customer commitment to the next step
- Interpersonal tact and diplomacy
- Voice inflection and enthusiasm
- Enunciation
- Ability to articulate thoughts
- Correct use of language
- Style and tone

An effective role play process would start with the candidate's receiving and reviewing the background information in preparation for the role play. Typically, the candidate is given twenty to thirty minutes to review the background and prepare for the call. If the candidate is being interviewed for an outside account manager position, the role play is conducted in a face-to-face interview. If the candidate is being interviewed for an inside account manager position, the role play is conducted over the phone. This most closely simulates actual working conditions and will some times result in a significantly different conclusion. (Some candidates will communicate with significantly different levels of effectiveness and confidence in different environments. For example, a candidate who is confident, outgoing, and enthusiastic over the phone may appear timid and withdrawn in person.) With the candidate in the role of the account manager and the assessor in the role of the customer, the candidate then manages the role play call with the "customer." The call is completed within a set time limit, usually twenty minutes. After the role play call, the assessor evaluates the candidate's ability to work within a sales process.

Other important elements of the role play process and issues to be considered in the process include the following:

1. A statement, either in writing or verbally, of your expectations for the role play. You are looking for skills and for the candidate's response to particular situations. You don't want the candidate to be guessing what your expectations are and adjusting his or her behavior accordingly. The statement should indicate that the candidate is expected to:

- Introduce the purpose of his or her call
- Discover any needs the customer may have
- Determine the value of the product to the customer
- Use objections as an opportunity to persuade the customer
- Verify the customer facts provided
- Attempt a close
- Obtain a verbal commitment for products or services closed

2. An appropriate amount of depth in the role play customer's background. The customer background information provided to a candidate needs to be thorough enough to allow all candidates to reasonably manage a knowledge-based sales process call with a customer. Background information provided for the role play is typically four to five pages in length (plus an additional one to two pages of role play instructions) and includes the following types of information:

Company Information

- Your (the candidate's) company's products and/or services
- Product features, packaging, and pricing
- Product benefits
- Any other advantages your company may have

Competitor Information

- Competitor products and/or services
- Competitor product features, packaging, and pricing

- Competitor product benefits
- Other competitor advantages

Customer Scenario

- Customer company name
- Type of company
- Length of time as customer
- Product purchase history
- Name and title of key contact (contact in role play)
- Changes in the customer's business situation that might suggest new needs, and therefore provide an opportunity to add value and close a sale (e.g., significant business growth, aging equipment or technology, relocation, new competitive situation, new customer products or services)

3. A tightly managed focus:

- Role plays taped for review and further evaluation (candidate notified that role play is taped and tapes are later erased)
- Extensive training for assessors, and their candidate evaluation and scoring periodically calibrated
- A maximum of twenty minutes allowed for role play calls

Behavioral Interview

The behavioral interview is conducted over the telephone by a trained assessor to determine whether a candidate for account manager has the required behavior traits. It is important to standardize as much as possible all interviews and all role plays so that each candidate is evaluated systematically. Standardization minimizes adverse testing conditions such as noise and provides an equitable testing environment for all candidates. Standardization also means asking candidates the same interview questions, administering test questions in the same order under the same conditions, and putting all candidates through the same simulation exercise. This minimizes the chance of some information being used to select one candidate and other information being used to select other candidates.

It typically takes between fifteen and forty-five minutes, depending on how candidates respond. The interview is usually tape recorded, after securing permission to record from the candidate. Taping is also valuable if there is concern about assessor bias, because multiple assessors can listen to the tape.

The format is such that the interviewer states the question and the candidate responds—there is no give-and-take—and the focus is on having the candidate give examples so that the assessors can look for evidence of behavioral traits in the responses. Figure 8-3 illustrates evidence that is observed for each of the behavioral traits specifically linked to the questions asked of candidates. The questions are asked as open-ended/situational questions, and the scoring is based on trait evidence that appears in the response. Because they are designed to gather evidence, appropriate questions have three characteristics:

Figure 8-3. Evidence of behavioral traits.

Question	Evidence	No Evidence
[Achiever] What have you been personally the most motivated by in your job?	Gives specific example that cites either freedom to work independently OR praise or special recognition for high achievement.	I'm always motivated [no differentiation]. I like my boss [general pleasant work environment].
[Competitor] Most companies set goals or expectations for their employees. What role do those goals or expectations play in how you set your own specific performance goals?	Takes their goals and makes them higher.	Discredits importance of goals or expectations.
Mission of Service] What will fundamentally motivate you in you in your role?	Mission- or service-oriented response or opportunity to serve.	Stereotypical or ego response.
[Discerner] Think back to a situation that required an ability to think on your feet. What was the situation, and how did you respond?	Example demonstrates an ability to gather and sort information and act appropriately.	No example or example does not demonstrate such ability.
[Prospector] What factors would you consider in determining whether or not a customer has additional potential for your products/services?	Customer's need, budget, and how our service will solve a problem they have. How other customers with similar circumstances use our products/services.	General or nonbusiness criteria, e.g., "I look to see if they are willing to buy more from me."
[Proactivity] What do you think is the most difficult obstacle you have had to overcome? How did you handle it?	Names obstacle and did something to prevent it from becoming a bigger one.	Nothing proactive.
[Intensity] Do you often find that elements of your work intrude upon your free time? (If yes) can you give me a recent example? Why does that happen? How do you feel about it?	Agrees and indicates that although it may be part of the job, it's also part of his/her individual makeup: "I'm never really removed completely from my work."	Doesn't agree; prefers to keep work and free time separate; reply indicates success in keeping them separate.
[Persuader] What have you found to be the best ways to get someone to agree with your line of thinking on a particular subject?	Response clearly demonstrates finding out the other's perspective, e.g., "I find out what their view is and either show how mine fits in with or is more effective than theirs."	Facts or logic only, e.g., "I state my case and show them why it makes sense."

- They are open-ended, frequently beginning with the words *what, how, would.*
- They are situation-based. They suggest that the candidate discuss responses in the context of a certain type of situation.
- They suggest (or specifically request) examples of situations and responses from the candidate's experience.

A standardized interview sheet is developed for each trait question. An interview sheet (Figure 8-4) provides the interviewer with the question, space to record key phrases (those that provide evidence of a trait or evidence of a lack of a trait) from the candidate's response, a definition of what evidence to look for in the response, and a definition of what type of response indicates no evidence or negative evidence of a trait.

Let's look at an example of a question and the related observable evidence.

Figure 8-4. Interview sheet.

Persuader Trait

Question: *What have you found to be the best ways to get someone to agree with your line of thinking on a particular subject?*

Responses/key phrases: _____

_____

_____

_____

_____

Score: _____		
	Positive evidence	2 pts.
	Partial evidence	1 pt.
	No evidence	0 pts.
	Negative evidence	–1 pt.

Evidence:

- Finds out the other's perspective
- Asks questions
- Listens intently for objections and rationale

No evidence:

- Restates their case or opinion
- Depends on facts and logic in their case

Question:	Could you give me an example of a time when you've done a good job? How did you know that you did a good job?
Answer 1:	I knew I did a good job because I achieved my goal. I knew I did a good job because I won an award.
Answer 2:	I knew I did a good job because the customer was happy.
Answer 3:	I knew I did a good job because I won—I beat the competition.

Each of the above responses provides evidence to support a different behavioral trait. Answer 1 is clearly the response of an achiever, a candidate who is motivated to achieve at a high level, takes pride in accomplishments, and wants and expects recognition for those accomplishments. The second answer is the response of a candidate with a high mission of service, someone who is motivated by serving others. Answer 3 is the response of a competitor, a candidate who is motivated by winning in a competitive environment.

Scoring the Candidates

Although the selection process is never an exclusively quantitative exercise, scoring of the behavioral interview and role play is an important step, and the score is a strong indicator of a candidate's fit to the account manager position.

The behavioral interview scoring system work as follows:

1. A minimum of two questions is asked for each desired trait.
2. Each question is scored against a four-step scale:

   —Positive evidence of trait   2 points
   —Partial evidence of trait   1 points
   —No evidence of trait   0 points
   —Negative evidence or counter evidence of
      trait   −1 point
3. Scores are summed by trait. Assuming two questions are asked for each trait, each trait has a potential of four points (although the scale goes from −2 to +4).
4. A total score is tallied and compared to a total acceptable score. Assuming the eight critical account manager traits, there is a total possible score of 32 points. With this number and set of traits, qualification ranges are as follows:

Total Score

26 and above	Highly qualified candidate
22–25	Qualified candidate
21 and less	Not qualified

A sample scoring sheet is provided in Figure 8-5.

5. A qualitative review of the behavioral screen is done. Two issues are addressed in this review. The first issue is balance, or
lack of balance, in the traits. A candidate could have a good
overall score, but have an unacceptably low score in one or
more individual traits (a score of less than a 2 in any trait
could be considered an unacceptably low score). The second
area reviewed is the "Concerns" column on the scoring sheet
(Figure 8-5). If one of these two areas indicates a concern, the
interviewer/assessor can go back to the candidate to confirm
the evidence with additional questions, disqualify the candidate, or qualify the candidate because of the mix of behaviors
and the total overall score. You would probably qualify a candidate with an overall score of greater than 26 and one trait
score of less than 2. You would probably disqualify a candidate with an overall score of 22 and one or more individual
trait scores of less than 2.

In addition to the behavioral interview, the role play is scored.
The role play is structured as a sales process, and the scoring is linked
to this structure. Each sales process step is scored on a 1–5 scale. The
structure, assessment items, and scale are as follows:

Role Play Outline

	Section	Assessment Item(s)	Point Scale
1	Introduction	Ability to make an effective in-troduction and get customer's interest.	1–5
2	Probing	Intuitive questioning skills	1–5
3	Information gathering and application	Listening skills and the ability to apply information gathered	1–5
4	Benefit positioning	Ability to speak in terms of ben-efit to the customer	1–5
5	Persuasiveness	Ability to turn objections into positive sales opportunities	1–5
6	Closure	Ability to secure customer com-mitment to next step	1–5
7	Customer sensitivity	Rapport building skills	1–5

Figure 8-5. Sample scoring sheet—behavioral interview.

Name: _____   Position: Account Manager

Interviewer: _____   Date: _____

Rank order of behavioral traits	A. Screener scoring	B. Additional information & observations	C. Concerns	D. Final score
Achiever • Confident and self-assured • Seeks independence & recognition • Driven to high levels of accomplishment				
Competitor • Energized by competition • Responds to measurable performance goals • Driven to produce				
Discerner • Skilled in self-appraisal • Quickly sorts the critical from the superfluous • Acts appropriately				
Mission of Service • Service-oriented • Team player • Committed to family and community				

Persuader • Skilled listener who identifies motivations • Probes and questions others' agendas • Strives to influence others			
Proactivity • Looks for solutions • Initiates change and improvement • Doesn't blame or shift responsibility			
Prospector • Targets accounts carefully • Continually probes and penetrates accounts • Methodical assessment of "fit" between prospects and his/her company			
Intensity • High stamina and endurance • Focus on work activities • Active hobbies			

TOTAL SCORE: _____

KEY:					
Positive evidence	+	2 pts.	TOTALS		
Partial positive evidence	P+	1 pt.	26 or above	Highly qualified	
No evidence	?	0 pts.	22–25	Qualified	
Counter evidence	—	-1 pt.	21 or less	Not qualified	

| 8 | Voice | Ability to use voice to show in-terest and enthusiasm | 1–5 |
| 9 | Speech enunciation and correctness | Ability to pronounce words, ar-ticulate thoughts, and correctly use language | 1–5 |

Total points   9–45

After a candidate completes the role play, a total score is tallied. This score is then used as an additional selection screen using the follow-ing qualification ranges:

Total Score

36 and above	Highly qualified candidate
27 to 35	Qualified candidate
26 and less	Not qualified

Evaluating the Candidates

The combined score from the in-depth behavioral interview and role play are then tallied and evaluated to get an overall picture of the candidate.

A strong behavioral score may offset a low role play score. For example, one candidate may possess the behavioral traits needed for the job but may not have a strong background in sales. Nonetheless, this person may be a good long-term fit for the position if his or her behavioral traits indicate potential sales ability. Another candidate may have slightly lower behavioral scores but do better in the role play. This person probably has more sales experience and may get up to speed more quickly. Although this candidate's long-term potential may not be as high as that of the candidate who is a better behavioral match, this candidate may still be successful in the job because of the skills he or she has developed.

A successful IAM program is simply not possible without highly competent account managers. An investment on the front end in se-lecting the right account managers is an investment in the overall success of IAM in the organization.

9

Defining Customer Contact Value: The Customer Workshop

"Chances are you're serving highly specialized needs. So why take a chance? Involve your customer directly in the product or service development. Make sure the product or service satisfies the desired core benefits and that it's user-friendly."

Robert E. Linneman and John L. Stanton, Jr.
Making Niche Marketing Work

A Day in the Life . . .

Just think about the number of marketing and sales contacts that the average customer, or would-be customer, can get in just one day. Let's take a typical businessperson.

On the way out of town for a business trip, she drives to her office first. During the drive, she hears some ten radio commercials. She stops at the office to pick up her mail. Of the fifteen pieces, probably thirteen are unsolicited. Two are invoices from suppliers that she needs to approve.

Driving to the airport, she hears another ten or so radio commercials and sees the same number of billboards. On the way to her departure gate, she walks past a half-dozen back-lit display ads. While waiting for her flight, she opens up the *Wall Street Journal*, which has an average of three ads per page. Once on board, she skims through the in-flight magazine, which has an average of five ads per page.

When she arrives at her destination, she checks her voice mail. It contains fourteen messages, eight of which are from suppliers or potential suppliers. There is also a message from her administrative assistant saying that three suppliers called but did not want to leave a voice mail message.

At the end of the day when she checks into the hotel, the clerk asks if she is a member of the hotel's frequent guest program. He then asks her what airline she traveled on. When she gets to her room, she checks her e-mail. There are seventeen messages, five from suppliers, two of which are prospective suppliers. Just before turning in, she makes a telephone call to her travel company to book a future trip. To relax a bit before falling asleep, she watches television for half an hour, during which time she sees about a dozen commercials.

So in the course of just one day, our beleaguered businessperson has been contacted by suppliers, or would-be suppliers, at least 300 times, at a cost of over $300 (see Figure 9-1).

Out of these 300-plus contacts, how many does the average businessperson notice? How many actually get their intended message conveyed to a customer? How many would customers say are of value to them? How many are consistent with, and supportive of, a strong relationship with customers? The sad reality is that only a small percentage are even noticed, and an embarrassingly low percentage of those are of customer-perceived value. In their 1986 book

Figure 9-1. Marketing and sales investments in one customer in an average day.

Type of Contact	Average Per-Contact Cost	Total Cost Per Day
Radio ad (15)	$ .15[a]	$ .225
Direct mail package (15)	.73[b]	10.95
Airport back-lit display ad (22)	.001[c]	.022
Newspaper ad (100)	.04[d]	4.00
In-flight magazine ad (150)	.15[d]	22.50
Telephone call (11)	23.25[b]	255.75
E-mail message (5)	5.00 (est.)	25.00 (est.)
Hotel check-in message (1)	unknown	unknown
Phone call to travel agent (1)	7.00[a]	7.00
Television commercial (1)	.009[a]	.18
339 Total Contacts		Total $325.63

Sources:
a. Jack Z. Sissors and Lincoln Bumba, *Advertising Media Planning* (Chicago: NTC Business Books, 1993).
b. Helen Berman, "Cost-Per-Contact Efficiency Pays Off," *Folio,* May 1, 1993, pp. 45–46.
c. (Milwaukee, Wis., rates). Interspace Airport Advertising.
d. *The Leo Burnett Worldwide Advertising and Media Fact Book* (Chicago: NTC Business Books, 1994).
e. Bob Stone, *Successful Direct Marketing Methods,* 5th ed. (Chicago: NTC Business Books, 1994).

Positioning: The Battle for Your Mind, Al Ries and Jack Trout estimated that "during the course of a single year, the average human mind is exposed to some 200,000 advertising messages." Do you think this number has increased in the last decade? How many of these ads from last year do you remember?

When Value Is Not Provided

Most of the contacts mentioned in the previous section are not only a waste of money, in some situations—such as account management—they can convey a message that is inconsistent with the relationship expectations you want to establish with your customers. Just think about how this plays out in a relationship: You make a contact with one of your customers (this example could apply to any medium, but let's use direct mail for this example). Your customer opens the mail, and the information is simply not relevant. Now, let's say that this happens fairly frequently. How does this affect the relationship? A common customer train of thought on receiving successive irrelevant contacts:

1. An irrelevant contact: ". . . is a waste of my time."
2. Another irrelevant contact: "What a waste of my time."
3. Another: "What a waste! . . . These people don't respect my time or really understand what I need. . . . Or care what I need."

The result is that, over time, customers become trained not to pay attention to your contacts: "They're a waste of my time." They are also trained not to trust you: "Why would I trust a company that either doesn't know or doesn't care about what my needs are?"

It should be no surprise, then, that there are so many skeptical customers in corporate America thinking, "The only time they call me is when they want to sell me something." One of the areas covered in the workshops you will learn to conduct later in this chapter is an exploration of negative contacts and the ways in which they undermine relationships with customers. Some themes tend to appear over and over in these workshops, pretty much irrespective of industry. Here is sampling of these themes taken from actual workshops with verbatim comments from participants.

Skepticism

"The rep pretended to know my industry, but as I got to know him, it was clear that he didn't."

"She was trying to sell me all the time . . . never took time to listen to what I had to say."

"The only time they call me is when they want to sell me something."

"I couldn't put my finger on why, exactly, but he just seemed insincere."

Ethics

"She gave me deceiving information. The product didn't perform at all like she promised it would."

"The dealer lied about how quickly he could ship, probably just to get my order."

"He tries to get through the receptionist by saying I've asked him to page me."

Lack of understanding of customer's needs

"The rep was very sympathetic, but he didn't have a clue about what would really help me with my business."

"She called me just about every week to 'check in,' but her calls met no need of mine. They were a waste of time."

Lack of respect for customer's time

"He kept launching into these presentations that were much too detailed."

"The salesman thinks I don't have anything better to do than sit around and chew the fat with him."

"Her timing was almost always bad. Her visits were very intrusive."

"He interrupted my work for no good reason."

Lack of knowledge and skills, either about product, industry, or interpersonal interactions

"She just didn't know her stuff."

"His recommendations were rarely on target."

Obviously, over time these reactions will have a significant negative impact on the business relationship. When you are not providing value, you cannot make it up in volume. Just the opposite: each additional contact serves to further deteriorate the relationship. It takes a multitude of positive contacts to offset one negative contact; and to remain competitive, businesses today simply cannot afford to continue investing in contacting customers when those contacts are more likely to deteriorate the relationship than to build it.

The Importance of Providing Value in Customer Contacts

This skepticism and the inefficiencies in the business system described above—as well as the actions and attitudes of businesses that feed it—are the antithesis of world-class account management. To overcome this, IAM programs have an inherent set of rules that govern all customer contacts:

• *Do not contact a customer unless you have a good reason to think that the contact will be of value to the customer.* Unvalued contacts drive a "peddler" perception, are at best confusing to customers, and are a waste of marketing dollars. "Good reason" in this rule means more than having an intuitive *feeling* that this contact could be of value. It means that there is *evidence* that this contact will be of value. Such evidence could be, for example, that the customer has requested similar information in the past, the customer responds positively to the contact, or the information provided is consistent with your detailed understanding of the customer's needs.

• *Seek first to understand, and then convey, an understanding of the customer and of his needs.* Nothing makes a customer more skeptical than a call that he perceives to be intended only to "sell something," especially something he is not sure he needs. If you do not have an in-depth understanding of customer needs, the delivery of value in marketing and sales contacts becomes at best a crapshoot.

• *Do not attempt to sell prematurely.* Prematurely trying to close a sale is the epitome of insensitivity. There is some risk in every business-buying decision, and customers resent feeling as though they are being manipulated to buy before they have become comfortable with the risk inherent in the buying decision. More often than not, contacts in IAM programs sell by not "selling." In IAM, contacts work to strengthen the relationship. As Victor Hunter of Hunter Business Direct often states in his workshops to marketing and sales professionals, "Never put the relationship at risk to get the sale."

• *Use the lowest-cost contact medium that can deliver the value to the customer.* Do not use a face-to-face visit if a telephone call will do; do not use the telephone if mail will do. The issues here are efficiency, convenience, and preference. Not only does a face-to-face contact cost at least ten times what a telephone contact costs, in some situations and for some customers, a telephone call is preferred. This concept seems so simple: I will spend one-tenth of my previous sales budget, and the customer will appreciate the contact more. It is appalling and amazing how few companies actively practice this thinking.

• *Provide continuity in the relationship.* Obviously, marketers want a relationship of some duration with customers. For their part, customers want one trusted, reliable, consistent, and empathetic source for product and information.

Defining Value

Do most marketers and salespeople know what their customers perceive as value? Not only in the products and services, but in the relationship? "Left to our own devices, we pay more and more attention to things of less and less importance to the customer," states Ron Zemke, author of *Service America.* This suggests that there is a risk in defining value-based contacts by using inside-out thinking, that is, defining for customers how you will add value based upon what you think is good for them and what you think they should buy. The reality is that an inside-out approach is a hit-and-miss proposition. Perpetuating such a random system is ultimately a prescription for failure. The most powerful tool—and the only one that consistently delivers an accurate definition of value—is the voice of the customer.

The rest of this chapter offers you a specific tool, the customer contact workshop, that provides a structured way for you to "hear" the customer's voice by allowing customers themselves to define what is of value to them and how you can deliver it. The workshop is one that has been conducted over a number of years across a variety of industries, including telecommunications, insurance, agriculture, computer equipment, and building supplies distribution. The following sections describe the methodology for conducting a workshop; this includes the philosophy behind the workshop, the workshop framework, and how to use the outputs of the workshop to build a foundation for adding value in relationships with customers.

The Customer Contact Workshop: Methodology

The Philosophy Behind the Workshop

The best answers to the challenge of defining value come from customers themselves. But this truism carries with it an inherent drawback: it is not possible to customize every contact for each customer.

You cannot, for example, create separate direct mail pieces for each customer because that would drive the cost from $1 per contact to $10, $20, and even $40 per package. For economic reasons, you need to have some standard types of contacts to use with customers.

To develop those standard contacts, you need to have a formal way to (1) gather input from customers about what is of value to them, (2) assimilate that information, and (3) create a formal way to drive that information into the organization, that is, turn it into tools that your marketing and sales staffs can use. One of the best tools for obtaining this information is a workshop that brings customers together in small groups and gives them a structured opportunity to tell you what they need and how you can add value to the relationship. If the market segments in the account management plan have very different needs (either product, service, or communication needs), separate workshops should be conducted for the different segments.

Overview

This is typically a three-hour, participatory workshop. Participants include customers, corporate sales staff, and marketing staff. The most effective workshops involve a minimum of six and a maximum of twelve customers. Through group discussion and consensus building, you define marketing and sales contacts that add value from the customer's perspective. At the end of the workshop, you will have a solid foundation for a meaningful and efficient customer contact plan.

Preparation for the Workshop

First, there are some logistics to administer in setting up the workshop:

1. Invite customers by telephone to participate four to five weeks in advance.
2. Coordinate arrangements with the facility:
   - Have a room large enough to comfortably hold at least fifteen to twenty people.
   - Arrange tables and chairs to facilitate the session; a U-shaped room or small conference table works best.
   - Obtain a flip chart, tape, and markers.
3. Fax or send a letter to participants one week in advance to:
   - Confirm attendance.
   - Confirm time and location of the workshop.

- Provide a telephone number to call with questions.
- Restate why this is important to you and them.

4. Call customers to confirm their participation. (You can expect some drop-off from the initial number of confirmed participants.)

5. Provide an incentive. An incentive not only encourages customers to participate, it also tells them that you value their input enough to compensate them for it. A common incentive is $50 cash. Other good incentives include a certificate good for $50 (or more) of services (this works particularly well in situations where you are a regular service provider to these customers), promotional merchandise, or free related products. The incentive that you use depends on who the customers are and what your relationship with them is. Small business customers typically respond well to cash incentives; large business customers respond well to a gift or some other indication that you appreciate their time and input.

The Workshop Framework

The workshop is designed to get customers to bare their souls—to tell you what they hate about marketing and sales contacts and why, and to tell you what they really like (i.e., value) about marketing and sales contacts and why. You, in turn, will apply this information to your relationship with customers and define specific marketing and sales contacts that will provide value to them. Figure 9-2 provides a more detailed agenda for the workshop, with objectives and questions for each agenda topic.

The agenda for this three-hour workshop looks like this:

Topic	Approximate Time
1. Introduction and orientation	10 minutes
2. Discussion of valued contacts	25 minutes
3. Discussion of negative contacts	25 minutes
4. Definition of performance requirements	30 minutes
BREAK	10 minutes
5. Identification of specific valued contacts	25 minutes
6. Rating of contact importance	15 minutes
7. Media identification and frequency definition	25 minutes
8. Summary and feedback from participants	10 minutes
9. Close and thank you	5 minutes

1. *Introduction and orientation.* The customers/participants start arriving for the workshop one by one; a total of eight to ten customers

Figure 9-2. Value-based contact customer workshop agenda.

Topic	Objectives	Questions	Time Frame
1 Introduction & orientation	• Set participant expectations for workshop • Set tone for workshop • Provide a contextual framework for participants • Orient participants -- Facilities -- Informal nature of workshop • Encourage involvement • Convey appreciation for participation		10 min.
2 Discussion of valued contacts	• Develop a common understanding of what a value-based contact is • Provide examples to broaden participants' thinking • Illustrate why contacts are of value	• I'd like each of you to share at least one experience where a contact from a supplier was of value to you. *[If necessary, provide examples of value, e.g., help you solve problems, make decisions, save money, manage costs better, etc. Flip chart examples.]** • *[After each example]* Why were these contacts of value? *[Flip chart "why" in different color next to example. Capture at least 15 to 20 examples. Work with participants in a round robin or open participation format.]*	25 min.
3 Discussion of negative contacts	• Develop a common understanding of what a negative contact is • Provide examples to broaden participants' thinking • Illustrate why negative contacts undermine customer relationships	• Now I'd like you to think about an experience where a contact from a supplier wasn't of value (and maybe even an annoyance). *[Flip chart examples.]* • Why were these not of value? *[Flip chart "why" in different color next to example. Capture at least 15 to 20 examples.]*	25 min.
4 Definition of performance requirements	• Define what the characteristics of a good/ value-based contact are	• We've already discussed the conditions or requirements for a good contact from a supplier *[Point out "whys" from examples given earlier and list on separate flip chart.]* Are each of these required conditions for a good supplier contact? • Are there additional requirements? *[Test the list by reading the list and asking.]* • If these conditions are met, would all contacts be of value?	30 min.

(continues)

Figure 9-2. *Continued.*

Topic	Objectives	Questions	Time Frame
Break			10 min.
5 Identification of specific valued contacts	• To build a list of specific contacts that will be of value to customers	• I'd like you to think about a relationship with your best supplier or an ideal relationship with a supplier. What types of contacts do you get or would you expect? *[Give examples of types of contacts.]* • How could Our Company provide an "ideal supplier" level of service? *[Flip chart all contacts identified. Number contacts. Probe for clarity when necessary.]*	25 min.
6 Rating of contact importance	• Determine the relative value of each of the contacts identified	• I would like you to review these contacts we have identified *[Point to flip chart]* and for each assign a rating using this scale. *[Written on flip chart.]* A = Very important. Adds significant value. B = Nice to have. Helpful. C = Don't bother. No value. An annoyance. *[Get ratings from participants and flip chart to sort out As, Bs, and Cs.]*	15 min.
7 Media identification and frequency definition	• Determine how frequently each of the contacts can be made and still add value • Determine how customers would like to receive each contact (face-to-face, phone, mail, fax, advertising, retail, etc.) • Determine which other media would be acceptable for each contact	• Now let's go through each of these contacts. For each one I will ask you for #1, frequency: in the next year, how many times would you like to receive a contact like this? And #2, media: how would you like to receive this contact (face-to-face, phone, mail, fax, advertising, retail)? *[Flip chart annual frequency and media for each A- and B-rated contact (number of contacts and time permitting).]*	25 min.
8 Summary and feedback from participants	• Get participant feelings on value-based contacts as defined	• How do you feel about the contacts we've defined?	10 min.
9 Close and thank you			15 min.

*Instructions to facilitators appear in brackets and italics.

arrive. If they have been offered cash compensation, it is given to them when they arrive. The room is set up to allow the facilitator to work comfortably with the customers, engaging them in discussion and charting their input. The atmosphere is relaxed, maybe even casual, depending on the audience. The facilitator asks questions, charts customers' responses, manages the agenda, encourages all customers to participate, keeps the energy level up, and maintains a relaxed yet productive and fast-paced atmosphere throughout the workshop.

The session starts with the normal introductions and orientation. Customers are thanked in advance for their participation, and the value of their input is highlighted.

2. *Discussion of valued contacts.* The facilitator then leads the group in a discussion of contacts they have received from suppliers that were of value. One at a time each of the customers shares his or her specific contact example with the group while the facilitator charts and asks questions to clarify and add depth.

The participants work hard to think of examples. A participant at one workshop, for example, enthusiastically described how the sales rep followed up after an equipment purchase. "He stopped by about a month after the equipment arrived to check and make sure the shipment was okay. Then he let me know about an upcoming sale on a compatible product, which I realized I could use. I appreciated that he inspected the shipment in such a timely fashion. And the entire visit was a good use of my time because he provided me with information to help run my business."

Another participant had this to say about an inquiry she made about a possible software purchase: "When I called, the sales rep had on-line a profile of my business and my whole sales history with his company. He was able to give me personalized information about what software I might want, and it saved a lot of time."

Yet another talked about how the sales rep responded after his service repair request. "First, he came within three hours after I called for service—I really didn't expect him to show up so quickly. Then he called three weeks later to make sure everything was still working all right. I was really impressed that he cared enough to follow up. He's got my business for sure!"

Phrases such as "personalized service," "listens well," "takes notes," "saved me time," "understands my business," "took the initiative," "knew my industry," "knew his product line," "sees things down the road that would be valuable to my business," "followed through," "demonstrated concern," and "made the extra effort" tend to recur in the workshops. The total list usually includes twenty to twenty-five items.

As the facilitator lists each of these examples on the flip chart, he asks the participant to explain *why* the contact was valuable. These ''whys'' are written in the chart in a different color from the examples themselves. In the first example above, for instance, where the contact was a follow-up after an equipment purchase, there are three ''whys'': the rep informed the customer about an upcoming product that the customer could use, the customer appreciated the timeliness of the visit, and the visit was a good use of the customer's time. This list of ''whys'' will be used later as the basis for defining performance requirements for valued contacts.

3. *Discussion of negative contacts.* Next the group shifts gears and begins to discuss negative contact experiences. The facilitator asks them to think of those that have provided no value or, at their worst, were annoyances. This exercise seems much easier for participants and tends to generate more passion and intensity. One participant, for example, growled, ''When this salesman calls, he doesn't take 'no' for an answer. And he always begins the conversation with, 'Do you know who this is?' Not only does he usually have poor timing with his calls, but he doesn't listen to me. Sometimes he's actually rude. It's really a waste of my time talking to him!''

Another recalled, ''I was having a problem with my bills, so I called my sales rep. He came to see me, but he didn't have the answer. After he left, he had three different people call, so I had to explain the situation again to each one. One of these people was a consultant who wrote me a six-page report! How about just fixing the problem? The whole thing was very frustrating. The rep didn't take the time to understand my problem, and I certainly didn't need the overly detailed answer from the consultant. I just wanted results!''

Again, the facilitator asks participants to explain why each contact was not valuable and lists the ''whys'' on the flip chart along with the examples, again in a different color. In the first example above, for instance, the ''whys'' are the rep's bad timing, rudeness, and inability to listen. This list, which also contains between twenty and twenty-five items, will also be used to build the performance requirements, but in this case the inverse of the whys will be used. That is, if ''bad timing'' is the reason given for the customer's perception that a contact is negative, then the corresponding performance requirement would be ''schedule a contact at customer's convenience.''

4. *Definition of performance requirements.* After this exercise the facilitator then begins to move the group into developing draft performance requirements, that is, those conditions that should be met on each contact for the contact to be of value. These draft require-

ments will be refined and consolidated after the workshop(s). The resulting working performance requirements will be used to define ongoing value-based customer communications. The group then uses the two lists of "whys" (why contacts did or did not have value) charted in steps 2 and 3 and develops the performance requirements by turning the whys into generic statements that can apply to every contact.

For example, if a contact is valued because the rep has detailed knowledge of what the customer has purchased in the past, has an understanding of what the customer's needs are, and can recommend appropriate new and collateral products, the performance requirements might be "uses customer's time efficiently" and "offers personalized service." Conversely, if a contact is not valued because the rep is unfamiliar with the industry, the performance requirement might be "shares useful information with customer about the industry." Then the group will match contacts (direct mail, sales visits, phone calls, etc.) to these requirements. If a contact meets these conditions, there is a high likelihood that it will be of value.

After six to eight requirements are defined, the facilitator then "tests" the requirements: "If a contact met these conditions, (1) _____, (2) _____, (3) _____, there is a high probability that it would be of value to you." If the group answers "No, it may be of value or it may not," the facilitator continues to ask for additional requirements. In effect, he is testing the performance requirements for completeness. Some common examples of performance requirements are:

- The contact must be personalized.
- The purpose of the contact must be stated at the beginning.
- The contact should convey appreciation of the customer.
- The contact should convey an understanding of the customer's unique business needs.
- The contact should be efficient and concise.

A list of performance requirements is a tool with several ongoing benefits: (1) It can be used to assess specific types of contacts that are being considered when developing an overall customer contact plan. (2) It can be used as the basis for a training program for account managers. (3) It is helpful in designing contacts such as a direct mail campaign or electronic contacts such as World Wide Web pages or e-mail.

5. *Identification of specific valued contacts.* The first three steps in the workshop—the identification of valued and nonvalued contacts

and the development of performance requirements—have accomplished a number of things. They have

- Focused the thinking of the customers/participants on value-based contacts
- Broadened perspectives about what contacts could be
- Developed some common understanding of what types of contacts are positive and what types are negative
- Focused participants' thinking about what they value and why, and what they do not value and why.

This gives the facilitator an excellent foundation to move to the next step, which is defining specific valued contacts. The facilitator asks participants to think of specific contacts they would like to receive and would receive value from. Each participant shares two to three ideas for specific contacts he or she would like to receive, and the facilitator lists them on the flip chart. The facilitator should keep the group focused on the content of the contacts, not the medium. (There seems to be a tendency in these groups for participants to jump to the medium.) For example, one participant keeps sharing his direct mail ideas. After tactful questioning by the facilitator, these "direct mail" contacts become "new product introductions," "new release/version information," and "product application case studies." When the participants finish this section, they have a list of about twenty to twenty-five specific contacts. See Figure 9-3 for examples of value-based contacts.

6. *Rating of contact importance.* Once again the facilitator turns to the flip chart in order to set up a grading scale for each type of contact:

A = Very important. Adds significant value.
B = Nice to have. Helpful.
C = Don't bother. No value. An annoyance.

The facilitator asks each participant to write down how important each contact is, and the participants share their ratings with the group. In one workshop, for example, for the contact "new product information," six participants rated the contact A while only one rated it B. For "follow-up after installation of product," three participants rated it A, two B, and two C.

7. *Media identification and frequency definition.* To wrap up the workshop, the facilitator then takes from the flip chart the list of contacts and their ratings. For each one he asks participants to state

Figure 9-3. Examples of valued contacts.

- Advertising information and support materials

- New product information

- Information about new processes
  –New to customer

- Order confirmation before shipment
  –Acknowledgment (especially when faxed)
  –Notification of shipping date and back order (and substitute products)

- Technical support/questions
  –Have someone available immediately
  –Answer question(s)

- On-line ordering

- Information on changes in industry regulations
  –Relevant to my business
  –In plain English
  –Summary format

- Technology
  –Especially changes within specific industry
  –Application to specific industry

- Policy changes
  –Billing
  –Product packaging
  –Timely fashion

- Electronic catalog (on CD-ROM)

- Documented case studies
  –All industries

- Make aware of conventions & when they take place

- New product offerings

- Discontinued products

- Samples/literature/specifications

- Price sheets

- Discontinued/changes in products

- Product/service satisfaction survey
  –Follow-up to determine quality of service

- Back order information

- Product demonstrations

which medium (or media) would be best (or at least appropriate or acceptable) and how often they would like to receive each contact. Also discussed is what events drive each contact and the preferred frequency of the contacts. Figure 9-4 illustrates how this information is documented.

For example, a type of contact the participants in one workshop identified as valuable was information about new product releases. After questioning by the facilitator, the participants decided that their preferred method of being contacted was through the mail, and no more than four times per year. They also agreed that a follow-up telephone call to make sure that the mailing had been received was

Figure 9-4. Value-based contacts.

Contacts	Frequency	Mail	Phone	Field
1. New product announcements	4	P ✉	A ☎	
2. Follow-up 1 week after equipment purchase	1		P ☎	A ☞
3. Product application information	4	P ✉	A ☎	A ☞
4. Product upgrades/new releases	4	P ✉	A ☎	A ☞
5. Case studies • Product application • Results	4	P ✉		
6. Industry research	1	P ✉		
7. Article reprints	6	P ✉		
8. Program specials	12	P ✉	A ☎	A ☞
9. Industry trends	2	P ✉		
10. Product use/performance assessment	4		A ☎	P ☞

P = Preferred medium   45 total contacts
A = Acceptable medium

acceptable, but that a face-to-face visit would be appropriate only if requested by the customer.

As another example, the type of contact participants identified as valuable was a follow-up contact after an equipment purchase, either by telephone or face to face. In this case participants indicated that the preferred frequency was event-linked, that is, a week to two weeks after the equipment was installed.

8. *Summary and feedback from participants.* The facilitator then asks each of the participants how they feel about the contacts that were defined. One after another, they respond positively and with enthusiasm.

9. *Close and thank-you.* After a brief statement of appreciation, the facilitator sends the participants home.

Using the Workshop Outputs to Build a Foundation for Adding Value

The two primary outputs from this workshop are the set of performance requirements and the list of specific valued contacts. These two outputs should be powerful drivers of how contacts with customers are designed and implemented. The performance requirements get refined and are used as guidelines for how you and your customer wish to communicate, becoming the checklist used to assess all customer contacts. This process of refinement needs to happen in a way that balances what customers have requested and what your organization wants to do and can deliver. Successful refinement—not only drafting a good set of requirements but also getting them used in the marketing and sales process—includes all of the groups that have contact or define contact with customers. This includes sales (both inside and outside), customer service, product management, and marketing communications. This group refinement leads to selecting and changing performance requirements so that they adhere to the following guidelines:

1. Each of the requirements is consistent with or supportive of the company's business objectives.
2. The company is able to fulfill the requirements.
3. The requirements are consistent with defined market and product positioning.
4. The consequences of implementing the requirements (cost, process change, personnel impact, etc.) are more than offset by the incremental value realized by customers.

Once these performance requirements are defined and agreed to, they become (1) a checklist for account managers to use to plan and assess their sales calls, (2) a training tool to drive the culture and response process in customer service, and (3) a checklist for use in the development of all printed communications with customers, including product literature.

It is essential that you communicate these two tools—performance requirements and specific valued contacts—to all company entities that contact customers, including the account management organization. This should be done through training materials, internal communications (see Figure 9–5 for an example of communication of these tools at Phone Power, a division of Stentor Telecommunications in Canada), job aids, and/or procedures manuals.

The summary list of specific valued contacts provides the framework for adding the customer's perspective to the contact-planning process. It is important to remember here that frequently one is trying to change from a "tell-sell" culture to an adding-value culture. Obviously, habits get in the way of this change. In addition, the skills and knowledge of the current sales and marketing staffs can be obstacles to creating this change. Salespeople have worked for years calling on customers to sell them something, to tell them about a product, or simply to make a courtesy call. The list of specific contacts provides the account manager with reasons and objectives for calling on cus-

(text continues on p. 158)

Figure 9-5. Performance requirements and specific valued contacts at Phone Power.

Checklist
The 8 criteria of value-based contacts

When we asked customers to define the conditions that must be met for a Phone Power contact to be considered valuable, the following seven requirements emerged as the most critical. The first applies to the initial contact with the customer, while the others should be inherent of all our on-going communications with them.

☑ Ensure Customers Understand what Phone Power is

Call it basic, but by their own admission, customers don't have a good understanding of the Phone Power organization, our mandate, what they can expect from us and the range of services we offer. (The Phone Power 'Building Profits through Partnerships' brochure provides this information.)

☑ Understand the Customer's Business Needs

As much as customers expressed a need to understand our organization, they also want the Phone Power Consultant to demonstrate a clear understanding of their industry, their needs, and how Phone Power can fulfill these needs. (A 'Customer Profile Worksheet' will be developed in the 1st quarter of '96.)

☑ Ensure Customers Understand the Reason for the Contact

The purpose and desired outcome of every communication should be stated up front and must contain information of value to the customer. As a rule of thumb, a phone call or 'drop-in' visit for the sole purpose of keeping in touch with the customer should be avoided.

☑ Personalize and Target Your Communications to the Customer

Information that is relevant and specific to the customer is considered most valuable. Customers also appreciate personalization in all written communications. (A brief handwritten note addressed to them personally accompanying printed material is sometimes all that's required.)

☑ Make Time for the Customer on an On-going Basis

Customers value an immediate response to a request, and want their Consultant to be accessible. Some expressed a need for an internal rep, someone they could get in touch with at the office when the Consultant is unavailable.

☑ Provide Information in a Timely Fashion

Contacts should be brief, to the point and timely. Information must not only be relevant to the customer, but must also be available on request. (Sales Support will implement a 'fax-on-demand' service in the 1st quarter of 1996 to respond to the customer's need for accessing information as required.)

☑ Reflect the Customer's Culture and Way of Doing Business

Investing the time to understand the customer's culture and way of doing business allows us to 'speak their language' and be sensitive to their challenges and processes. For example, many participants stated that Phone Power Consultants should have industry specific expertise, and suggested that the Consultant be committed to learning their business. (Industry portfolios will be available in 1996. Some telcos are also shifting to consulting by industry group.)

☑ Present Quantitative Competitive Value of Phone Power Services

Even though many Phone Power services are still offered free of charge, customers expressed a need to know the dollar value of those services so they can compare them with competitive offerings.

Value-Based Contact Matrix
(As Defined by Phone Power Customers)

Content	Frequency	PREFERRED COMMUNICATIONS MEDIUM (ACCEPTABLE*)					Telco/PP Resources
		Communiqué	Mail	Phone	Field	Elctr	
1. Regulatory information	Monthtly	✎				💻	**Fax-on-demand (1996)**
2. Updates and changes to services, policy/billing, technology	Monthtly	✎				💻	**Fax-on-demand/ Tele-Direction**
3. Case studies (in-depth)	As requested	✎	📬			💻	**Tele-Direction/ Testimonials**
4. Industry trends	Monthly	✎				💻	**Tele-Direction**
5. Network Management - usage analysis, blockage analysis	Monthtly		📬*	☎*	🏃 as required		
6. Account team/contacts introductions, updates, and the value of each	Beginning and when team changes		📬				**Letter/ Personalized Mailing**
7. Phone Power follow-up after installation of services	1 to 2 days later			☎*	🏃		
8. Market research and call centre statistics (Coopers & Lybrand study, etc.), + benchmarking	As available		📬				**Call Centre Marketplace profile**
9. Economic model and business case for call centre applications (revenue and cost spreadsheets)	As required		📬				
10. Tips and techniques on running a call centre	Monthly, on request	✎	📬	☎*			**Tele-Direction**
11. Training updates and information: standard and customized to training manager/call centre manager, develop a "training catalog", for agents	Quartely		📬	☎*			**Training Catalogue 2Q '96 & Tele-Direction**
12. Post-training follow-up and evaluation	3-6 mos. after training			☎			**Consultant call**
13. Phone Power services portfolio	Annual update, or on request		📬				**Building Profits Through Partnership**
14. Business needs and process assessment	As required			☎*	🏃		
15. Call centre operations review	As required				🏃		**Operations review/Jan. '96**

tomers that are consistent with this value approach to the relationship. It is important to remember that these specific contacts are only a starting point. Actual contacts to add value to your customers could be as varied as your customers.

With these two tools—the set of performance requirements and the list of specific valued contacts—account managers can call on customers with the confidence that they will be adding value. Better yet, account managers can be assured that they will be consistently developing relationships that will result in high-worth and highly productive customers. These performance requirements and the list of specific contacts are core elements used in a well-structured methodology for working with accounts.

Note

1. Al Ries and Jack Trout, *Positioning: The Battle for Your Mind* (New York: McGraw-Hill, 1986), p. 196.

10

The IAM Process

Business processes have been addressed at great length in the reengineering literature available in the business press. Definitions abound:

- A systematic series of actions directed to the achievement of a goal
- A particular method of doing something, generally involving a number of steps or operations
- A set of linked activities that take input and transform it to create output

Each of these definitions either explicitly or implicitly describes two important attributes of a business process.

1. It takes inputs and produces an output (or outputs) of more value than the inputs.
2. It is a series of steps or tasks designed to achieve a goal.

Let's look at the process of introducing integrated account management to a base of customers and look at how the process explains, initiates, and demonstrates this new way of doing business. We will also examine the way IAM sets new performance and relationships expectations with customers and begins to develop the win-win relationships between customers and account managers that are the hallmark of effective IAM programs. Figure 10-1 provides an illustration of an IAM program launch as an input/output model. The inputs in this model include knowledge acquired, analysis conducted, tools developed, existing customer relationships, and customer and marketplace perceptions. The outputs consist of profitability and strong customer relationships leading to customer loyalty. The critical output during this introduction phase is the customer relationship.

How do we design a process that strengthens customer relation-

Figure 10-1. IAM as a process.

Inputs	Process	Outputs

• Customer knowledge
  - Needs
  - Objectives
• Customer database
• Account management software
• Customer worth/grades
• Existing customer relationships
• Customer & marketplace perceptions
• Customer loyalty factors
• Products & applications
• Economic models
• Contact tools library
	Process
	• Gather information
	• Apply customer & product knowledge
	• Customer communications
	• Make customer investments
	• Overcome skepticism
	• Provide value
		• Profits
		• Strong customer relationship
		  - Trust
		  - Willingness to commit
		  - Cooperation
		  - Continuity
		• Customer loyalty
		  - Customer retention
		  - Referrals

Tools Used
in the Process

• Customer database
• Account management
  software
• Economic models
• Contact tools library

ships so that customers trust us, are willing to invest their time, feel they can depend on us, and are willing to make a commitment? There are some obstacles to overcome in developing this kind of customer relationship. For the most part, these obstacles are included in two of the inputs to the process—existing customer relationships and customer and marketplace perceptions. Too often the introduction of an IAM program is viewed as a simple communication step. It would be nice if you could just *tell* customers that you will add value, that they can depend on you and should just trust you. Unfortunately, it is not that easy. The perceptions that are barriers in the marketplace have been developed and reinforced over a long period of time. They are ingrained in customer and supplier behavior, sometimes to the extent that customer responses seem like automated reactions. These perceptions are subtle, almost insidious, in the way they work to prevent strong supplier-customer relationships. Let's consider some of the barriers resulting from these perceptions.

• *Skeptical customers.* These customers believe your self-interest is so great that it prevents the development of a win-win relationship. This skepticism is sometimes so strong that it offsets the value provided by suppliers. It cannot be overcome by telling customers that in this new way of doing business you will both win. It can only be overcome by demonstrating win-win behavior in situations over a period of time. You will never overcome this skepticism in some customers. After the first few contacts, perceptive account managers can usually identify those few skeptical customers with whom the development of a win-win relationship will be a long, arduous, and expensive task. Continuous significant investments in these customers with the goal of changing their skepticism and developing a better relationship are usually not good economic decisions. You need to manage these customers appropriately in the account management mix, servicing them to sustain the relationship you have but not investing in incremental contacts to significantly broaden or strengthen the relationship.

• *Adversarial tone of buyer-seller relationships.* This perspective, that a buyer-seller relationship is adversarial, is equally shared and equally a problem for both buyer and seller. Buyers may believe they need to be tough negotiators to get a fair price and that it is to their advantage to work with multiple suppliers, pitting one against the other. Many industrial buyers still take great pride in their ability to negotiate the lowest price. They believe that every price provided by the seller is artificially high to allow room for negotiation. Sellers often believe that all the customer is after is the lowest price and treat the sale as a conquest. In these kinds of relationships, even after the sale is made, both sides feel dissatisfied. The negotiation too often ends with one or both parties thinking, "I could have gotten a better deal." This adversarial attitude almost always results in each party continually trying to get a little bit more from the other and once receiving it thinking they should have asked for even more.

• *Customers waiting for the sales pitch.* This perception was best characterized in a customer's comment in a survey conducted for a high-tech company: "The only time they call me is when they want to sell me something." What happens when customers see the relationship this way? They literally keep waiting for the sales pitch. They regard questions with caution, concerned that their response will give the supplier ammunition to "sell" them something. They don't listen well to benefits explanations, assuming that they are only the set-up for the sales pitch.

• *Tell-sell expectations.* These expectations are perpetuated by suppliers that explicitly tell customers what they need or implicitly tell them what they need by trying to sell a product without having a conversation that at least confirms the customer's needs. At its worst, this leads to sales of products for which the customer has no need.

One humorous way a good salesperson is described shows how in-grained this perception is: "He could sell ice cubes to Eskimos." When customers have these expectations, they are reluctant to invest time on the front end of the relationship to help a supplier under-stand their needs.

• *Unwillingness to spend time.* It is surprising to many companies how frequently their customers say they see value in a contact from a supplier that asks them questions and gets at their needs. This re-luctance to spend time with suppliers comes out of previous unsuc-cessful efforts. Customers say the time invested does not provide a value in return because the seller does not retain the information or there is too much turnover in the seller's sales force for the investment of time to provide long-term value. From the customer's perspective, the frustration in this issue isn't spending the time, it's spending the *same* time over and over. In our workshops, customers say their num-ber one annoyance is having to train a new sales rep.

• *Doubts that value can be provided.* In some cases, customers be-lieve the intent but doubt that suppliers have the ability to deliver the value promised because there is no historical evidence that the sup-plier can provide that value.

• *A perceived gap between rhetoric and reality.* Unfortunately, over-promising is still sometimes a successful selling tactic. You would be hard-pressed to find customers who have never experienced this with at least one of their suppliers.

The baggage that comes with these obstacles cannot be overcome with more rhetoric. Simply telling customers that you are going to do business differently is not enough. The only way to overcome these obstacles is to have an IAM launch process that demonstrates how different, and how much more valuable, this new way of doing busi-ness will be. Adapting to an IAM program is not easy. In addition to the marketplace barriers, some sales habits prevent easy internaliza-tion of the program. The launch process cannot be left to chance; IAM should be defined and communicated in great detail. In a launch that is designed to effectively deal with these obstacles, each step demon-strates the new way of doing business. Each step adds incremental evidence to ultimately build a strong case for IAM that will secure customers' trust and commitment.

Let's use a representative launch process to demonstrate how such a process works to overcome these obstacles and uses the com-munications performance requirements to ensure that each contact in the launch delivers value to the customer. (The customer contact workshop discussed in Chapter 9 illustrates how communications performance requirements are developed.) For our example, let's use the most frequently occurring performance requirements.

- Contacts must be personalized.
- The purpose of the contact must be stated at the beginning.
- The contact should convey appreciation of the customer.
- The contact should convey an understanding of the customer's unique business needs.
- The contact should be efficient and concise.

Introducing IAM: A Sample Launch Process

For the most part, the introduction of IAM to customers is accomplished in a series of conversations. However, it is of value to include printed introductory materials in the launch process. Because of the nature of printed materials, this introduction package, as used in step 5.0 of the launch process (outlined later in this chapter), provides a number of additional benefits in the IAM launch, including the following:

• It serves as a confirmation and clarification of the conversation(s) that the account manager had with the customer. In most cases, IAM is a new and significantly different way of doing business with customers. The introduction package clarifies, reinforces, confirms, and even demonstrates this new way of doing business. It highlights new expectations that customers should have in an IAM relationship, describes the value that customers should anticipate receiving, demonstrates the use of mail as a value-adding contact medium, and demonstrates the continuity between contacts that customers should expect.

• It starts to build a relationship between the customer and the account manager. The package should make it clear to customers that all future contacts, including mail, are part of their relationship with their account manager.

• It becomes a reference tool for the customer. This introduction package is a great opportunity to add value at the start of the IAM process. IAM will make it easier for customers to do business with your company. Use this introduction package as a way to teach customers how to do this.

The IAM Introduction Package

A package delivering these benefits should typically contain the following components:

• *Envelope.* Obviously, this package needs to go out in an envelope. Not as obvious is the opportunity to highlight this package as an important piece to the customer coming directly from the account manager. It should be clear to the customer upon seeing the envelope that this is a package from the account manager.

• *Letter.* The package should contain a personalized letter to the customer from the account manager. The letter should convey appreciation of the customer, list the other materials included in the package, summarize IAM as a new way of doing business, invite the customer to contact the account manager at any time with further questions or needs, and set up the next contact by the account manager (e.g., "I will call you to follow up on our conversation regarding . . .").

• *Brochure.* A brochure or circular that announces the new IAM program is usually included. The brochure should explain
   —The reason you are implementing IAM
   —How IAM will work from the customer's perspective
   —How IAM will benefit the customer
   —The new or increased expectations that customers should have
     of you
   —The steps customers can take to get the most value from this
     way of doing business

• *Reference materials.* These are value-adding pieces that are intended to be retained and used by customers over a long period of time. They should help customers understand how best to do business with you. These materials could include company telephone directories, product reference information, and easily referenced information about the customer's individual account manager (e.g., Rolodex card with phone numbers, account manager introduction piece).

This package, once developed and used, is informative, not promotional. It is personalized to the customer from the account manager. As part of the IAM launch process, it confirms the information discussed in the previous contact and sets up the next contact. It efficiently communicates this way of doing business with customers by demonstrating a number of the operating principles that define IAM.

A process walk-through is the most effective way to get an in-depth understanding of the launch process which is diagrammed in Figure 10-2.

0.0   *Before the launch, gather and consolidate customer data.* Some
        customer information is gathered by the account manag-

Figure 10-2. IAM launch process.

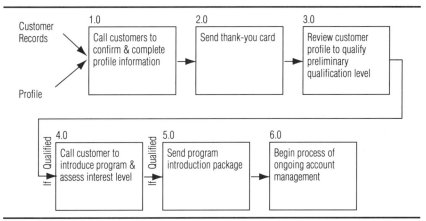

ers. In addition, a substantial amount of customer information is provided by different parts of the organization.
For example, there may be billing information in accounting, service information in the customer service group,
and ordering and shipping information in an order processing and fulfillment system. The gathering and provi-
sion of this data to account managers can, depending on
the accuracy and completeness of the data, allow account
managers to demonstrate to customers that their previous investments of time to provide information were not
wasted. The data also provide a framework to drive the
most efficient contact.

1.0   *Call customers to confirm a complete profile.* This is not a
        sales call. This call is intended to allow the supplier to
        gather information about the customer and the custom-
        er's needs so that the supplier can better serve those
        needs. There is no sales pitch. If a sale is made, the discus-
        sion is initiated by the customer. The attitude conveyed
        is one of listening and understanding. The caller asks per-
        mission for the customer's time and states the intent of
        the call at the beginning of the call.

2.0   *Send a thank-you note or letter.* The account manager sends
        the customer a thank-you note conveying appreciation
        for the time spent by the customer, reaffirming the value
        of the information provided by the customer, and ensur-
        ing the customer that the information provided will be
        used to service the customer better. An effective format is
        a personalized, handwritten note from the account man-
        ager. Although not as personal, a system-generated letter
        signed by the account manager can also be effective.

3.0   *Review customer profile and conduct preliminary qualification assessment.* In preparation for a relationship where there is a greater investment in customers and where incremental value is added to customers, account managers assess the fit of each customer. At this point, customers have already been assigned to an account manager's module based on the segment and grade of the customer (the design of modules is covered in Chapter 7; the segmentation and grading of customers is covered in Chapter 6). To some degree, this already qualifies them as customers you want to include in your IAM program (assuming the information you have compiled is accurate; it is not unusual for this confirming call to identify inaccurate customer information). However, there are typically some qualifying criteria that can only be captured and identified in the actual call or conversation with the customer. These criteria include the customer's future plans (e.g., growth objectives) and the customer's attitudes regarding particular issues that are important to the relationship. For example, if you are selling technology products and services and the customer has an aversion to technology, you may want to remove this customer from the module or change the customer's grade level. Some customers won't provide enough revenue to make the investment worthwhile, some customers won't value the relationship, and some customers simply won't have needs that you can address. This off-line step allows account managers to make that assessment. It is a relatively loose screen that removes from the program customers that obviously do not fit the conditions necessary for a mutually beneficial relationship.

4.0   *Conduct customer introduction calls.* Again, the account manager contacts the customer, this time to introduce the IAM program and to explain the benefits of the program. The account manager conveys knowledge and understanding of the customer's needs (gathered or confirmed in step 1.0) by explaining how the program supports some of the customer's needs. Again, this is not a sales call, and a sale is transacted only if initiated by the customer. The account manager commits to sending an introductory package to the customer explaining the program in more detail. The account manager then attempts to schedule a follow-up call to discuss in more detail a particular need or set of needs that he has confirmed to be of some importance and urgency to the customer. If there are no immediate needs, the account manager commits to a follow-up call with the customer in approximately three months.

5.0 *Send the introductory package.* Figure 10-3 contains components of the introductory package for the Lexmark Authorized Typewriter Dealer Support Representative Program (an IAM program). The package contains a personalized letter to the customer, a brochure explaining the program—what customers can expect and what's expected of them—a card with a picture of and introduction to the account manager, and a Rolodex card with names and phone numbers of company contacts.

6.0 *Begin the ongoing process (calling on customers) of IAM.* Finally, the account manager enters into a value-based selling process that loosely works through the following steps:

- Reaches decision maker
- Makes introduction
- Clarifies and confirms needs as identified in previous contacts
- Asks questions to determine business needs
- Identifies appropriate services; explains value proposition
- Makes sales presentation
- Handles objections, receives feedback
- Repositions—explains how product can add value given the customer's objections, or suggests alternative
- Closes presentation; thanks customer
- Sets expectation for next contact
- Completes postcall, wrap-up, documentation work

This six-step IAM launch process is effective at meeting the performance requirements and overcoming the obstacles that come out of marketplace perceptions because:

- Each written contact is personalized. Both the thank-you note and the introductory package are addressed to the specific customer, both are signed by the account manager, and the thank-you note is handwritten by the account manager.
- In each of the three phone contacts, the purpose for the contact is stated at the beginning of the call.
- The two written contacts explicitly state appreciation for the customer.

(text continues on p. 172)

Figure 10-3. Sample introductory package brochure.

Questions and Answers About
The Lexmark Dealer Support
Representative Program

1. *Q) What is the Dealer Support Representative (DSR) Program?*

    A) This is a program that provides all Authorized Typewriter Dealers (ATDs) with additional typewriter and supplies support from Lexmark. Through timely mailings and phone calls each ATD will receive sales support and information pertaining to Lexmark products and programs.

2. *Q) How does this program differ from what I am receiving today?*

    A) Inside marketing personnel will team up with Lexmark Dealer Account Representatives (DARs) to support ATDs nationwide. The support representatives will communicate with you primarily by mail and phone conversations. They will provide timely information and help make sure that Lexmark is providing the resources you need as you sell our products. This will free up some of the DARs time to concentrate on things like specific marketing programs, training and joint sales calls to increase typewriter sales within your business.

3. *Q) Which Lexmark distribution channels will benefit from the Dealer Support Representative Program?*

    A) Lexmark is announcing this program to the Authorized Typewriter Dealer (ATD) channel at this time. We will assess the effectiveness of the program and may introduce this program to other Lexmark resellers at a later date.

4. *Q) How long will this program be in effect?*

    A) There are no pre-determined time limits on this program. As long as this program is effective as a communications vehicle and provides a high degree of dealer satisfaction; it can be expected to continue indefinitely.

5. *Q) Will I see a change in Lexmark Dealer Account Representative (DAR) coverage?*

    A) In some cases, account coverage will change in an effort to provide a better balance across the United States and to increase specialization. Each ATD will be assigned a specific Lexmark DAR and Dealer Support Representative (DSR).

    (continues)

Figure 10-3. *Continued.*

6. *Q) Why is Lexmark introducing the Dealer Support Representative Program at this time?*

A) The primary reason is to enhance our responsiveness and support of all ATDs and to maximize the typewriter business through effective sales contacts.

7. *Q) How many times can I expect to be contacted throughout the year?*

A) The number of contacts throughout the year will vary by ATD. Some dealerships will receive a higher or lower number of contacts due to size, business potential, or geographic proximity. At a minimum, each ATD will be contacted by mail and/or phone on the average of once a month.

8. *Q) What are the responsibilities of the DSR?*

A) The DSR will work closely with your DAR to provide you with product or program information on a timely basis. The responsibilities will vary, but will include such items as product announcements, marketing programs and promotions, problem resolution assistance, performance tracking and sales assistance. This program will not replace any of the currently established Lexmark services (i.e., order assistance from Lexmark Order Management Center, technical help, and information from Technical Support Operations, etc.).

9. *Q) Will the Dealer Support Representatives (DSRs) be knowledgeable on all Lexmark products?*

A) The DSR will support all current IBM Typewriters and associated supplies. They may not be able to assist with questions or situations relating to non-typewriter related Lexmark products. You should call your DAR with these questions.

10. *Q) Who should I call when I have a question about a Lexmark product or program?*

A) There are several sources of assistance within Lexmark to answer various questions. If you have a sales related need or cannot find the answer to a question, call your Dealer Support Rep or DAR.

11. *Q) Will this service/program be offered to Lexmark Dealer Associates?*

A) The Dealer Support Representative Program is being offered only to active ATDs.

12. *Q) Are the DSRs available for dealer phone calls? If so, when?*

A) One of the benefits of the Dealer Support Representative Program is the day-to-day availability of the inside marketing support reps. Although much of their time will be spent on communications outbound, they are also available to accept your calls. The Dealer Support Reps will be available 8:30 a.m. - 7:00 p.m., EST/EDT.

13. *Q) Who will the Lexmark Dealer Support Representative contact within the dealership?*

A) The DSR will work with the people in your dealership who sell or support IBM Typewriters. During the initial calls, you will be asked to help identify the correct people and their responsibilities.

14. *Q) Will all of my authorized locations receive contacts as a part of the Dealer Support Representative Program?*

A) Initially, only your primary location will receive mailing and/or phone contacts related to this program. However, through communications with you and/or the DAR, other locations and individuals can selectively be included at your request.

15. *Q) Who is my primary Lexmark contact?*

A) The Lexmark DAR will continue to be responsible for dealer satisfaction within the ATD channel. However, some ATDs will find that the DSR will be the primary contact for their sales-related activities.

16. *Q) When will the Lexmark Dealer Support Representative Program begin?*

A) We intend for the program to be operational starting July 1, 1994. You may receive your first call as early as the later part of June. This will be an introductory call to verify that the information in our files is up-to-date.

- The customer's needs are confirmed and an understanding of those needs demonstrated in steps 4.0, 5.0, and 6.0.
- At no point in the process before step 6.0 does the account manager attempt to move the conversation to a sales discussion.
- Through a series of making and fulfilling commitments, the account manager has demonstrated the company's dependability.
- With a thorough up-front process and time investment, the account manager has demonstrated a willingness to make an investment in and commitment to the relationship.
- There is continuity in the process. Each step clearly leads to the next. The customer knows what to expect, and the account manager reliably delivers.
- Even when the selling process begins at step 6.0, it is consultative in nature, based on the customer's needs and built around a solution that helps the customer achieve objectives.

These steps engage the customer in the launch process and set a foundation for customer trust and commitment in the business relationship.

I remember a particularly insightful conversation with a client that was in the middle of implementing a launch process similar to this. We were discussing how it was working customers through the process, taking them through the first call, the mail contacts, the second call, and finally the third call. While discussing these, she almost apologetically said, "Mark, we can't help it. We're selling on the first and second calls." What happened was that there was so much value in the customer base, so much pent-up demand, and such an eagerness for this kind of relationship that customers were initiating sales discussions in the nonselling contact (the first and second calls).

Institutionalizing the Launch Process

Important steps in institutionalizing the IAM launch process include making the process tangible, making it visible, communicating it, and explaining the rationale, objectives, and benefits to account managers.

Short of stamping this process on account managers' foreheads, how do you ensure they follow a process like this? It is not necessarily easy; it takes patience, discipline, faith, and a thorough understanding of the rationale behind the process. There are a number of specific steps in building IAM that increase adherence to the process. Consider the following:

- The process is documented. The picture is worth a thousand words. The process is charted in a relatively easy to understand linear process diagram (see Figure 10-2).
- The process chart is posted in each inside account manager's workstation and is inserted in each outside account manager's planner. Additionally, the chart is posted on the wall at the account management center.
- The process is embedded in and is an integral part of training. In fact, much of the training is built around the process.
- Account manager-customer tracking systems monitor progress and visibly post results within the process.

Summary

Once institutionalized, the process becomes "background music" for account managers. It allows account managers to focus on their customers during the contacts, increases the probability that account managers will be able to overcome customer relationship obstacles, and provides account managers with leveraged tools to use in the process. Productivity and quality are both supported as customer relationships are developed.

11

Building the Contact Plan

Superior contact planning is the essence of world-class integrated account management. It is where you take what you have learned about customers and develop a plan that works. Let's review what you have accomplished up to this point.

- You have gone through segmentation, which has enabled you to develop an understanding of what your customers' needs and business objectives are and has provided you with a framework for associating specific customers with the needs identified.
- You have gone through grading, which has enabled you to determine what each customer is worth to ensure that you invest in customers in the right amount to run a profitable business.
- You have gone through a value-based contact workshop, which has helped you define what a value-based contact is. This knowledge enables you to understand what customers value in communication, that is, what kinds of contacts they want and how those contacts provide value to them.

You have spent a substantial amount of time getting smart about customers. It is now time to build the contact plan. This is the point at which you decide how you are going to build the plan that drives your communication with each customer.

Three Levels of Contact Planning

By its very nature, the management of many customer relationships is complex. Marketers continue to pose questions regarding who in the organization develops the contact plan and consequently who drives the communications with customers. Is it best planned by corporate marketing, sales management, or an individual account manager? Ultimately, you will need individual account managers to take ownership of and to implement contact plans for their customers. This suggests that account managers have to be involved in development of the contact plan. In addition, it is essential that the customer contact plan fit into the economic requirements of the company, sends a consistent message to the marketplace, and provides for achievement of minimal customer coverage goals. This suggests that sales and marketing management also need to be involved in the development of the contact plan.

To facilitate this involvement and address these issues, the contact plan as described here is developed at three levels: the overall corporate marketing, the module, and the individual customer levels. The overall corporate marketing level provides a basis for all communications with customers. The contact plan at this level provides a benchmark for how and how often all customers in the total customer base are contacted. The decisions made at this first level create a standard for all customers as well as an expectation for all of the account managers. At this level the plan provides a guideline that underlies the economics for all of account management.

For example, if you have an IAM program center with ten account managers, you start by developing a contact plan for the whole program. Of primary interest is the number of contacts, their grade levels, and ways to make those contacts profitably (specifically, what contact medium to use).

The next level of contact planning is the module level. At this level the goal is to create an appropriate balance of customer coverage, account manager productivity, value to customers, and profitability within each module. The module level, more than any other, deals with the allocation of limited marketing resources, the most limited of these resources being the account manager. Perhaps most important is to drive a degree of ownership for the contact plan into the account manager level by having each account manager develop his or her own contact plan using the overall plan as a guideline. In some cases the overall plan specifies minimum contact levels, but in all cases it serves as a template to determine what the account managers do with their individual modules as they develop a contact plan for their set of accounts and for each individual account.

The third level is the individual customer level. At this level individual contact plans are developed for each customer by the account manager or account management team. An individual account strategy is developed to ensure that relevant value (that is, value that specifically deals with the customer's individual business situation and addresses the customer's individual needs) is being provided to the customer through the solutions sold and through the contacts known to lead to sales.

The Rationale Behind Contact Planning

Why bother going through this process? Consider the benefits of effective contact planning:

• Contact planning provides, first and foremost, a degree of structure and control. It results in high degrees of productivity and builds tools that provide value to customers. Because contact planning is built into the module plan and moves it forward, it allows structure and process that are "background music" for the account manager, whose actual work, of course, is focusing on customers. Contact planning supports putting the structure in the background and the focus on individual customers in the foreground.

• Contact planning provides a framework for leverage and consistency in the way account managers work with customers. Leverage comes because the overall contact plan gives account managers a beginning frame of reference. Consistency results because all account managers are working from the same frame of reference. When the module is viewed from an overall level for all customers, the result is a set of guidelines that drives consistency in the organization and at a customer level. The consistency is applied at the module level and adapted to accommodate the uniqueness of each individual module in a manner that is supportive of the account manager's knowledge of his or her module and is compatible with the way each account manager wants to work that module.

• Contact planning ensures customer coverage and service across the total account base. When trying to build some "stretch" into a module (and have an account manager cover a number of accounts that exceeds any historical precedent), it is easy for some accounts to get lost in the shuffle. This approach to contact planning protects accounts from neglect. It provides checkpoints through the use of minimal contact levels for all account grades to ensure that there is coverage across the total customer base rather than just the portion of the customer base that offers immediate opportunities for sales.

• Contact planning creates common expectations and encourages ownership of the process itself. Building the contact plan at all three levels provides common expectations for all the account managers and does so in a way that places ownership of the entire process at the account manager level. This ownership ensures that what gets planned gets implemented. The common expectations set through this contact planning process ensure that the ownership is experienced within an appropriately controlled model. Corporate marketing management can comfortably give up customer contact control and know that an acceptable contact level with customers is being maintained.

• Contact planning helps account managers adapt more easily to a new way of doing business. Typically, when a new IAM program is being implemented, there are a lot of obstacles to overcome. A whole new productivity standard is being set. Contact productivity in IAM programs is maintained at a level significantly greater than has ever existed in most organizations. Combined with this is a whole new expectation around how to provide value to customers. Providing more value to more customers at a faster pace is virtually impossible without a plan.

• Contact planning helps allay the fears that "just come with the territory" of selling. These can include the fear of getting in front of a customer, the fear of getting on the telephone with a customer, and the fear of rejection. All of these dynamics can make the situation fairly complex for a new account manager or someone moving into the position from a different role. It is important to provide direction by assigning some very specific tasks that will allow account managers to be productive. An overall contact plan provides this direction.

A Core Principle: Optimizing the Mix

One of the basic principles of world-class IAM is that of optimizing the mix (introduced in Chapter 2, operating principle 12, which states: Each contact with a customer is part of a larger system of contacts. Excellence is achieved through integration of these contacts. This optimization is a relatively simple yet extremely powerful process. It works as follows:

Old Contact Plan (Mix Not Optimized)

Let's use a grade B customer as an example. As illustrated in Figure 11-1, this B customer is one of 250 such customers, and each one is worth $20,000–$40,000 in annual sales volume. While not the highest graded customers, B customers are excellent customers with significant worth. In the old model contact plan, this customer was contacted twelve times annually in the field. At a field contact cost of $400 per contact, the annual customer contact investment in each of these customers is $4,800.

Figure 11-1. Old contact plan—mix not optimized.

Grade/Sales ($000)	1000 Accounts	Contact Frequency		Average Annual Customer Contact Cost
		Field		
		Per acct	Total	
AA $60 +	50	20	1,000	$8,000
A $40-60	150	15	2,250	$6,000
B $20-40	250	12	3,000	$4,800
C $10-20	250	6	1,500	$2,400
D < $10	300	6	1,800	$2,400
Total contacts	68,550 =	+6,550		
Average contact cost	$47.28	$400.00		
Total cost by medium ($000)	$3,241	$2,620		

New Contact Plan (Optimized Mix)

In the new contact plan (Figure 11-2), the mix of contacts by contact medium is adjusted. Field contacts are adjusted down from twelve to eight. Twenty-five phone contacts are added to the mix. These phone contacts are tightly linked to the field contacts. The inside account manager works closely with the field manager or outside account manager. Their calling patterns are well coordinated, their focus on

Figure 11-2. New contact plan—optimized mix.

Grade/Sales ($000)	1000 Accounts	Contact Frequency						Average Annual Customer Contact Cost
		Mail		Phone		Field		
		Per acct	Total	Per acct	Total	Per acct	Total	
AA $60 +	50	12	600	50	2,500	20	1,000	$9,060
A $40-60	150	12	1,800	40	6,000	15	2,250	$6,860
B $20-40	250	12	3,000	25	6,250	8	2,000	$3,760
C $10-20	250	18	4,500	12	3,000	4	1,000	$1,030
D < $10	300	24	7,200	10	3,000	1	300	$720
Total contacts	68,550 =	41,250		+20,750		+6,550		
Average contact cost	$47.28	$5.00		$20.00		$400.00		
Total cost by medium ($000)	$3,241	$206		$415		$2,620		

value has consistency, and their respective contacts complement one another. Twelve mail contacts are also added. Again, these are focused on value and are approved by both the field and inside account managers. At a field contact cost of $400 per contact, a phone cost of $20 per contact, and a mail cost of $5 per contact, the total annual investment in each of these customers is $3,760.

Let's look at the results from this "optimized contact plan."

• The total contact cost for this customer was reduced from $4,800 to $3,760. This represents a savings of $1,040 on this one customer—a savings of almost 22 percent over the old contact cost. Applying this 22 percent savings across all B accounts represents a total savings of $260,000 (and this is only the B accounts: 250 out of 1,000 total accounts).
• The total number of contacts for this customer has increased from twelve to forty-five. This increased contact level makes customers feel they are getting a higher level of service. In my experience, the customer's perceived service level is more impacted by the frequency of contact than by the contact medium.
• The leverage provided by integrating phone and field contacts allows the field account manager to handle a significantly greater number of accounts. The four contacts saved on this one account can now be applied to other accounts.

This principle is applied at both the overall and module contact planning levels to simultaneously increase customer perceived service levels, increase customer satisfaction and loyalty, and decrease the cost of selling.

During the transition of the Shell Oil Company TBA business to TeamTBA (Shell's aftermarket sales organization, discussed in Chapter 1) the field account manager in the Chicago North District, Bob Johnson, had a module planning and implementation challenge. His was a district that contained approximately 100 Shell Autocare dealers. It was managed in the old contact plan model by twelve field sales territory managers. In 1993, Bob was taking over this district as the only field account manager, with one inside account manager. Incidentally, this inside account manager also had responsibility for 100 other accounts shared with another field account manager. Bob focused on a module plan that delivered contact frequency to all dealers, allocated his time primarily to the upper account grades, and delivered significant value and leverage through coordinated phone contacts.

The obstacles here were attitudinal. The Shell district office was doubtful that the plan would deliver enough value to dealers and presumed that this integrated contact strategy would ultimately result in a decrease in sales volume. Some dealers were also skeptical. They doubted that phone contacts would be valuable, and some were concerned that the decrease in face-to-face contact would have a significant negative impact on service. Interestingly, the higher-worth dealers tended to think they could get by with less contact than Bob's plan called for, and the lower-worth dealers thought they would need more contact (especially face-to-face) than the contact plan indicated.

In a relatively short time the value delivered changed, the worth of customers changed, and, consequently, perspectives changed. Dealers appreciated the fact that the inside account manager had their detailed purchase history, could help them track their inventory, help with sell-through of product, and could be relied on to be there whenever the dealer called. They no longer looked at the inside account manager as a telemarketer trying to sell them something or simply calling to take an order. Both sales and customer satisfaction levels increased. TeamTBA was actually able to win back some of the TBA business that had been lost to local suppliers. Bob's role with customers became increasingly consultative. He was helping the dealers understand how to improve their businesses, specifically the sale of tires, batteries, and accessories, through merchandising, sell-through support, recommendations, and training.

The remainder of this chapter is devoted to a detailed description of the three levels of contact planning.

Level 1: The Overall Customer Contact Plan

The overall level is the highest level of the planning process. It is at this level that company policy is set for IAM. The goal is to develop a benchmark for how and how often the customers in the total customer base are contacted. A good customer contact plan ensures coverage so that customers will be insulated from the competition. It demonstrates, step by step, the achievability of targets. Guidelines are developed to support the customer contact policy, and tools are identified to accomplish the sales objectives for account management. The message sent to account managers is, as a business unit here is how we intend to do business with customers.

A good example of this is the overall plan developed by Shell's TeamTBA (see Figure 11-3). The customer contact matrix was defined to manage account contacts—that is, to balance getting the maximum return from each account while providing optimal value using a mix-

Figure 11-3. TeamTBA customer contact matrix annual data.

Average Revenue		Field Contacts	O/B Phone Contacts	Mail Contacts
$10,000+	A	40–50	24	24
$2,500-$10,000	B	24	18	24
$1,000-$2,500	C	15	12	12
$250-$1,000	D	2	6	12
$0-$100	E	1	4	6
Cost per contact		$175	$30	$5

ture of contacts, each with vastly different costs, with some contacts being delivered by limited resources.

The contact policy for outbound contacts was as follows:

- Field account managers call on the A, B, and C accounts at a frequency that depends on territory size and the needs of the customer. A accounts should be called on most frequently, up to once per week if the customer needs it (contacts are generally face-to-face but would also include quality phone contacts). B accounts are generally contacted twice a month, and C accounts generally once every three to four weeks.
- Field account managers must complete the prospecting appointments set by their inside rep, regardless of grade. These are mostly lower-worth accounts, C and also D and E accounts.
- Inside account managers call on all account grades, but at very different frequencies than field reps do. Inside reps contact the A and B accounts at most two times each month. C accounts are contacted once per month, and D and E accounts (mostly prospecting calls) should be set up to utilize the remainder of the available outbound calling time.

Developing the Overall Contact Plan

The steps to develop an overall contact plan are as follows:

1. *Determine contact costs.* To allocate contacts effectively across the various grade levels of customers, it is necessary to determine the cost of each field, phone, and mail contact. Contact costs are calcu-

lated determining the fully burdened cost (a fully burdened cost includes all the expenses, direct and indirect, associated with putting an account manager in the field or on the phone) of the contact resource, determining the number of contacts delivered by or through that resource, and then dividing the fully burdened cost by the number of contacts delivered. When working through these costs for both inside and field account managers, all expenses (such as automobile, equipment, suppliers, training costs, and management time) are included in the calculation.

Let's use a hypothetical company, Acme Office Machines, Inc., a provider of office equipment and maintenance services to the business marketplace, to demonstrate this contact planning process. Figure 11-4 illustrates the components and the fully burdened cost of a field account manager for Acme Office Machines. Figure 11-5 illustrates the components and the fully burdened cost of an inside or telephone account manager.

Once the fully burdened cost is calculated, the next step is to determine the average number of contacts that can be made in a year. Account manager capacity, as reflected by the number of contacts that can be made annually, can vary substantially from industry to industry and even from company to company within an industry. In our example, you can see that Acme Office Machines field account managers spend 190 days per year in the field and at four contacts per day have an annual capacity of 760 customer contacts (see Figure 11-6). Phone account managers spending 210 days working the

Figure 11-4. Acme Office Machines field account manager estimated fully burdened cost.

Base compensation	$60,000
Estimated variable compensation	$30,000
Benefits	$25,000
Auto expenses	$10,000
Equipment & usage (phone, computer, fax)	$12,000
Travel & entertainment	$25,000
Training	$20,000
Direct management (also an allocation of a fully burdened cost)	$20,000
Support resources	$20,000
Supplies	$5,000
Miscellaneous	$5,000
TOTAL	$232,000

Note: These costs are used to demonstrate the model and calculations. They are not intended to necessarily reflect actual industry costs.

Figure 11-5. Acme Office Machines telephone account manager estimated fully burdened cost.

Base compensation	$30,000
Estimated variable compensation	$10,000
Benefits	$10,000
Equipment	$12,000
(phone, computer, software, allocated office equipment)	
Training	$5,000
Direct management	$10,000
(also an allocation of a fully burdened cost)	
Support resources	$5,000
Supplies	$3,000
Miscellaneous	$3,000
TOTAL	$88,000

Note: These costs are used to demonstrate the model and calculations. They are not intended to necessarily reflect actual industry costs.

Figure 11-6. Acme Office Machines field account manager average contact capacity.

Number of days in year	Average vacation days	Holidays	Administrative and training days	Planning time/days (@3 hrs/wk)	Total calling days	Average contacts per day	Total annual contacts
260	15	10	25	20	190	4	760

phones at thirty contacts per day, have an annual capacity of 6,300 customers contacts (see Figure 11-7).

Next, calculate the contact cost by dividing the fully burdened cost (Figures 11-4 and 11-5) by the capacity numbers of contacts in Figures 11-6 and 11-7. The result of these calculations is as follows: $232,000/760 equals a field contact cost of $305; $88,000/6,300 gives a phone contact cost of $14.

2. *Estimate average account grade level distribution.* Account grades have usually been assigned at this point (Chapter 6 provides more detail regarding account grades). What is needed here is the average

Figure 11-7. Acme Office Machines telephone account manager average contact capacity.

Number of days in year	Average vacation days	Holidays	Administrative and training days	Planning time/days (@3 hrs/wk)	Total calling days	Average contacts per day	Total annual contacts
260	10	10	10	20	210	30	6300

account grade distribution across a module—specifically, the number of accounts and the percentages of accounts in grades AA, A, B, C, and D. The five-level grading model in Chapter 6 provides a frame of reference for this distribution: AA, 5 percent; A, 15 percent; B, 25 percent; C, 25 percent; D, 30 percent. Figure 11-8 illustrates this distribution for Acme Office Machines.

3. *Estimate account management capacity.* In Step 1, you estimated the capacity of an individual account manager. The IAM center capacity is simply the sum of the averages. For example, calculating this for Acme Office Machines, an IAM center with thirty-seven field account managers and fourteen phone account managers (using the individual account manager capacity numbers in Figures 11-6 and 11-7), total available contacts are 116,320, consisting of 28,120 field contacts and 88,200 phone contacts. In some IAM environments, capacity is calculated at a level higher than historical levels, assuming that with higher goals account managers will increase their productivity. While this is sometimes effective, the risk is that this tactic may leave the center underresourced and subsequently not provide either the service level required or the customer coverage desired. In other environments, capacity to service the existing customer base is calculated at a lower level, assuming that account managers will be bringing new accounts into the model.

4. *Build an overall contact matrix.* The intent in building the contact matrix is to determine how the contact resources will be allocated to accounts. The contact matrix provides a format for planning and communicating an integrated contact plan for the organization. Begin developing this contact matrix using any popular spreadsheet package (as developed and illustrated for Acme Office Machines in Figure 11-9) using the format in Figure 11-10.
   a. Insert predefined numbers.
     • Grade levels and worth of accounts at indicated grade

Figure 11-8. Acme Office Machines account grade distribution.

Grade/Sales ($000)	Number of Accounts	Percentage of Total Accounts
AA $60+	258	6%
A $40-60	774	18%
B $20-40	1,204	28%
C $10-20	1,075	25%
D <$10	989	23%
TOTAL	4,300	

Figure 11-9. Acme Office Machines overall customer contact matrix.

Grade/Sales ($000)	4300 Accounts	Mail Per acct	Mail Total	Phone Per acct	Phone Total	Field Per acct	Field Total	Sales Cost per Customer	% of Sales
AA $60 +	258	12	3,096	50	12,900	15	3,870	$5,335	8.89%
A $40-60	774	12	9,288	35	27,090	12	9,288	$4,210	8.42%
B $20-40	1,204	12	14,448	25	30,100	8	9,632	$2,850	9.50%
C $10-20	1,075	24	25,800	12	12,900	4	4,300	$1,508	10.05%
D < $10	989	24	23,736	6	5,934	2	1,978	$814	9.04%
Total contacts			76,368		88,924		29,068		
Average contact cost			$5		$14		$305		
Total cost by medium ($000)			$382		$1,245		$8,868		

levels. Refer to the grades that you created in Chapter 6, "Segmenting and Grading Customers," for your grade level definitions. Acme Office Machines' grade levels and corresponding customer worth levels are shown in the Grade/Sales column in Figure 9-9.

- Customer counts. These are the numbers of accounts that meet the definition of each particular grade level. For Acme Office Machines, there are 258 AA customers.
- Calculated phone and field costs (average cost each). In

Figure 11-10. Your Company overall customer contact matrix.

Grade/Sales ($000)	Accounts	Mail Per acct	Mail Total	Phone Per acct	Phone Total	Field Per acct	Field Total	Sales Cost per Customer	% of Sales
AA $									
A $									
B $									
C $									
D < $									
Total contacts									
Average contact cost									
Total cost by medium ($000)									

the Acme Office Machines example (Figure 11-9) these are shown as $14 and $305, respectively. The estimated cost of an average mail contact is $5 in the Acme Office Machines example.

- The estimated sales (average annual sales dollar volume for each grade level).

b. Insert formulas into the spreadsheet.

- Total contacts by medium, calculated by multiplying the number of accounts by the total contact frequency for each medium.
- Sales cost, a calculation of the total sales contact cost at each grade level and in total. This is calculated by multiplying the total contact frequency by the average contact cost for each medium (mail, phone, and field), and then adding the three together.
- Sales cost per customer, calculated by dividing the sales cost by the number of customers at each grade level.
- Total costs by medium, the sum of total contact frequency by medium multiplied by the average contact cost for that medium.

Having these formulas preinserted into the spreadsheet will allow you to immediately see the economic impact and the capacity impact of each contact frequency.

c. Define per-account field contact frequency by grade. This is part of the larger step of defining the per-account contact frequency by medium. The per-account contact frequency is the driving number of this matrix. Once you determine this frequency, all other numbers are calculated from it. Determining this frequency is a trial-and-error exercise that ultimately results in planned customer coverage in total and at each grade level, a contact cost balanced to revenue, a mix of media leveraged to manage accounts, and an effective allocation and use of limited contact resources. Use the following guidelines to determine field contact frequency:

- Field contacts should reflect the principle of investing in customers relative to their worth. This means that you can afford to spend significantly more on your AA customers than on your A customers, more on your A customers than on your B, and so on. In our Acme Office Machines example, fifteen field contacts are planned for AA accounts, and twelve field contacts are planned for A accounts. This means that Acme Office Machines is investing $4,575 in field contacts—or 7.63 percent of the

AA revenue—for each AA account and $3,660, or 7.32 percent of the A revenue, for each A account.

In many cases, these percentages will be similar at each grade level. However, there are a number of reasons why you would invest in a different proportion at certain grade levels in field contacts:

(1) Some grade levels simply don't need an equal proportion of field contacts. Twelve field contacts may be the maximum number that is needed and meaningful. This number is determined by what customers have indicated as value-based contacts (see Chapter 9) combined with the number of messages you want to get to the customers throughout the year. In such a case Acme Office Machines would plan twelve field contacts per year for both AA and A customers.

(2) You can frequently offset field contacts with phone contacts.

(3) There are particular planned marketing events (product introduction, product penetration campaigns, and so on) throughout the year that require field contact for a number of customers, irrespective of grade.

- The field contact volume should be consistent with the principle stating that all contacts provide value to customers. For Acme Office Machines, this means that it believes that each of the planned fifteen field contacts will add value to customers and that this belief has been confirmed in customer workshops (as outlined in Chapter 9).

- The total number of field contacts should be consistent with the total estimated field capacity. Acme Office Machines has planned field contacts at 29,068 versus an estimated capacity of 28,120. This is a reasonable difference, in particular because Acme Office Machines has initiatives planned during the year to increase the capacity of its account managers. This difference means that each field account manager needs to make twenty-five additional contacts—one additional customer contact every two weeks.

d. Define the per-account phone contact frequency by grade.
  - Determine phone contact frequency after you have completed field contact frequency. Again, as with field contacts, you need to stay focused on two goals: (1) investing in customers relative to their worth and (2) ensuring that

all customer contacts add value. In the Acme example, per-account phone contact frequency is set at fifty contacts per year for AA accounts. The combined per-account investment in phone and field contacts to AA accounts is now $5,275, or 8.79 percent of the revenue generated for an average AA account.

- Also, as in field contacts, you have to stay consistent with the phone IAM contact capacity. However, it is usually easier and less expensive to increase phone capacity than it is to increase field capacity. A particular tactic used when defining phone contacts is to assess and ensure customer coverage. If, at any grade level, you are not comfortable that you have adequate coverage to protect customers from competition, phone contacts are a substantially more economical way to increase coverage than field contacts.
- At this point, you have a mix of field and phone contacts. This mix of contacts will probably represent an extremely high percentage of your total investment in customers (Acme Office Machines' plan shows phone and field contact expenses at 96 percent of total contact expenses).

e. Define the per-account mail contact frequency by grade. Mail contacts are added to the mix for a number of reasons, including:

- They increase the productivity of field and phone contacts. Mail contacts can be used to set up a field or phone contact (setting the customer's expectations for the call) or used as follow-up contacts after a phone or field contact.
- They incrementally increase customer coverage. There may be some grade levels at which it is not economically viable to contact customers often enough in person or by phone to protect them from competition. In these situations, mail can be used to decrease your vulnerability with these customers.
- They deliver customer-preferred, value-based contacts. In most markets, there are a set of contacts that customers simply prefer to receive through the mail (you have identified these in the customer workshop in Chapter 9).

5. *Assess economics and achievability.* After you have defined the frequency of all contacts, your next step is to assess and modify, if indicated, the overall contact plan. You have worked through the ini-

tial definition of contact frequency one medium at a time. Your focus is broader here as you assess the overall plan, addressing the following questions:

- Is there a reasonable mix of mail, phone, and field contacts at each grade level? Does the contact plan use the resource capacity that you have? Are you getting enough leverage from lower-cost contacts?
- Is the cost of selling in line with the revenue generated at each grade level, both as actual cost and as a percentage of revenue?
- Is the cost of selling percentage reasonably close across grade levels? If not, is there a specific marketing strategy or tactic to support this?
- What is your gut feeling? Does it make sense? Do you think it can work?

The result of going through these planning steps should be a solid overall contact policy for IAM that provides contact planning and implementation guidelines, sets organizational expectations, provides a framework for consistency, and provides a foundation that the account managers can work from to create their module contact plans.

Once the overall contact plan has been developed and provided to account managers as a frame of reference, the next step is for account managers to build their own plans to define how they will work with their customers. These plans are called module contact plans.

Level 2: The Module Contact Plan

The goal of building a module contact plan is the for the account manager to create an appropriate balance of customer coverage, value to customers, profitability, and their own productivity. When this balance has been achieved, it provides the foundation for working with individual customers to service their unique needs and for running specific campaigns through the modules. It is also at this level that limited resources must be allocated to specific accounts. An account manager must realize that he or she is the most expensive contact resource and as such needs a module plan to support the most effective use of time and to determine how to leverage other company resources and activities.

Let's go through the steps for creating a module contact plan.

Figure 11-11. Acme Office Machines module planning process IAM workload model: inside account manager example.

Number of days in year	Average vacation days	Holidays	Administrative and training days	Planning time/days (@2 hrs/wk)	Total calling days	Average contacts per day	Total annual contacts
260	15	10	15	12	208	35	7,455

1. *Define account management workload.* Given that account managers are a company's most important and limited resource, module planning starts with development of an account manager workload model. Figures 11-11 and 11-12 are samples of account management workload models for both inside and outside account managers. As you can see, the models start with the number of working days in the year, subtract vacation days, holidays, time spent on administrative procedures and training, and time needed for planning. The result is the total number of days available for making calls. The total number of calling days times the average number of contacts per day equals the number of contacts per year. Account managers can figure their own total calling days by modifying the numbers to fit their particular situations. Seasoned account managers usually have more vacation days. Newer account managers typically need more administrative and training time. In our experience, a conservatively low estimate of two hours per week for planning is a bare minimum. This planning time is typically time that pays high dividends in productivity. The examples for Acme Office Machines are two workload models for their more seasoned account managers, one an inside account manager (Figure 11-11) and the other an outside account manager (Figure 11-12). Use the format in Figure 11-13 to develop your workload models.

2. *Review the module profile.* Reviewing the module profile is a step account managers go through to get a better understanding of the makeup of their module. This step consists of first requesting (most IAM groups have access to a support group that could pull these reports off the database) and then reviewing a number of mod-

Figure 11-12. Acme Office Machines module planning process IAM workload model: outside account manager example.

Number of days in year	Average vacation days	Holidays	Administrative and training days	Planning time/days (@2 hrs/wk)	Total calling days	Average contacts per day	Total annual contacts
260	20	10	15	12	203	4	812

Figure 11-13. Module planning process IAM workload model.

Number of days in year	Average vacation days	Holidays	Administrative and training days	Planning time/days (@2 hrs/wk)	Total calling days	Average contacts per day	Total annual contacts

ule profile reports that provide counts of customers in modules that meet a certain set of conditions (for example, customers who have purchased certain product lines, have installed particular equipment, or are in specific industries). Module profile reports allow account managers to take a broader view of their modules and are used to identify opportunities for leverage in a module. Typical module profile reports include:

- Customer counts by needs-based segments (defined as part of the segmentation process described in Chapter 6)
- Counts of customers with specific installed equipment
- Customer counts by location or zip codes
- Customer counts by size of company
- Customer counts by grade (see Figure 11-15)

Account managers at Acme Office Machines will use an installed equipment by segment profile report (Figure 11-14), shown for Module 1, to identify leveragable activities. These reports are reviewed as background information for subsequent steps that will assess needs, define contact levels at different grade levels, and define campaigns that can be run through the module. Profile reports allow account managers to identify pockets of opportunity for leveraged contacts to sets of customers that have similar needs. In the sample report (Figure 11-14), the account manager might identify tax accounting firms as a seasonal target for a pre-tax season letter campaign or might identify

Figure 11-14. Acme Office Machines sample module profile report: customer counts by installed equipment*—module 1.

Type of Business	Installed Equipment				
	Copy Machines	Fax Equipment	Multipurpose Equipment	LANs	Modems
Medium-sized law firms	27	31	8	20	28
Real estate offices	33	25	9	13	22
Tax accounting firms	53	41	5	18	21
Totals	120	97	22	51	71

* Number of customer accounts.

Figure 11-15. Acme Office Machines sample module profile report: customers by grade—module 1.

Grade	Number of Customer Accounts
AA	10
A	19
B	31
C	27
D	26

all customers with LANs as a target for a new product introduction campaign.

3. *Develop the module revenue plan.* This is a fairly complex step for account managers. They start by planning how they are going to work with their accounts, specifically how they are going to contact their accounts. Second, they determine how they are going to allocate their contact resources (the most significant, expensive, and limited resource is their own time). Third they estimate how they intend to work in terms of frequency of presentations and then estimate close rates. This revenue plan (as illustrated in the Acme example in Figure 11-16 and as shown in a blank format in Figure 11-17) builds up from the basic calling activity and looks at the following factors, which ultimately impact revenue:

- Number of customers in module. This figure would come out of the grading profile report that was provided in step 2 (Figure 11-15). It is the number of customers in a module at the specific grade levels.
- Average number of contacts per year. This is the frequency of contact as planned by account managers. The frequency levels for field and phone contacts in the overall customer contact matrix (Figure 11-9) are used as a frame of reference and a starting point and are modified as the account manager sees fit. The overall customer contact matrix was developed based on an average of all modules and an overall anticipated way of doing business for each grade level of account. Account managers will have a more complete understanding of their modules and will determine how best to do business with customers in their modules based on this understanding. The contact frequencies in this module revenue plan could differ from the contact frequencies in the overall contact matrix for a number of reasons, including:
  —The number of accounts in the module is different from the

(text continues on p. 196)

Figure 11-16. Module planning process: module revenue plan (Acme example).

Grade	Number of Customers in Module	Avg. No. of Contacts per Year	Total Contacts	Proposal %	No. of Proposals Presented	Estimated Close Ratio on Proposals	No. of Orders per Year	Average Order Value Low	Average Order Value High	Revenue Generated Low	Revenue Generated High	Revenue per Contact Low	Revenue per Contact High
AA Phone Field	10	65 50 15	650 500 150	33%	215	15%	32	$17,000	$22,000	$546,975	$707,850	$842	$1,089
A Phone Field	19	47 35 12	893 665 228	33%	295	15%	44	$14,000	$19,000	$618,849	$839,867	$693	$941
B Phone Field	31	33 25 8	1,023 775 248	33%	338	15%	51	$8,000	$14,000	$405,108	$708,939	$396	$693
C Phone Field	27	16 12 4	432 324 108	33%	143	15%	21	$5,500	$9,000	$117,612	$192,456	$272	$446
D Phone Field	26	8 6 2	208 156 52	33%	69	15%	10	$1,500	$5,000	$15,444	$51,480	$74	$248
Total	113		3,206							$1,703,988	$2,500,592	$531	$780

Total phone contacts: 2,420
Total field contacts: 780

Figure 11-17. Module planning process: module revenue plan (blank form).

Grade	Number of Customers in Module	Avg. No. of Contacts per Year	Total Contacts	Proposal %	No. of Proposals Presented	Estimated Close Ratio on Proposals	No. of Orders per Year	Average Order Value		Revenue Generated		Revenue per Contact	
								Low	High	Low	High	Low	High
AA Phone Field													
A Phone Field													
B Phone Field													
C Phone Field													
D Phone Field													
Total													

Total phone contacts:
Total field contacts:

average module size that was represented in the allocation of contacts in the overall customer contact matrix.

—The capacity of the account manager(s) is different from the average capacity used in the overall customer contact matrix because they have different levels of experience, they have different customer audiences, or simply work at a higher productivity level.

—The grade level distribution in the module is different.

—They have a specific strategy to upgrade accounts or anticipate some declining accounts in the next year.

—They are going to alter the mix of contacts through increased use of phone and mail and through leveraged multipurpose field contacts (where you attempt to achieve multiple objectives; for example, demonstrating a product, presenting a proposal, and delivering a "mail" package in one field contact).

—The needs of customers in their module require a lower, or higher, contact frequency.

• Total contacts. Calculate by multiplying the number of customers by the average number of contacts per year.

• Proposal percentages. These are the account managers' estimates of how frequently they will be making specific product and/or service recommendations to customers (as a percentage of total contacts).

• Number of proposals presented. Calculate by multiplying total contacts by the proposal percentages.

• Estimated close ratios on proposals. These are the account managers' estimates of how often they will close as a percentage of proposals presented. This ratio, in conjunction with proposal percentage, is reflective of an account manager's individual style. Some account managers will propose every time they have any indication of a fit to a potential customer need. Other account managers will only propose when they are certain that the customer has needs that make the proposed solution a good fit. This style will be reflected in a lower proposal percentage and a higher close ratio. These examples illustrate different approaches to produce the same results; both are acceptable in the context of IAM.

• Number of orders per year. Calculate by multiplying the number of proposals by the estimated close ratio.

• Average order value. The last thing account managers do is estimate the order size. In this model they have a high and a low value. Historical order sizes provide the basis for this estimate.

- Revenue generated. Calculate by multiplying the number of orders per year by the average order value.
- Revenue per customer. Calculate by dividing the revenue generated by the number of customers in the module.

This module revenue plan is the account managers' (or IAM team's) plan for how they will achieve their revenue goals. It is owned by the account managers, reflects the account managers' preferred ways of working with customers, and reflects the needs of and nuances of customers in the module.

4. *Assess module customer needs.* The assessment of module customer needs comes out of a basic understanding of what the module profile is, and this assessment is a precursor to defining module campaigns. In the assessment, account managers are looking for a set of customers with a common set of needs that create a compelling reason to buy, allow them to provide unique value, or at this point in time are unfulfilled needs. The account managers, working with the needs-based segment documentation (Figure 6-7 in Chapter 6) and the module profile reports (Figures 11-14 and 11-15), identify needs that they feel they can address and complete the industry needs and applications worksheet (Figure 11-18 shows a completed worksheet and Figure 11-19 provides the basic worksheet). These needs will then be applied to campaigns in step 5.

Figure 11-18. Customer contact planning process: industry needs and applications worksheet (completed).

Associate : _____   Date completed: _____

A. Segment: Tax accounting firms

1. Segment demographics: *SIC code — 20–50 tax accountants*

2. Segment needs: *Increased copy & fax capacity during tax season*

3. Competition: *Other local suppliers*

4. Segment — target applications: *Short-term equipment leases*

5. Benefits and rationale: *Allows customer to increase capacity during short time frame needed*

6. Specific campaign(s) *Pre-tax season capacity campaign*

Figure 11-19. Customer contact planning process: industry needs and applications worksheet (blank).

```
┌──────────────────────────────────────────────────────────────────────┐
│                                                                        │
│  Associate :_____    Date completed: _____ │
│                                                                        │
│  A. Segment: Tax accounting firms                                      │
│                                                                        │
│     1.  Segment demographics:       _____ │
│                                     _____ │
│                                                                        │
│     2.  Segment needs:              _____ │
│                                     _____ │
│                                                                        │
│     3.  Competition:                _____ │
│                                     _____ │
│                                                                        │
│     4.  Segment — target applications:  _____ │
│                                     _____ │
│                                                                        │
│     5.  Benefits and rationale:     _____ │
│                                     _____ │
│                                                                        │
│     6.  Specific campaign(s)        _____ │
│                                     _____ │
│                                                                        │
└──────────────────────────────────────────────────────────────────────┘
```

5. *Define module campaigns.* In IAM, campaigns are run as a way to obtain leverage within a module. Campaigns are defined as a targeted set of contacts with a similar value and message to a set of customers with similar needs. Of course, the larger a set of customers the campaign appeals to, the greater the leverage value to account managers; this value then provides the opportunity to achieve improved productivity. Leverage in a campaign is achieved through:

- A similar set of needs that the account manager understands well and discusses with customers throughout the campaign
- A similar product offer/solution to fill the customer's need
- Printed communications packages that can be used for multiple customers
- Accumulated knowledge (during campaign contacts) of customer objections and repositioning statements that address objections

Figure 11-20 is an example of a completed campaign definition worksheet. This module-planning process and these worksheets focus account managers on campaigns that are driven by the needs of their specific customers. They define which customers are targeted by the campaign and define campaign strategy, objectives, and tactics.

By definition, a campaign results in greater productivity than general individual customer calling. As such, campaigns should be

Figure 11-20. Module planning process campaign definition worksheet.

Audiences:	*All tax accounting firms*
Campaign strategy:	*Address customer capacity needs with short-term copier & fax leases*
Campaign objectives:	*Close new equipment leases with 20 out of 54 tax accounting firms*
Campaign tactics: (activities, e.g., identify support requirements):	*Set up call with initial mail package, qualify and close using scheduled phone & field contacts*
Number of customers (by industry/product applications):	*53 tax accounting firms*
Average contacts per customer:	*2*
Number of contacts (by industry):	*106*

assessed from a productivity perspective, using a reporting tool similar to the module revenue plan. Use the module planning chart shown in Figure 11-21 to get a clear picture of all aspects of performance and productivity, including revenue performance, average order size, close ratio, proposal ratio, and customer contact level productivity. The revenue per contact in Figure 11-22 indicates a revenue of $1,089–$1,444, compared to an average revenue per contact of $531–$780 from the total line in Figure 11–16. The contacts used here are no more expensive than other contacts, so this campaign appears to be a better investment of contacts than general individual customer calling.

6. *Assess and reconcile the module plan.* In complex business processes it is necessary to include an evaluation step. In module contact planning, this step is essential. In this step, an account manager reviews the module plan, first alone and then with the sales manager, to ensure that:

- A balance of campaigns and individual customer contacts is used so that the highest value is delivered with the most productivity. This is a subjective evaluation on the part of the account manager and the sales manager. Do they feel that more campaigns can be defined that could provide leverage in the module plan?

Figure 11-21. Module planning specific campaign definition.

Campaign	Industry & defining characteristics	Number of customers	Avg. No. of campaign contacts	Total campaign contacts	Proposal %	No. of proposals	Close ratio	No. of orders	Average order value		Revenue generated		Revenue per contact	
									Low	High	Low	High	Low	High
1. Accountant Pretax season	Tax accountants	54	2	108	45%	49	25%	12	$9,800	$13,000	$117,600	$156,000	$1,089	$1,444

- Campaigns are run that provide *value* to customers—not just sales. The industry needs and application worksheets and the thinking that account managers put into them provide evidence that campaigns are value driven.
- In the revenue planning process the numbers balance so that the process has integrity. Is the sum of the revenue in module revenue plans approximately equal to the total revenue planned?
- There is historical evidence that the numbers in the revenue plan are achievable so that goals are realistic and motivating. Are average order sizes realistic based on historical customer order sizes? Have the planned contact levels been achieved (or nearly achieved) in the past? Is there any historical evidence for the projected close ratio?
- There is motivation for the account managers to achieve and surpass their goals. The plan provides a goal, the tactics to achieve the goal, and some evidence that supports the achievability of the goal. This achievability combined with the account managers' ownership of the process are the two factors that influence account manager motivation.

Level 3: The Individual Customer Contact Plan

The goal of the individual customer contact plan is to ensure that you (the account manager) are providing relevant value to each customer through the solutions you provide and the contacts you deliver. Customers have already told you, through the value-based contact workshop, about the kinds of contacts that are of value to them. You already have an understanding of the needs that businesses like theirs have from the needs-based segment documentation (Figure 6-7 in Chapter 6). You already have a good understanding of the worth— both actual and potential—of the customer from the grading work that was done (also in Chapter 6).

All of this previous work has given you a great foundation for understanding your customers—their worth, their needs, the communication they value. As you work with individual customers, you need to take this understanding, confirm its applicability to each customer, discover the unique needs of your individual customers, assess how much you're willing to invest in them, and plan the specific contact tactics you will use to manage the relationship.

At times, the process of individual customer contact planning requires you to reconcile the conflicts that occur as a result of previous work. The segmentation work may indicate certain needs, yet the account grades do not indicate that there is enough revenue to warrant the investment required to fulfill the defined needs. The module campaigns defined may cause the contact frequency for any individual customer to exceed the contact frequency for that grade of customer in the module revenue plan. These conflicts are resolved based on the judgment of the account manager. For any given contact, an account manager needs to make sure (1) that the customer needs the contact, (2) that the customer will perceive value in the contact, and (3) the investment required to make the contact is justified, either through actual sales or anticipated sales.

Let's look at an example of these conflicts. The segmentation work at Acme Office Machines may have indicated that tax accounting firms have a need for increased copying capacity during the tax season. However, that particular need may not apply to every tax accountant—Acme account managers may find that some specialize in serving customers who file their taxes at other times of the year. Additionally, the grading work the account managers have done has estimated the total potential worth of each tax accounting firm. However, as they talk with each customer firm, the account managers find one that is planning rapid, aggressive growth (indicating a much higher potential worth) and another that is planning to retire next year (indicating much lower potential worth). Each customer has a unique set of characteristics and plans that define its worth. Each individual customer has a unique set of needs. And each customer will value different contacts that provide communication in the relationship. In individual customer contact planning, Acme's account managers take what they have learned from previous work, apply the unique needs and characteristics of each of these customers, and define a specific plan for how they will work with each customer.

The process of building the individual customer contact plan is broken down into four parts that draw upon this previous work and upon subsequent contacts with each customer. The steps in the process are: (1) account needs assessment, (2) account objectives, (3) account strategy, and (4) engagement strategy.

1. *Understand the customer and identify the business needs.* Because account managers and their companies provide business value, a detailed understanding of business needs is essential. These needs are initially identified through a review of the needs-based segmentation documentation (see Chapter 6) and through a review of your company's transaction history with the customer (orders, quotes, shipments, invoices, payments, service records, and so forth). Then these needs are validated and further needs are identified through your discussions with the individual customers. These discussions are in-

tended to uncover the unique needs and plans of each individual customer.

What is the customer's current business situation? Include some understanding of their customers (who they are, what their demographics are), some understanding of the products and services they provide to their customers, some understanding of who their competitors are and the relative strength of their competitors, and an understanding of why their customers do business with them.

In each individual customer's business situation, what are their needs? Do they have product issues, service problems, competitive threats, or cost/profit problems? This in-depth understanding of the customer could help you address a number of issues. The following list of questions is a helpful tool to further this understanding. Some of these questions are answered by information about customers in the database, some are answered by an account managers' knowledge of the industry, and some are answered through dialogue with individual customers.

- Where is the account in its life cycle?
  —Is it a new or old business?
  —Is the business growing or declining?
  —Is the industry hot or cold?
- What are the characteristics and attributes of the business (grade, number of products in use, level of advertising, industry, and so on).
  —Understand its important business issues (growth, customer satisfaction, productivity, reduction of costs, or others).
- What are the industry trends? Is it a seasonal business? Is the product popular, highly differentiated, or a commodity? Is new technology affecting production in a way that will influence costs? Is demand usually steady or does it fluctuate?
- How much impact do competitors have? What are they doing that would specifically impact the business (new products, new services, cost changes, change in market share, entry into new market segments, new geographies, new products, new channels, for example)? This information is gathered and, ideally, stored in the database for each individual customer to help define the individual customer contact plan and to be used as a future reference.

In the business-to-business marketplace, marketing success is a result of addressing the customer's business needs. This first step in individual customer contact planning gets at those needs.

2. *Determine the account's business objectives.* Find out what specific business objectives the customer has. Does the customer plan to expand the business, add new products or services, change the focus of the business, improve a particular service area, or downsize the business? An understanding of the customer's business situation and needs and the customer's business objectives form a framework on which you, the account manager, can build an account strategy.

3. *Select a specific account strategy to help the customer achieve business objectives.* Now that you have collected this information on your individual accounts, it is time to condense it into a strategy. The essence of an account strategy is finding product, service, and applications solutions that address customer needs and help the customer achieve business objectives. Some questions to ask yourself are:

- Where do I see this customer in two to three years?
- Is my company planning any applications or solutions that would relate to this customer?
- Are there any positioning tactics necessary with this customer that can help me and/or the customer understand the benefits in the account strategy?

Any account strategy should take into consideration:

- Incremental products, services, and features. This is the obvious intent and result of any sales or account management process. It is absolutely essential. However a balanced strategy is critical, and incremental products and services is simply a part of that balanced strategy.
- Your understanding of how to use existing products and/or services. There is little customers appreciate more than an account manager who helps them address a business problem through the use of some product or service they have already purchased. In some industries this type of solution offers a huge opportunity to add value because many customers have products and services they don't understand how to use. (In many companies, account managers frequently find customers with services or equipment that they just do not understand how to use to help solve their business problems.) Using this kind of customer strategy has a significant positive impact on customer loyalty. It develops a strong bond of trust and typically develops a long-term commitment from the customer perspective. It is not an effective short-term revenue increasing strategy; however, over the long term its impact can be enormous.

- Product retention. This is somewhat related to how to use existing products or services, because that is obviously one of the tactics that can be used to increase product retention. Product retention has one spin in some industries, like telecommunications, where the customer keeps the service for a long period of time and pays a monthly fee for the use of that service. In other industries product retention might be the continual repurchasing of a stocked product. In any case, product retention is a consideration for an account strategy with a customer. At the core of this strategy is your belief that your company's products help customers achieve their objectives. This strategy is then used to help customers understand how staying with your company's products best addresses their needs.
- Replacement strategy. Sometimes the best solution for a customer is to completely remove existing equipment, services, or products, and replace them with new products.
- Product migration. This is related to replacement strategy. In some industries, like high-tech products—both hardware and software and telecommunications—sometimes a phased-in approach to replacing the product is appropriate. This is beneficial to the customer because frequently it makes the transition to new products and services less stressful and possibly less expensive in the short term. It is beneficial to you as the account manager because it guarantees a customer bond, minimally through the end of the migration.

4. *Select an engagement strategy.* Here is where you develop a specific plan for working with individual customers. This plan defines the frequency of contact, the tone of discussions, and the intent and objectives of each individual contact with the customer. It provides a qualitative perspective that is combined with the quantitative perspective from the module revenue plan to help you define what you will do with a customer in the very short term. It requires specific account tactics where a minimum of the next two contacts are designed and scheduled.

- Partnership. This is a very effective strategy in that it fosters a win-win environment. A partnership engagement strategy is the epitome of IAM. It assumes that what is good for the customer is also good for the account manager. Working together in a partnership implies a high level of commitment by both parties. While some degree of partnering should happen in every account relationship, a full partnership engagement and the level of commitment it requires isn't always appropriate for the account manager or for the customer. In this kind of strategy, you need a customer with a high worth to justify your investment in the account, and you need a customer that sees value in and is willing to invest time in this type of relationship.

- Trolling. This is one of the less aggressive approaches. It is one where an account manager keeps in touch with the customer, staying aware of needs, objectives, and potential opportunities to add value and/or sell products and services. This approach is a little contradictory to the kind of relationship that is typified by an IAM approach. However, it may be exactly the kind of relationship that the customer wants. This approach is a fit when the customer does not see value in, or is not willing to commit their time to, developing a partnership, or when the total potential worth of a customer does not warrant the investment required in a partnership-type relationship.

- Hit and run. This kind of strategy is usually applied in an IAM environment where home-run productivity is the optimization model. The implication in this environment is that opportunities at an individual customer level are few and far between. The approach to engaging suggests a heavy sales focus on the "home run" and a service focus afterward—until the next big opportunity surfaces.

Summary

Contact planning is completed at three levels. Account managers confidently manage the moment of truth (time with customers, face-to-face or on the phone), conduct weekly planning against their module plan, adjust their module plan as appropriate, create and use leveraged contacts and campaigns, continue to test and push the economics of the module, and ultimately provide a lot of value to a lot of customers.

Contact planning offers an interesting set of paradoxes. It allows simplicity within a complex system. It provides order within chaos.

12

Developing Account Managers

The work force is indisputably our principle asset.

Tom Peters

At this point in the process of developing a world-class integrated account management (IAM) program, you have invested quite a bit in making sure that you have the right infrastructure—the right systems—in place. Your selection process, as detailed in Chapter 8, "Profiling and Selecting the IAM Team," has focused significantly on getting people who have the right behaviors and the right raw abilities in place. The next component is making sure you equip those people with the right knowledge, the right attitudes, and the right skills to be successful in the account manager position.

The Account Manager Position: A Demanding Job

As we have defined the account manager position, it is a very demanding job, and your expectations for the person holding the job are high. There is a complex set of knowledge, skills, and attitudes that account managers need to develop in order to be successful. Good account managers:

- Are grounded in the vision and mission of IAM and of the company.
- Are able to do some level of both strategic and tactical planning.
- Understand how to run a business; that is, they understand how to make an investment in customers and get a return on that investment.

- Have a thorough understanding of their customers and their customers' businesses. They know what makes their customers' businesses successful.
- Have a certain level of listening and communication skills that they use to develop productive relationships with customers.
- Have product knowledge, which sometimes involves having technical expertise. They understand how their company's products and services can be applied to help their customers be successful.
- Are able to work effectively in a sales process—talking with customers to understand their businesses, identifying customer needs and objectives, understanding how products can be used to fulfill customer objectives and needs, presenting recommendations, positioning product and application benefits against these needs, negotiating where appropriate, and closing sales.

This chapter explores ways to help transform people with raw talent into well-functioning, highly productive, and, eventually, seasoned account managers. This process will not work for everyone, however, which is why it is critical to select the right candidates in the first place. Further, simply providing account managers with an initial training program, as is sometimes done, is not likely to produce the desired results. The complexity of the account manager position requires a process that consists of three modes of development—training, monitoring, and coaching—within the context of an overall account manager development process.

While training is an important mode in this development, it is sometimes inaccurately viewed as a panacea for all performance problems. At times this perception drives overuse or ineffective use of training to address performance issues. There are three things that occur in organizations that cause this ineffective use of training. The first is that many managers view training as a formal, one-time event. Training is often set up as a quick solution to fix a specific problem, with the expectation being that people will come out of the training with the knowledge and skills they need to deal with the specific problem area that originated the need for the training. The second is that most training sessions try to get across too much information and try to impart too many skills at one time. The third is that the training often occurs before people are ready to fully absorb the experience, either because they are too new on the job or because they are too far removed from the opportunity to put into practice the new skills they have just learned.

The goal, at the completion of this development process, is to

Figure 12-1. Development goals.

Knowledge, Skills & Attitudes
• Understanding of vision & mission
• Customer knowledge
• Product knowledge
• Product application knowledge
• Ability to link product to customer knowledge
• Module planning
• Customer contact planning
• Business knowledge
• Customer empathy & focus
• Ability to work within sales process
• Relationship skills
• Ability to use account management system
• Productivity
• Time management
• Communication skills

have independent, competent, and confident account managers who are able to build relationships with their customers within the context of their module/business plan (Chapter 11 discusses the development of an account manager's module plan). Figure 12-1 lists the knowledge, skills, and attitudes you need to cultivate in account managers during this development process.

The Four Phases of Account Manager Development

A development approach that I recommend takes an account manager through four phases of development (as illustrated in Figure 12-2):

1. Foundation phase
2. Initiation phase
3. Accountability phase
4. Readiness phase

These four phases and this approach are based on the following premises:

• Learning is best facilitated when the account managers have already experienced situations where the knowledge, skills, and attitudes can, or could have been, applied.
• Account managers become more ready to learn when they have

Figure 12-2. Phases of account manager development life cycle.

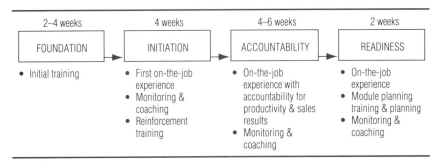

2–4 weeks	4 weeks	4–6 weeks	2 weeks
FOUNDATION	INITIATION	ACCOUNTABILITY	READINESS
• Initial training	• First on-the-job experience • Monitoring & coaching • Reinforcement training	• On-the-job experience with accountability for productivity & sales results • Monitoring & coaching	• On-the-job experience • Module planning training & planning • Monitoring & coaching

felt a need to gain the knowledge to improve their performance.

• Training will "stick" better if applied shortly after the training is completed.
• Absorption and retention is enhanced when training is delivered in smaller (digestible, bite-size) pieces.
• The concepts in the learning become a way of doing business when coaching and consequences reinforce the learning.
• Learning is facilitated in an environment where sales managers (the managers and coaches of account managers) are active participants in the learning process.

The intent of this development approach is to have an account manager operating with full responsibilities and accountabilities (with a broad set of developed competencies—as outlined in Figure 12-1—supporting these responsibilities and accountabilities) at the completion of this development life cycle.

Foundation Phase

In this phase, you (company marketing and sales management) are preparing to get account managers in front of customers (face-to-face and/or over the phone)—fast. This is designed as a relatively short phase to give account managers the minimal level of knowledge and skills they need to be comfortable beginning to work with customers and that you need them to have in order to feel comfortable *letting* them get in front of customers.

There is temptation to try to train account managers in everything they need to know during this phase. Account managers will perform at a higher level if the development process combines some training with on-the-job experiences that allow them to apply the learning from the training.

The foundation phase is a two- to four-week training phase. This timing could vary in any organization and could be less than two weeks or more than four weeks, depending on the complexity of the products, the complexity of the customers' buying process, the complexity of the organization's internal systems, and the experience level of the account managers being trained. For example, it may take less time to train an existing employee from a different department than an account manager hired from outside the company, simply because the existing employee has more company and product knowledge.

This training provides account managers a grounding in company knowledge, customer knowledge, products (especially the customers' use of products), and the basics of IAM (including use of the software/database within the context of IAM).

There are four training courses built into this foundation phase. In sequence they are

1. Company training
2. Customer training
3. Product training
4. IAM training

Company Training

This training provides a company overview to account managers, highlighting what the company is about and why it exists. In the following example, these are conveyed as the mission statement and value proposition.

Additionally, a brief overview of IAM is provided to illustrate how it supports the mission and value proposition.

Company Training Outline

Learning Objectives

- Account managers understand the mission.
- Account managers understand the value proposition to the marketplace.
- Account managers demonstrate an understanding of the rationale and basic concepts behind IAM.

Content Outline

- Mission statement
- Company overview
  —Company history

—Company finances
—Company demographics
—Customers served
—Value proposition: a discussion of products and services pro-
  vided to customers
• Value and importance of IAM.

Customer Training

Customer training is conducted before product and IAM training because it provides a context for each of these subsequent training courses. The products and service provided through IAM are
important because they meet customers' needs and have a positive
impact on each customer's business; therefore the focus in customer
training is on customer business processes and customer needs.

The customer segments defined in Chapter 6 provide detailed
information about the various customer segments, the defining characteristics of those segments, and the set of needs associated with
customers in those segments. The needs identified in that segmentation work become training materials in customer training.

Additionally, you will want to assign account managers specific
customer roles for their role plays in IAM training. This assignment
sets the expectation that they will role-play customers in a specific
segment while other account managers take the account manager
role during this exercise. This assignment at this point in the training
creates a need on the account manager's part to understand the customer's perspective. If at all possible, you will want to assign account
managers to customer segments that are included in their customer
modules.

Customer Training Outline

Learning Objectives
• Account managers have a basic understanding of how customers' businesses are run (enough so that they can see how the
  products they provide support running the business).
• Account managers understand the product and service needs
  of customers and can relate those needs to the company products and services offered.
• Account managers develop empathy toward customers.

Content Outline
• Customer segments overview
  —Different segments served
  —Demographics of each segment

- Account manager customer roles selected for role play in IAM training
- Customer business processes
  —All processes related to use of your products
- Customer needs
  —Common needs across all segments
  —Unique needs by customer segment

Product Training

The specific topics that you need to address in product training build upon the customer training and upon each other. In sequence, the specific topics addressed are: the customers' business processes and needs; use of your products within those business processes; business benefits that result from the use of products; ways in which specific product features and product support address customer needs; and ways customers make buying decisions about your products.

The content and the sequence of content is intended to encourage account managers to view products and product features from the customer's perspective.

Product Training Outline

Learning Objectives

- Account managers know how the company's products are used in the customers' business processes.
- Account managers can explain how the products can have a positive impact on customers' business processes, and subsequently, on the customers' businesses.
- Account managers understand the product features for each of the product lines.
- Account managers understand what product support is offered for each product line and why that support is offered.
- Account managers understand how customers make buying decisions for each product line.

Content Outline

- Product application overview
  —Review of customers' business processes from customer training
  —Discussion of product usage within each business process

- Potential business impact of product usage
  - —By product within business process
  - —Benefits for each product line or product category
    - Improved business processes
    - Improved through-put processes
    - Reduced downtime
    - Economic benefits
    - Improved service to their customers
- Discussion of product features
  - —By product lines
  - —How product features address customer needs
  - —How features are priced and packaged
  - —Technical aspects of product features
- Product support
  - —By product line
  - —Product warranty information
  - —Technical support (manuals, help desk, web-site, and so on)
- Customer buying process
  - —By product line
  - —Steps in the buying processes
  - —Decision makers and influencers

IAM Training

This training is the final preparation before actual customer contact. After an IAM overview, you teach account managers how to work in account management teams, how to manage their customers, how to provide value to customers, how to be effective in a sales process, and how to use the system. Additionally, it is helpful if you begin to set performance expectations with your account managers at this early point in the development process.

IAM Training Outline

Learning Objectives

- Account managers understand the objectives and intent of IAM.
- Account managers demonstrate an ability to work in IAM teams.
- Account managers demonstrate an ability to conduct a customer contact within the defined sales process.
- Account managers are able to use the IAM system to manage and conduct customer contacts.

- Account managers have an understanding of the expectations that management has of them.

Content Outline

- Review of IAM vision and objectives
- Account management team ownership of customers and process
- How to work in teams
- Discussion of communications between account managers on IAM teams
- Review of customer-defined contact performance requirements (defined in Chapter 9)
- Review of customer-defined value-based contacts (defined in Chapter 9)
- Use of other media to contact customers
- Overview of the IAM sales process
- Discussion of and exercises to demonstrate customer contact skills
  —Identifying decision makers
  —Questioning/probing skills
  —Listening skills
  —Identifying needs
  —Positioning a product
  —Understanding objections
  —Closing
  —Setting follow-up expectations
- Role plays and diagnostics of customer contacts
- Review and usage of customer grades and customer worth
- Overview of individual customer contact planning process
- Development of individual account plans (theory and exercises)
- Overview of IAM system
- Review of functionality
- Hands-on exercises to use system
- Practice of system use within a simulated customer contact
- Discussion of management expectations
  —Revenue results to be achieved
  —Productivity expectations
  —Quality of the contact
  —Quality of module planning and management
- Discussion of how account manager expectations support IAM vision and objectives

At the end of the foundation phase, account managers are ready to begin planning for and contacting customers in the field and/or over the phone.

Initiation Phase

In this phase, you give account managers their first on-the-job experience while closely monitoring, providing extensive coaching, and providing periodic reinforcement training. This on-the-job experience is extremely valuable at this step in account manager development because it takes the foundation training from theory to practice.

Extensive monitoring of customer contacts is essential early in this phase of account manager development. Monitoring of inside account managers is conducted as silent telephone monitoring. Monitoring of outside account managers is conducted as joint sales calls. Different elements of the customer contacts are observed, and feedback is provided to the new account managers. This exercise is typically guided by a monitoring checklist.

Following is an outline for an IAM monitoring checklist.

1. Contact planning
2. Contact of decision maker(s)
3. Call introduction
4. Effective questioning and understanding of customer's needs
5. Customer recommendations
6. Objection management
7. Closing
8. Contact completion and postcontact work

As sales managers monitor contacts, they evaluate account manager performance in each of the above categories. Monitoring helps identify strengths and weaknesses of individual account managers, identify account manager training needs, ensure the quality of individual customer contacts, and acquire specific examples of account manager performance as input for coaching sessions.

The sales manager looks at specific elements of performance in each of the monitoring categories.

1. *Contact planning.* Sales managers don't actually monitor the precontact planning that an account manager does. They look for evidence of precontact planning within the customer contact. Evidence in the contact includes an account manager referring to a previous contact, having an objective for the contact that is apparent early in

the contact, and use of and reference to previously gathered customer information.

2. *Contact of decision maker(s).* The intent here is to evaluate how effective an account manager is at identifying and contacting the decision maker(s) and influencers for product purchase decisions. In the call, sales managers evaluate how account managers work through assistant, secretary, or receptionist screens, whether they confirm that they have reached a decision maker (by asking the person, "Do you have responsibility for . . . ?"), and whether they identify other decision makers or influencers ("Who else in your organization would be involved in this decision?").

3. *Call introduction.* This monitoring category evaluates the front end of a customer contact. Does the account manager confirm an appointment if the current contact is a follow-up to a previous contact? Ask permission for the customer's time and set an expectation with the customer for length of the contact? Convey their appreciation to the customer? State the purpose of the contact? This category looks at how the call is positioned at the beginning to provide value to the customer and provide continuity in the relationship.

4. *Effective questioning and understanding of customer needs.* Product and service recommendations that are of value to customers are based on their needs. This monitoring category assesses an account manager's effectiveness at gathering and confirming those needs. Specifically: Does the account manager gather information about those needs through open-ended, nonleading questions (typically, questions that begin with what, how, or why)? Does he or she confirm stated needs? Confirm assumed needs (i.e., needs identified in segmentation work as discussed in Chapter 6? Identify and focus on needs that are relevant (i.e., needs where the account manager can add value through expertise or through product and service offerings)?

5. *Customer recommendations.* The "customer needs" information gathered ultimately leads to specific product recommendations. The sales manager evaluates the product and/or service recommendation(s) made by the account manager. Does the recommendation address the customer's needs? Does the account manager restate the customer's needs when presenting the recommendation? Link the recommendation to business benefits? Convey or demonstrate the economic benefits if appropriate?

6. *Objection management.* Customers object to product recommendations for a number of reasons, including the following:

- They don't have the money.
- They don't have the authority to make the buying decision.

- They don't see the recommendation as a solution to their prob-
lem(s).
- They disagree with the account manager's perception of their
needs.
- They simply don't want to make a decision.
- They don't understand the recommendation.

This monitoring category evaluates how well an account manager handles these objections. Does the account manager clarify and
confirm the objection? Ask why the customer is objecting? Deal with
the specific objection and the reason(s) for the objection? This clarification will lead to an acceptance of the objection, a resolution (which
will probably lead to an attempt to close), or a repositioning of the
recommendation using new knowledge gained through the objection
management step.

7. *Closing.* An effective understanding of needs results in good
product recommendations (ones that provide value to customers).
Good product recommendations lead to sales. This category assesses
an account manager's effectiveness at turning recommendations into
closed sales. Does the account manager ask for the order when appropriate (after having identified and confirmed a need that is addressed
by the product)? Restate the benefits? Gather the necessary information to take the order and review the next steps?

8. *Contact completion and postcontact work.* At the end of each contact, an account manager needs to end the call, convey appreciation to
the customer (regardless of the outcome of the call), and set customer
expectations for the next contact. At the completion of the contact,
the account manager updates the database with information learned
during the contact, such as company or individual demographic
changes or corrections, further needs, or other individuals involved
in the buying process. The account manager then schedules the next
contact in the database and completes the work required to place the
order taken into the order processing system.

Coaching Account Managers

The monitoring checklist is used to document the sales manager's evaluation of a customer contact and as input into coaching sessions with individual account managers. A contact or set of contacts
is monitored by a sales manager, and coaching regarding those contacts is conducted immediately after the contact.

With each new account manager, you will want to conduct at
least one or two monitoring sessions each week. If an account man-

ager is struggling during customer contacts, you will want to increase the number of coaching and monitoring sessions. If an account manager is performing well in customer contacts, you should still conduct at least one monitoring and coaching session per week through this initiation phase.

These coaching sessions are relatively brief—twenty to thirty minutes. They focus on the specific behavior that is documented on the monitoring checklist. The sessions identify and communicate effective performance in the contacts as well as areas of performance that need to be improved. Recommendations to improve these areas are discussed. These identified areas for improvement are then observed and discussed in subsequent monitoring and coaching.

Reinforcement Training

During the initiation phase, account managers can be overwhelmed by the volume and diversity of issues they are managing. In this environment, it is important to provide a set of smaller, reinforcement training sessions. These reinforcement training sessions focus on specific, relatively narrow topic areas and ensure that core concepts and related skills are not lost or ignored in the press of day-to-day activity and learning.

Your reinforcement training plan should focus on areas that are most at risk of being ignored or not practiced in your organization. A typical reinforcement training plan might consist of four two-hour training sessions delivered each week for the four weeks in the initiation phase.

In most organizations, reinforcement training is needed in the following areas:

- Customer needs questioning and probing
- The business applications and business impact of products
- The use of customer-defined value-based contacts in individual customer contact plans
- The individual customer contact planning process

Accountability Phase

Until this phase, the emphasis in the development of account managers has been largely qualitative, focusing on working within the process, understanding the needs of customers, applying product solutions to customer needs, providing value in the contacts with customers, and working at managing customer relationships and contacts in an IAM team environment.

The accountability phase emphasizes the sales and productivity requirements that account managers are accountable for. The four- to six-week time frame for this phase allows a "ramp-up" in both sales expectations and productivity expectations. The intent is to have account managers running at 100 percent of their sales and productivity objectives on a weekly basis at the end of this phase.

Readiness Phase

After account managers have developed an understanding of their customer base, have developed a set of IAM skills, and have demonstrated an ability to operate with acceptable levels of sales results and productivity, they are ready for module management training.

Module management training gets at the essence of IAM. One of the operating principles of IAM (actually the first of the principles described in Chapter 2) is that account managers act as small business owners. An outcome for module management training is a module contact plan, which, for all intents and purposes, is the account manager's "business plan." This training teaches account managers how and where to invest resources to run a successful business; it deals with the development of module campaigns and with the integration of contacts and contact media.

This is typically a two-day training session.

Module Management Training Outline

Learning Objectives

- Account managers demonstrate an ability to assess and adjust an account grade using both quantitative and qualitative criteria.
- Account managers make appropriate contact media selections for customer contacts that provide value, balancing customer needs, customer preferences, and customer worth/economics in their media selection.
- Account managers create customer contact plans.
- Account managers demonstrate an ability to define and document campaigns to run in their modules.
- Account managers demonstrate an ability to develop a realistic revenue plan for their modules—with supporting background and rationale.
- Account managers build an effective overall module plan.

Content Outline

- Overview of module planning process
- The account grading model

- Assessing and assigning probability of achieving potential incremental worth (as described in the grading process in Chapter 6)
- Review of the process of individual customer contact planning
- Development of individual account plans (theory and exercises)
- Overview of the module contact planning process (as defined in Chapter 11)
- Building of draft module plans

Account Manager Development Summary

This four-phase development approach to account manager development is effective for several reasons.

- It explicitly links the training to the vision and mission of the organization. This is a powerful component of the training and provides a number of benefits. It enables account managers to make decisions around unfamiliar issues that arise because they understand the basic principles and values that the processes, procedures, and tools of IAM have been developed upon. The organization's vision provides a foundation so that account managers know why they are learning what they are learning. They understand not only what business results are desired in IAM, but what kinds of relationships and environment are intended to be created.

- It provides the training in bite-size, digestible pieces rather than as a formal one-time event. In this overall plan there are two more-formal, larger, training experiences: (1) the front-end training in the foundation phase that prepares account managers for their first on-the-job account management experience, and (2) the training in the readiness phase (module management training) that prepares account managers to plan and manage their modules as if they were running their own businesses. Between these two formal sessions there are smaller training sessions provided during the initiation phase.

- It makes the training as experiential as possible (as opposed to didactic).

- It provides the training in a time frame so that what is learned is applied immediately. This tends to have a positive impact on the ability of the training to stick in the organization, to have an impact on performance that goes well beyond the training time.

• It makes sure the training is supported by feedback systems, especially monitoring and coaching. Monitoring and coaching are powerful tools, especially in the hands of an effective sales manager. While training focuses on teaching the skill, monitoring and coaching focuses on applying the skill and ongoing incremental improvement of the skill and, ultimately, performance. Alignment of monitoring and coaching with training that is done is absolutely essential. Monitoring and coaching by sales managers should reinforce and amplify the training that was done.

• It builds the training around a process that institutionalizes what the account manager is learning. Adults enter a learning experience with a task-centered orientation to learning. A process-centered approach to training is consistent with this assumption. In the account manager training there are a number of processes around which the training is built. The first is the IAM launch process, outlined in Chapter 10. The second is the module contact planning process, and the third is the individual customer contact planning process, both outlined in Chapter 11. The use of these business processes provides a framework of steps and behaviors for account managers to operate within. This allows account managers to quickly internalize these processes. When this happens, the process becomes "background music" and account managers are able to focus on individual customers during contacts with those customers. This provides consistency around the process and variability where it is necessary in contacts and relationships with individual customers.

• It makes sure the training is supported by consequences. One of the important aspects of each training session is that it serves to set expectations for account managers. These expectations include productivity, call levels, contact levels, expectations around the quality of the contact with the customer, and expectations around sales levels. The measurement systems and reward systems are aligned with those expectations. When an account manager comes out of a training session and there is emphasis on calling productivity, that is tracked immediately, the results posted after that training session, and the rewards and consequences made immediate and visible. Lack of these measurement systems and reward systems creates inconsistency and dissonance in the environment.

Summary

When evaluating training and development materials, ask yourself what the customer would want account managers to know, to feel, and to do, and design the training and development accordingly. I refer to this as the last rule for developing account managers. Account managers will be successful only if they are effective in the moment of truth—in their contact with customers.

Successful development of account managers is a critical component of building and maintaining an IAM capability. Development is most effective when it is addressed as a multidimensional activity, providing multiple sets of formal training, on-the-job experience, and bite-size pieces of training to focus on immediate job skills, defining a ramp-up of performance expectations, and providing ongoing monitoring and coaching to promote account manager development.

13

What to Expect and How to Measure It

"You are what you measure." "If you can't measure it, it doesn't exist." "Hard (quantitative) always beats out soft (intangible)."

Corporate America has become infatuated with measurements. For the most part, this has been a positive trend that has been commented on in hundreds, maybe thousands, of business publications. For all of the recent business publications, I don't know if anyone has conveyed the value better than the character Sherlock Holmes in Sir Arthur Conan Doyle's story "Scandal in Bohemia," from *Adventures of Sherlock Holmes* (1891): "It is a capital mistake to theorize before one has data. Insensibly one begins to twist the facts to suit theories, instead of theories to suit facts."

One of the most intriguing and powerful characteristics of integrated account management (IAM) is its measurability. The high degree of measurability provides a tight framework for managing multiple aspects and multiple levels of IAM. The benefits of the measurement system, when applied, can be profound.

The measurement system shows you how well IAM is working and how different components of the process cause it to succeed or fail. For all the positives that result from a strong IAM measurement system, there is some risk associated with putting measurements in place and holding employees accountable for those measurements. This risk is amplified if measuring is not introduced as part of an overall system.

Too often, management does not consider the human behavior that will result from the use of measurements. Some years ago, while conducting a call center audit, I encountered an interesting mix of measurements and resulting human behavior. The management team at this large, high-tech company was focused on the balance between productivity and service levels. The service level, measured by percent of calls answered in one minute and percent of calls abandoned (i.e., the caller hung up before the call was answered), was declining in their call center, which consisted of some 50 telephone sales reps. Call volume was increasing, up to about 1,500–2,000 calls per day. Taking into consideration their service levels, this meant that each rep, on average, was taking about 35 calls per day. Let's work the numbers. At 35 calls per rep per day, assuming there are not significant fluctuations in call volume during the day, the call center could handle 1,750 calls. Now, if you could just get each rep to handle 5 more calls per day, you could manage the 2,000 calls without a head count increase and without a degradation of the service level. That was exactly what management decided to do. It decided to put in place two measurements that would allow it to effect this productivity increase. The measurements were number of phone calls managed per day and average call length. Management's assumption was that the reps would become more efficient, both during calls and between calls. Management believed that if it improved these measurements, service levels would increase, customers would be happier, and the company might even get a little additional revenue from calls that were no longer abandoned. Because it would be able to do this without an increase in head count, it would be able to hold present costs, and the net effect would be an increase in profitability.

The results: Reps found a way to be more efficient. They handled more phone calls each day and actually achieved a higher service level. However, they did this by reducing the length of each phone call, and none of the other results were achieved. Reps quickly discovered that the more products a customer ordered, the longer the phone call lasted. They also realized that at the completion of each call, they asked a few questions (Are there any other products that you need today? Have you considered product A? Do you know that if you order a larger quantity you'll receive a discount?) that invariably increased the length of the call. In addition, more often than not the customer replied "No, thank you" to these queries. Removing these questions from the end of the call resulted in a reduction in length of time on the phone that ultimately ended up decreasing the average order size, negatively impacting customer satisfaction (customers felt like they were rushed through the call), and negatively impacting profitability. The good intentions of management went awry, and the positive results were more than offset by the negative results.

Was this measurement tactic successful? The obvious answer is no. While the measurement was achieved, it did not lead to the anticipated and desired business results. What went wrong? Were these two measurements simply bad measurements? Like a measurement system, the answer to this question is complex. Management made three mistakes that contributed to the failure of these measures. By failure I mean they did not cause decisions that led to positive business results.

1. It did not treat these measurements as part of an overall system. In overall business systems, measurements have the potential to effect one another just as in the human body, where different measurements have an impact on each other. Losing or gaining weight can have an effect on blood pressure and pulse rate. Similar to this, one business system's measurement can affect others. Increasing productivity could decrease a service level or a sales level. In an IAM module, increasing the number of times that a product is recommended or proposed may decrease the close rate. Increasing the price may have an impact on customer retention and close rates. It is critical whenever core measurements are put in place that the interaction with other measures and the potential impact on other measures is anticipated. In this case example they were simply treated as independent entities that could be changed with no impact on the system. Obviously that wasn't the case.

2. It didn't anticipate the behavior that would be caused by these measurements. Again if we use the human body as a metaphor and talk about a measurement like losing weight, it is obvious that there are healthy ways to lose weight and unhealthy ways to lose weight. As in the example above, an unhealthy way to increase productivity was to decrease the average order size. Before you put measures into place, it is critical that you anticipate how employees might go about achieving those measures and that you think through both the healthy ways that people might accomplish those measurements and the unhealthy ways they might accomplish those measurements.

3. It did not provide employee training and education as part of the introduction of the measures. Too frequently employees are not given training or even provided with rationale that allows them to understand why new measurements are put into place, what the company thinks it will be able to achieve with those measurements, and what positive behavior it anticipates toward achieving those measurements. In the call center example, the reps simply had the measures. They were not told what business results management expected, and they didn't think through what business implications might result from their actions. They simply focused on achieving the measurements as provided by management.

Aligning Measurements to IAM

Figure 13-1 illustrates a model for defining two sets of measurements. As illustrated, these two sets are results measures and process mea-

Figure 13-1. IAM measurement system.

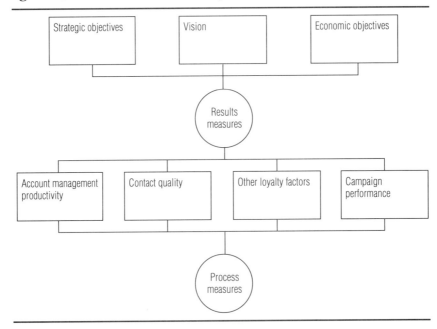

sures. The first tell us whether IAM is working; that is, whether it is achieving the objectives in a way that is consistent with the vision. The second set of measurements are process measures—key indicators of why something is or is not working. Process measures tell you what is driving results, both positive and negative. Examples of results measures are return on investment and customer retention. Examples of process measures are customer contacts per day and the quality rating of each contact.

The model illustrated is a top-down process, as follows:

1. Define the objectives. As the model indicates, these objectives for account management typically fall into three categories: (1) strategic objectives, or results you want to achieve in the marketplace (e.g., create a competitive barrier); (2) vision objectives, or how you want to do business with customers; and (3) economic objectives, which deal with the financial impact of IAM and include profitability, revenue and revenue growth, and return on investment calculations.
2. Define the results measures that are evidence that the objectives are being achieved.
3. Identify the business processes or process components that encompass the activities that will result in an impact on the objectives and results measures.

4. Define the measures within the business processes identified that are evidence of change within the processes—change that is directed toward realizing the results measures and achieving the objectives.

In this model, results measures are always explicitly linked to objectives, both strategic objectives and economic objectives. These measures answer a relatively simple question: "How will you quantitatively know that you have achieved your objectives?" Figure 13-2 illustrates some measures associated with strategic objectives that were outlined in Chapter 3.

When results measures are thoroughly and accurately defined, process measures can then be linked to process components that are in turn linked to results measures. Let's walk through an example to demonstrate. Let's assume the following objectives in a mature market:

Figure 13-2. Measuring strategic objectives.

Strategic Objectives	*Results Measures*
1. Create a competitive barrier	• Customer retention rates • Customer defection rates • Customer repurchase intent
2. Reduce the cost of selling	• Marketing & sales productivity (marketing & sales cost as a percentage of revenue)
3. Growth through account penetration	• Average number of divisions & sites/locations per customer account • Average number of buying customers per account • Share of customer at an account level
4. Growth through product penetration	• Average number of product lines purchased per account • Percentage of customer base with new product line purchases
5. Customer share growth	• Share of customer — percentage of available dollars (dollars spent on products offered by seller)
6. Harvest	• Marketing & sales productivity (marketing & sales cost as a percentage of revenue) • Overall cost of marketing & selling

- A strategic objective to reduce the cost of selling
- Economic objectives that include sustaining an existing revenue stream, increasing customer share, and increasing profitability
- A vision that focuses on maintaining strong relationships with customers by providing relevant value

What will you measure as evidence that you have achieved these objectives?

- Contribution (dollars and percent) after selling expenses—a measure of profitability and an indicator that highlights the cost of selling and its impact on profitability
- Marketing and sales productivity, or the cost of marketing and selling as a percentage of revenue—evidence that the cost of selling is being reduced
- Customer retention, or the percentage of customers that purchased last year and are still active purchasing customers this year—a measure of sustained existing revenue and evidence of strong relationships with customers
- Customer intent to repurchase—one of the most effective indicators of strong customer relationships and evidence, before the customer actually purchases, that the existing revenue stream will be maintained
- Average annual revenue per customer—an indicator of customer share

Note: There is a strong focus in these measures on keeping business that you already have—both customers and sales levels from those customers. That is because these are the least expensive sales you can make. As such, they have a positive effect on profitability and the cost of selling.

Which process components will you change or manage more closely to effect these results and achieve these objectives?

- An obvious area to consider is IAM productivity. IAM productivity will directly affect marketing and sales productivity and indirectly affect improvements in contribution margins.
- Contact quality is an area that will have an affect on relationships with customers.
- Loyalty factors not only have a positive correlation to the strength of customer relationships; they are also precursors to customer share, customer retention, and customer intent to repurchase.

The set of process measures might include the following:

- Customer contacts per day per account manager and/or time spent with customers, measured as hours per day. Marketing and sales productivity as a results measure suggests getting more out of existing resources. It's plain and simple, using a "bang for the buck" mentality. The account manager, as the most important and most limited resource, is usually the focus of this measurement. There could be two different approaches here: (1) a cost-reduction approach (maintain revenue and reduce cost, usually by downsizing) and (2) a growth approach (increase revenue using existing resources, especially IAM resources) to improve marketing and sales productivity. For our purpose, let's consider the growth approach. The questions in sequence are: How do you get more sales dollars through existing account managers? How do you increase the average size of each sale made by account managers? How do you improve close rates? How do you get account managers to talk to more customer decision makers? How do you find more customer time for account managers? The starting point for this stream of logic is the account manger's time with customers and how that time is used (number of customer contacts). Any other measures, including the result of marketing and sales productivity, ultimately flow out of these two process measures.
- Customer service problem occurrence (focus on factors that influence retention). This process measure is supportive of the results measure of customer retention. Reducing the frequency and severity of service problems can have a positive impact on customer retention and intent to purchase.
- Number of product lines purchased per customer or number of individual customers/decision makers per account. Both product penetration and account penetration are approaches to increasing annual sales per customer. Increasing annual sales per customer is evidence of increasing customer share. Product and account penetration are supportive of increasing sales per customer and are both different and additional pieces of evidence to support increased customer share.

A Revenue/Productivity Model and a Catalyst for Change

The revenue/productivity model provides a framework for understanding IAM measures as a system. A review of the model in Figure 13-3 illustrates how this works.

Figure 13-3. IAM revenue/productivity plan influencers.

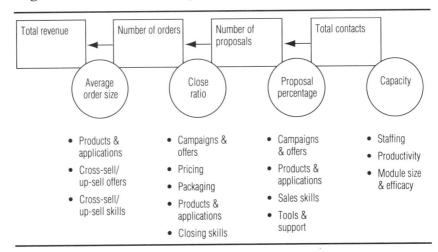

On the right-hand side of the model is capacity, a result of staffing levels, productivity of staff, and the ability to deal with the nuances in different market segments. We refer to it as module efficacy. In some markets it is simply more difficult to contact a decision maker. In some, account managers need to develop a very specialized set of skills to get through to decision makers. Building and getting leverage out of those skills is a consideration in module design. The factors that can be addressed and influenced by management to increase capacity are staff size, staff productivity, and module design. Capacity dictates the total number of customer contacts that can be made.

As contacts are made, some will result in proposals, or recommendations to customers. The percentage of contacts that result in proposals (reflected in Figure 14-3 as proposal percentage) is impacted by the effectiveness of the defined offers, the capability of the available products to meet customers' needs, the product support, the account managers' ability to link the products and the application of the products to customers' needs, and the sales skills of the account manager.

The next ratio that builds to revenue is the close ratio, which is defined as the percentage of proposals that are closed. Management affects the close ratio through: effectiveness of campaigns and offers, an appropriate pricing policy, creative packaging options, products and the applications of products, the ability to position these against customer needs, and the strength of account managers' closing skills.

The last ratio in this model that affects revenue is the average order size. Too frequently we see this one ignored. It is, for many organizations, the least expensive way to increase revenue because it measures additional revenue in a customer contact that you've already invested in, therefore leveraging the contact and contact cost.

With this model, it becomes apparent how a system of process measures leads to a result, and a result measure, in this case, leads to revenue. This model also illustrates how the key ratios can be influenced to change performance levels and achieve the desired result(s).

An additional benefit, possibly the most important, is the ability to use process measures to anticipate the result. In this model, if you begin to see a decline in contact productivity, proposal percentage, close rate, or average order size, you can soon expect to see a related decline in sales. The process measures in the model allow you to see potential, or actual, problems and begin to deal with those problems before they get to the results.

What to Do and What to Measure

IAM is a highly measurable business system. Like any strong characteristic of a business system, this measurability is both a strength and a weakness of IAM. As a strength, the measurability allows you to adjust tactics based upon what's working and what isn't, allows you to get out ahead of the curve and anticipate problems, allows you to focus on particular parts of the business system, and allows you to run IAM in a continuous improvement environment. The negatives are more subtle. They include excessive measurements (measuring everything simply because you can), fixing the measure without fixing the root cause, and managing exclusively by the numbers.

Let's discuss three common traps inherent in the measurability of IAM.

1. *The incrementality trap.* A few years ago, when I was in my early twenties (well maybe it was more than a few years, but who's counting?), I purchased and moved into a house that could probably be described as a "fixer-upper." One of my early projects was remodeling the bathroom. The most daunting part of that project was replacing the cast iron bathtub. I had to use a sledge hammer to break the tub apart before I could remove it. It took at least twenty-five sledge hammer hits before the tub broke, and most of those first twenty-five hits had no discernible effect on the tub. Now, if I applied the "incremental theory of marketing," and looked at each of those separate hits as campaigns, I would draw the conclusion that the twenty-fifth campaign was highly successful and the other twenty-four were miserable failures. In fact, I wouldn't be able to justify the

first twenty-four and I would end up running the twenty-fifth campaign as my first and only campaign.

In IAM you cannot justify every single contact or investment in a customer as a separate entity. The relationship with the customer is what provides marketing success (ultimately growth and profitability). It is typically a series of value-adding contacts with the customer that leads to the relationship. The measure of success is the measure of the relationship—the sum of all sales and profitability in the customer relationship minus the sum of all marketing and sales investments in the customer—not of each individual marketing activity.

Another aspect of the incrementality trap is trying to measure the value of IAM as the incremental sales that it generates. IAM, especially when first implemented, can generate a large volume of new incremental business with existing customers. Not as obvious unless it is measured is the impact on customer loyalty and current revenue streams. Over time, the economic impact of customer loyalty will dwarf the impact of incremental business that is generated.

The third and worst aspect of the incrementality trap is the "we could have got that sale without IAM" trap. The fact is, IAM will not work if you treat it as an incremental customer contact tactic. It only achieves full effectiveness when it becomes the relationship, which nullifies any attempt at measuring it incrementally.

2. *Managing by the numbers.* Because of the measurability of IAM, there is a temptation to try to get the numbers to make business decisions for you. The value in the measurements comes out of the analysis and interpretation and comes as a result of blending the numbers with your business judgment. Blind faith in the numbers to the exclusion of business judgment is a prescription for failure.

Another way that "managing by the numbers" plays out as an inordinate focus is in measuring subjective detail. This results in a phenomenon that was pointed out by Dr. Joseph Juran, a pioneer in the field of quality improvement, who said quality managers fail because they are "preoccupied with conformance to specifications rather than focusing on fitness for use."

There is a "tele-selling" theory being taught by some consultants that states that you "should use the customer's name at least three times in the first sentence of your call." Can you imagine trying to measure this as part of the process? What positive outcome will result from this measurement? "Fitness for use" implies a result. The desirable result in this case is the customer relationship. Is this measurement a good indicator of how a call improved a business relationship with a customer?

Most companies simply need to get more comfortable making

decisions with a blend of highly quantitative data and very subjective information (some information is subjective, but this in no way implies that it is superficial or that rigorous analysis was not done before drawing the conclusions).

3. Not defining *customer*. This one seems so simple that it is often overlooked. The answer is that a customer is someone who buys something from you. Okay. What if the customer bought something three years ago and hasn't purchased from you since then? What about the customer who never made a conscious decision to buy from you (like a utilities customer)? What if the customer only bought some ancillary product that sold for $1.99? Or bought one product and returned that product two weeks later? Are all of these still considered customers? Customers are at the heart of IAM. It doesn't work and its measurement systems don't work unless an *active* customer is clearly defined.

The Critical Measurement Categories

There are three critical areas of measurement that need to be considered.

1. *The income statement.* Because of the way the income statement has been discredited in the business press the last few years, this almost feels like a "pity vote." However, I feel quite strongly that the income statement is a viable and important measurement. The problem isn't the tool; it is the application of the tool. The income statement is clearly a results measurement tool. It will not provide the information needed to fine tune a business process. It is a valuable indicator of how you are doing. As such, I have included it here in the arsenal of IAM measurement tools. Over time, IAM should result in better financials—both top line (revenue) and bottom line (profitability).

2. *Customer loyalty.* By its very nature, a world-class IAM system is a customer loyalty producing system. While the income statement is a measure of short-term business viability, customer loyalty is the best measure of long-term business viability. The customer loyalty measurements, which are covered in more detail in Chapter 14, should address:

- Customer retention
- Product penetration
- Purchase volume
- Referrals

- Repurchase intent
- Willingness to refer
- Customer service factors

3. *Account management productivity.* Customer loyalty measures provide an "outside-in" perspective. They drive the customer's perspective into the organization. IAM productivity measures provide an "inside—out" perspective. The productivity model—available customer time × customer calls × customer contacts × proposal % × close ratio × average order size—provides an excellent framework for driving change in internal IAM processes.

Summary

Building these measurement systems is a sizable task. However, the benefits are also substantial. The measurement system is a veritable control panel that not only tells you how you are doing but in addition tells you what parts of the business system are working well and what parts aren't. It provides a framework for a system of continuous improvement in your IAM program.

14

Customer Loyalty as an IAM Measurement System

It's not how satisfied you keep your customers, it's how many satisfied customers you keep!

Frederick F. Reichheld
Bain & Company, Inc.

The Complexity of Customer Loyalty

There is a mistaken notion that a primary function and outcome of integrated account management is an increase in customer satisfaction, as measured by an overall satisfaction level. The flawed logic that supports this thinking is as follows:

Stronger customer relationships are a critical result of IAM.
An overall satisfaction level is a good indicator of the strength of customer relationships.
Therefore, an increase or decrease in the overall satisfaction level is an indicator of an increase or decrease in the strength of customer relationships.

Although the first statement above is obviously true (stronger customer relationships *are* part of the foundation that IAM is built on), the use of overall satisfaction as an indicator is filled with problems. For example: Two steps are typically taken in our IAM pilot to provide an accurate assessment and measurement of the program's impact on customer relationships. The first step is a customer satisfaction study conducted before the program begins to give management a baseline against which to measure. The second step is a follow-up survey conducted approximately six months later to measure the difference in customer attitudes and perceived service levels for customers participating in the IAM program. The survey gathers information on a number of factors that are seen as meaningful measures of the strength of relationships with customers, including the following:

- *Overall satisfaction.* A measure of the customers' overall satisfaction with the company's products, services, and service
- *Whether they would recommend the company.* The likelihood of customers recommending the company's products and/or services to a friend or associate
- *Whether they would stay with the company.* A measure of the likelihood that they would continue to purchase from the company (assuming that in all cases there are other suppliers available)
- *Personalized support.* A measure of how satisfied customers are with the level of personalized support they have received
- *Knowledge of my business.* The customers' perception (reflected in a rating) of the company's knowledge of their businesses
- *Recommends services/products that meet needs.* A measure of customers' satisfaction with the company's ability to recommend products and services that met their needs
- *Product knowledge.* A rating of the company's representatives' knowledge of their own products and services
- *Follow-up after a sale.* A measure of customers' satisfaction regarding follow-up
- *Responsiveness.* A customer-perceived rating of the company's responsiveness when they needed assistance
- *New product information.* A measure of effectiveness at updating customers on new products and services
- *Speak to appropriate person.* A measure of the ease of contacting the person at the company who could address the content of the customers' calls

A recent IAM pilot, and the corresponding customer satisfaction study, demonstrates the complexity of these measurements.

If the issue here was purely satisfaction, this IAM pilot failed. The "overall satisfaction" results (illustrated in Figure 14-1) did not justify a rollout of IAM. The pilot simply did not have a positive impact on customers' overall satisfaction levels. In fact, overall satisfaction decreased by two percentage points, which is not a statistically significant difference.

On the other hand, it appears that the pilot did have a positive impact in a number of other areas (Figure 14-1). Two of these areas—intent to stay with the company and willingness to recommend the

Figure 14-1. Satisfaction results—change from pretrial to midtrial.

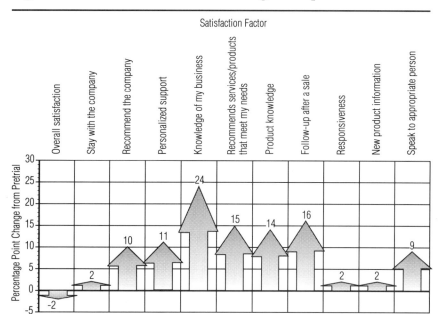

company—are indicators of some interest. Intent to repurchase (stay with the company) shows some slight, but not significant, increase. Willingness to recommend shows a significant increase.

Additionally, all of the factors that typically are thought of, and used, as value indicators show a positive, and in most cases significant, increase. The improvement in these factors ranged from two percentage points (responsiveness and new product information) to twenty-four percentage points (knowledge of my business).

These results seem paradoxical. The customers experienced approximately six months of a new type of relationship. They had their own account manger, who proactively managed the relationship, focusing on providing value, working to enhance the use of company products and services in their businesses, providing personalized attention, and working to ensure that customers received excellent service. In response to this, customers reported in the survey that they received a higher level of personalized support, that the reps understood their business better, that they received better product recommendations, that there was a higher degree of product knowledge, and that there was better after-sale follow-up. Additionally, customers said they are likely to recommend the company to friends and associates. And yet, after all of this, their overall satisfaction level stayed the same. What the heck is going on here?

The Theory of Rising Expectations

Richard Farson, in his book *Management of the Absurd* (1996), provides some insight. In the chapter titled "The Better Things Are, the Worse They Feel," he discusses the theory of rising expectations. "When we managers take action to improve situations, we expect that our efforts will produce satisfaction for those we try to help," Farson writes. "But they seldom do—not for long anyway. The paradox is that improvement in human affairs leads not to satisfaction but to discontent, albeit a higher-order discontent than might have existed before."[1] Farson goes on to give the history of revolutions as an example, pointing out that revolutions start not when conditions are at their worst but only after they have begun to improve, reforms have been instituted, leadership has developed, and the poplace has come to have a new vision of what might be. This is what historians have labeled the theory of rising expectations. This theory fuels the fires of revolution and change because it creates a discrepancy between what people have and what they see is possible to have. That discrepancy is the source of discontent and the engine for change.

"Absurd as it seems," Farson concludes, "the way to judge your effectiveness is to assess the quality of the discontent you engender, the ability to produce movement from low-order discontent to high-order discontent."

Let's look at how this applies to the above example, from one customer's perspective: "I'm getting more attention, personalized service, more value—I'm more likely to recommend your company to others. What's that? How do I feel? What's my overall satisfaction level? Well, I guess I feel pretty good. I always have. The difference is that I now have different and higher expectations."

Let's state this very clearly now: Increasing an overall customer satisfaction level is not a primary objective of an IAM program.

This does not in any way reduce the necessity for a measurement of the strength of customer relationships. What is needed is a multidimensional customer loyalty measurement that focuses on customer behavior (specifically retention and referral), helps you understand what factors drive repurchase and referral behavior, and ultimately allows you to identify how you can create barriers to competition in your customer base.

The Loyalty Measurement System

There are three areas of focus that are absolutely essential in a loyalty measurement system:

1. A focus on customer behavior, with an emphasis on buying and referring behavior
2. An emphasis on the economic impact that illustrates the effect of loyalty on sales, profitability, and number of customers
3. A focus on identifying, defining, and driving pragmatic change that results in competitive advantage

When these areas of focus are combined with three categories of measures: (1) customer behavior, (2) intended customer behavior, and (3) the factors that impact customer behavior, the result is a potentially powerful loyalty measurement system.

These three categories of measures are embodied in an effective customer loyalty system and are valuable as independent measures and as integrated measures. The relationships between the measures can help you identify and understand attitudes and behaviors in your customers that you can't get at any other way.

All three of these categories are important. Let me illustrate. I am a frequent customer of a local bookstore. If I buy three books a week from this bookstore, they are going to look at me and think, "He is a good loyal customer." What they do not realize is that I get frustrated every time I go into the store because I have to wait in line for twenty minutes just to check out. The only reason that I continue to go to that store is because it is the only one close to the office. My behavior says I am loyal, but my intended customer behavior tells a different story. My intended customer behavior is to buy books from any other bookstore that opens up near my office. I am a psychological defector with loyal behavior traits. Suddenly a new bookstore opens up, and I immediately defect. The original bookstore I went to can't figure it out. What went wrong? Why did Mark stop coming? He used to buy three books a week. Maybe we should lower our prices; maybe we should implement a better frequency program. The managers have no clue why I left because they never asked me why I bought from them when I was a customer. Now not only do I go to this new bookstore, but I tell all my friends and associates to go there. The original bookstore has not only lost a customer; it has created an advocate for the competition.

In this example, my historical purchase of three books per week is customer behavior. My intent to purchase from another bookstore as soon as one is conveniently available is my intended customer behavior. The current bookstore service level and my twenty-minute wait to check out are factors that impact customer behavior. If the bookstore is tracking and managing all three of these categories it will understand what its customers are doing (to help it identify problems and validate forecasts), what its customers are planning to do (to identify potential/anticipated problems, to forecast retention and repurchase), and why they are planning to do it (to identify things that need to change to improve actual and intended customer behavior).

Let's discuss these three categories in more detail.

Customer Behavior

Customer behavior relates specifically to actual customer buying and referral activity. (Please see Figure 14-2 for measurements and information sources by category.)

One could make a case for buying behavior's being the only true measure of customer loyalty, and in a sense that would be correct. Historical buying behavior is the irrefutable evidence that customers were loyal. It is a measure of how effective your customer loyalty efforts were. The only problem with relying on buying behaviors is that it is a backward-looking rather than a forward-looking perspective. Is historical buying behavior an important factor in understanding future customer behavior? Absolutely. Is historical buying behavior the only, or in most cases even the primary, factor in understanding future customer behavior? Absolutely not. In the planning process, relying too heavily on historical buying behavior is a little like driving by watching the rearview mirror.

In addition, an overreliance on this behavior as a sole or independent measure can be deceiving because sometimes customers buy from you because they feel they have no reasonable alternative. If there are factors in the relationship that create frustration with customers, they can have an extremely negative impact on the relationship. These customers may feel they are not being serviced, yet may feel that they are in a captive relationship (this frustration is illustrated in the foregoing bookstore example). Customers experiencing this kind of situation are typically looking for the first opportunity to defect to a competitor.

In this sense, customer behavior is not an independent measure that allows you to look forward and plan future customer loyalty efforts. It is an important historical measure that needs to be assessed with intended customer behavior and the factors that drive customer behavior.

The most effective loyalty measurement systems use customer buying behavior to measure effectiveness of their customer management efforts, to assess the impact of product/service/delivery factors, and to validate previous intended behaviors and the economic models developed. Use of this actual buying behavior as a validation of

Figure 14-2. Customer loyalty measurement system.

Category	Measurements	Calculation	Source
Customer Behavior	• Repurchase/ retention rates	• Percentage of repurchasing customers from one buying period to the next (typically 1 year)	• Customer purchase history
	• Product penetration	• Average number of product lines purchased by customer	• Customer purchase history
	• Dollar volume purchases	• Dollar value of sales within a given buying period (typically 1 year) • Rate of change in buying period (annual) purchases	• Customer purchase history
	• Referrals	• Number of referrals within a time frame	• Customer database
Intended Customer Behavior	• Repurchase intent	• Percentage of customers definitely and probably intending to repurchase	• Customer loyalty study
	• Willingness to refer	• Percentage of customers definitely and probably likely to refer friends and associates	• Customer loyalty study
Factors That Affect Customer Behavior*	•Knowledge of customer needs • Product and service knowledge • Appropriateness of product recommen- dations • Postsale follow-up • Effectiveness of communication	• Percentage of customers with very satisfied and satisfied satisfaction levels combined with correlation to buying and intended buying behaviors • The correlation between customer buying behavior and service problem occurrence	• Customer loyalty study • Real-time service tracking system

*These are representative and may vary by industry.

intended behavior is critical. This checkpoint allows a marketer to deal with the phenomenon of customers not behaving exactly the way that they said they would. For example, customers who defect to a competitor even though on the last loyalty survey they indicated that they would continue purchasing from their current supplier.

The specific measurements of customer behavior as illustrated in Figure 14-2 are the following:

• *Repurchase/retention rates.* For many companies this is a relatively simple measurement; it is represented as the percentage of buying customers from last year that are still buying this year. In some industries, using consecutive years in this measurement is not meaningful; for example, if the customer's buying cycle is much greater than one year in length. In this case the stated retention rate is much lower than the actual. If the buying cycle is much less than one year, the stated retention rate is still reasonably accurate. In this situation, customer retention is a good indicator of effectiveness. It is not a good measure for identifying individual customers at risk in this situation, however, because it does not necessarily identify these customers early enough.

• *Product penetration.* This is a relatively simple measurement. In concept, it tells us that product breadth is evidence of the extent of commitment that a customer has made, evidence of trust in the relationship, and evidence that there is an economic benefit to the customer's staying with your company (reflected in the economic investment already made in the relationship and in potential switching costs). A single product purchase can happen because the purchase was convenient or because the customer had a specific need that was fulfilled by the product. Second and third product purchases indicate that there is something more than coincidence in the relationship—trust and credibility. Product penetration is usually a good measure of the strength of the relationship.

• *Dollar volume purchases.* As customers become increasingly comfortable with the relationship, they tend to spend more. This suggests that there are two separate dollar volume purchase measurements of loyalty: the actual dollar volume and the rate of change in purchase volume, typically from one year to the next. All other things being equal, a customer who spends more with you is usually a more loyal customer. Additionally, a customer whose annual dollar volume purchases have increased from year to year is more loyal, and a customer whose annual purchase amount has decreased is less loyal.

• *Referrals.* Referrals have obvious benefit: they are an excellent source of prospective new customers. In addition, referring others is an excellent indicator of loyalty on the part of the referring customer. When a customer recommends your company to friends and associates, she demonstrates a high level of trust and increases the commitment she has made to the relationship. Customers who give you referrals typically have higher retention rates and higher lifetime value.

This suggests two tracking requirements. The first is the ability to track the referrer as the source of the new prospect. This is important because it allows you to track the return, and subsequent value, from referrals. The value can be used to encourage internal behavior that generates referrals and to justify expenditures in referral-generating campaigns.

The second requirement is the ability to track referring behavior of the referring customer. A customer who gives you referrals is one that is typically more loyal, has a higher lifetime value, and provides additional value through the potential new business from referred prospects. Tracking this behavior allows you to treat that referring customer differently and supports a higher investment in that customer based upon the additional worth that results from the referral(s).

Tracking this referral activity doesn't have to be complex. It requires that the information be captured at the source when new prospects and new customers are first identified. This information should later be stored in a database, where it will allow you to update the referral information on the new prospect/customer record and update the referring activity data on the existing customer record.

As part of implementation, the questions that gather this referral data (How did you hear about us? Were you referred to us by anyone?) become part or the call guide(s) and monitoring checklists for all account managers handling new prospects and customers. Performance standards are put in place to ensure that there is a mutual understanding of the importance of capturing this information, and the use of this information in referral campaigns is shared so that account managers see the value and outcome from this information.

Intended Customer Behavior

The second category of measures, intended customer behavior, is what customers tell you they intend to do. The specific measurements of intended customer behavior (as illustrated in Figure 14-2) are the following:

• *Repurchase intent.* As a consultant, I frequently have the opportunity to ask marketing and sales executives how they can tell if they are providing value and high-quality goods and services to customers. Too often I hear the response, "Customers pay their bills, even though we have a money-back guarantee." This response only deals with the previous purchase. The line of questioning regarding repurchase intent gets at how customers feel relative to their next purchase. This comes out as, "How likely are you to purchase from ABC company the next time you have a need?" This line of questioning allows you to anticipate customer defections before they occur and provides the information to drive remedial action to prevent those defections.

• *Willingness to refer.* Additionally, there is a need to understand a customer's willingness and intention to recommend your company to others. This line of questioning gets at one of the best indicators of customer loyalty. Customers who have a high likelihood of referring others are your most loyal customers. Incidentally, this idea of providing referrals is not a bad seed to plant in your customers' minds by asking the question, "Would you recommend our company to others?"

This intended behavior not only allows you to gauge the seriousness of any customer discontent, it also allows you to gain a level of understanding of how, from the customers' perspective, you stack up against the competition.

Factors Affecting Customer Behavior

Customer behavior is an excellent historical record that indicates how you have performed in engendering customer loyalty. Intended customer behavior is an excellent indicator of what is likely to happen in the short term. The factors that impact customer behavior are the measurements that allow you to get ahead of the curve, drive appropriate process change into your business, and identify customers at risk or soon to be at risk. A good metaphor is that customer behavior is the damaged engine in your automobile, intended customer behavior is the oil light on your dashboard, and factors are the regular preventive oil pressure checks that you do. Figure 14-2 illustrates some common factors that impact customer loyalty in an IAM environment. Although these factors may vary from one industry to another, or from one company to another, some representative factors are quite common in all industries and companies (illustrated in Figure 14-2):

• *Knowledge of customer needs.* I've discussed at some length the importance of understanding customer needs (in the operating principles in Chapter 2 and in the needs-based segmentation in Chapter 6). This measurement is designed to get the customers' perspective regarding your knowledge of their needs. Your knowledge of customers' needs doesn't provide value unless customers see that knowledge in what you say and do.

• *Product and service knowledge.* This is the customers' perception regarding how well you know your own products and services. This would typically include features of your products, usage or application of products, and benefits of products.

- *Appropriateness of product recommendations.* From the customer's perspective, this is both a competency and a trust issue. From a competency perspective, the issue is how well you apply your knowledge of customer needs and your knowledge of your products and services when making recommendations. From a trust perspective, customers must feel that your product recommendations are in their best interests.
- *Postsale follow up.* This is an important factor to measure because it is a key step in the business process and because short-cutting this step can feed the skepticism in many customers, giving them the feeling that "the only time they contact me is when they want to sell me something."
- *Effectiveness of communication.* Most organizations spend an enormous amount of money on communicating with customers. This line of questioning gets at the customers' perspective of how effective that communication is.

In addition to these general factors, there is a need to identify and quantify two other specific types of factors that influence loyalty—differentiating satisfiers and dissatisfiers. Differentiating satisfiers are those positive factors in your relationships with customers that define why customers buy from you. Dissatisfiers are the negative factors in your relationships with customers that they identify as problems or barriers to doing more business with you.

The identification of these types of factors allows you to determine how well you are performing in general product, service, and relationship areas; allows you to determine why customers choose you over the competition; and allows you to understand your areas of vulnerability in the marketplace.

These sets of factors are a significant component of the three categories of measurements.

A loyalty measurement system that is built on these three categories of measurements is essential at the outset of an IAM program. It is the primary tool that allows you to ensure that the IAM program is built and managed in a way that drives customer loyalty and the resulting profitability.

IAM Applications of Customer Loyalty

Customer satisfaction and customer loyalty studies almost always provide interesting and potentially valuable information. The problem is that way too many of these studies end up sitting on someone's shelf gathering dust. Again, the key is action. Satisfaction and loyalty studies that don't drive action create dissatisfaction and decreased loyalty. When done in context of an IAM program, there are some very specific applications of the studies.

Five specific applications are: (1) assessing and quantifying the impact of IAM, (2) targeting loyalty segments, (3) identifying and perpetuating satisfiers that positively impact customer behavior, (4) identifying and removing dissatisfiers, and (5) building an early warning system.

1. *Assessing and quantifying the impact of IAM.* Integrated account management is not of value unless it has a positive economic impact in areas such as profit, revenue, share, productivity, and customer retention. A loyalty study helps you understand and quantify that impact by:

- Identifying the number of customers at risk and the corresponding revenue at risk in the current environment. The study specifically asks customers what their likelihood of repurchasing or continuing to purchase is. In Figure 14-3 the data indicate that a significant percentage of the customer base is at risk. Counting "definitely would not," "probably would not," and "might or might not," 41 percent of the customer base is at risk.

At-risk amounts would be calculated as follows:

Percentage of customers likely to defect	13%
Percentage of customers at risk to defect	41%
Total customer base	133,000
Average annual customer revenue	
—likely-to-defect customers	$636
—at-risk-to-defect customers	$489
Total customers	
—likely-to-defect	17,290
—at-risk-to-defect	58,520
Total revenue at-risk	
—from likely-to-defect customers	$10,996,440
—from at-risk-to-defect customers	$28,616,280

Figure 14-3. Intent to repurchase.

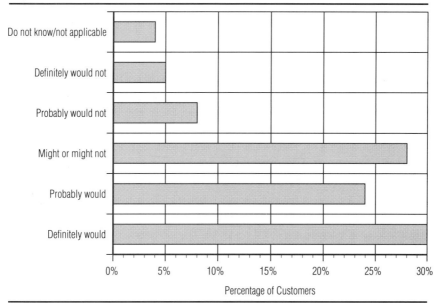

While these numbers may appear shocking, I have seen companies run with customer retention rates of less than 40 percent, which means a customer defection rate of greater than 60 percent. This quantification is important because it induces companies to invest in areas that will have an impact on the economics, highlighting situations where customers have low expectations. Customers who have low expectations generally feel good about your products, service, and the relationship. However, there is not enough strength in the relationship nor in the customers' perceptions of your products and services to compel them to continue to do business with you. When customers have low expectations, they are very susceptible to competitive offers. These customers may indicate that they are satisfied or even very satisfied. This degree of overall satisfaction is not necessarily an indicator that these customers are protected from competition. In fact, in industry after industry 65 to 85 percent of defecting customers indicate that they are either satisfied or very satisfied—and stated such on the most recent customer satisfaction survey they had participated in. There are a number of conditions that indicate low customer expectations, including the following:

- A significant difference between satisfaction levels and repurchase levels. If 65 percent of customers say they are very satisfied, but only 40 percent say they would definitely repurchase from you, that indicates an expectation problem.
- A significant difference between satisfaction levels and willing-

ness-to-refer levels. Willingness to refer is one of the best indicators that customers have a high degree of trust and have
made a commitment to the relationship. This dissonance indicates a problem.
- A significant difference between overall satisfaction levels and
  satisfaction levels for particular factors. When customers tell
  you that overall they are very satisfied but that they are not
  very satisfied with your understanding of their business, your
  ability to recommend products, or the availability of products,
  you have an expectation problem. The expectation problem is
  even more of a concern when there is a high correlation between these individual factors and repurchase intent.

The identified revenue at-risk becomes the basis for a justification of an investment in IAM. In the illustrated example, there
is a revenue total of $39,612,720 that could be lost as a result of cus-
tomer defections ($10,996,440 from likely-to-defect customers and
$28,616,280 from at-risk-to-defect customers).

At the start-up of an IAM program, integrated account management is positioned to reduce this defection level, and the dollar value
of that reduced defection is easily determined to justify the up-front
investment in IAM and to set specific retention (or defection preven-
tion) improvement goals for IAM.

Over time, the loyalty study is repeated. It can vary based upon
industry, but a commonly used time frame and one I recommend is
six months after start-up and annually thereafter.

You now have two economic comparisons to measure IAM impact. The first is a comparison of anticipated/intended customer behavior to actual customer behavior. In our example, 17,290 customers
indicated that they were likely to defect. Out of those indicating that
they were likely to defect, how many that are managed through IAM
are still purchasing and what is the corresponding revenue that was
retained with these customers?

The second economic comparison is a measure of the change in
customers' attitudes in the time frame from one loyalty study to the
next. A reduction in the number of customers likely to and at risk to
defect is linked to a specific economic benefit.

2. *Targeting loyalty segments.* Loyalty segments are defined as follows:

- Secure customers. Customers who demonstrate a high degree
  of loyalty through their buying behavior, satisfaction levels,
  and referrals. These customers are typically most unlikely to
  defect to competition.

- Complacent customers. Customers who demonstrate some evidence of loyalty. The general sense is that although these may be good customers, they also may be targets for competition, and the relationship with these customers may not be strong enough to overcome a competitive action.
- At-risk customers. Customers who demonstrate little or no evidence of loyalty. The right competitive offers are likely to get these customers to defect. In fact, many of these customers typically have already defected in their minds, as reflected in their intentions.
- Defector customers. Customers who have bought or intend to buy from competition or customers who have not repurchased or are unlikely to repurchase. Some of these are already psychological defectors. They want to defect and will if the conditions are right.

Conducting this analysis as follows provides a loyalty scorecard for the business:

- A loyalty survey is completed. Customers are assigned to loyalty segments based on satisfaction level, intent to repurchase, and willingness to refer.
- Customer loyalty segments are then quantified as part of the overall customer base (Figure 14-4).
- Loyalty segments are then quantified with respective revenue and share of business (Figure 14-5).
- The two tools are used to understand the current situation. Assuming annual sales of $159 million to a base of 133,000 active customers, the following observations are made.
  - —17,290 customers, worth approximately $11 million, have already defected. Can these customers be identified and tactics put in place to attempt to reactivate them?
  - —23,940 customers, worth approximately $27 million are vulnerable to competition. Can action be taken that will move these customers up to the next loyalty level?
  - —25 percent of customers (33,250) are secure, representing 48 percent of revenue. Investing in these customers to retain their business is a top priority.

3. *Identifying and perpetuating satisfiers that positively impact customer behavior.* In a business relationship there are both positive and negative characteristics that drive the strength of the relationship. Identifying and understanding the positive characteristics, in particular those that differentiate you from the competition and those that posi-

Figure 14-4. Customer loyalty segments.

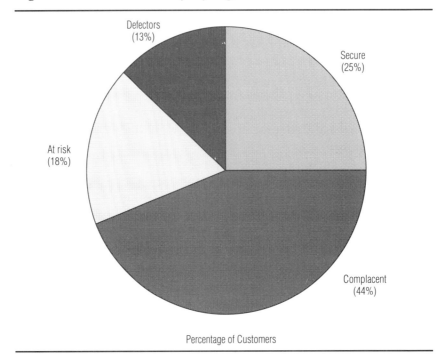

Percentage of Customers

Figure 14-5. Loyalty segment revenue and share of business.

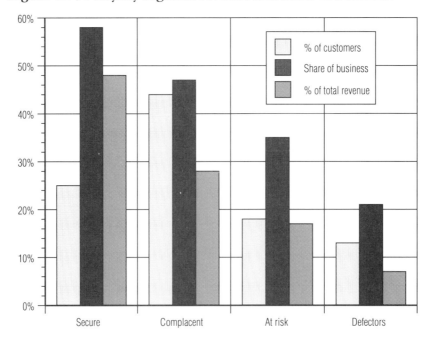

Figure 14-6. Differentiating satisfiers: account/customer loyalty analysis.

Differentiating satisfiers	Secure	Complacent	At-risk	Defector	Total
Technical support	25%	26%	39%	23%	31%
Personal relationships	20%	9%	9%	15%	12%
Superior customer service	16%	14%	3%	8%	12%
No differentiating satisfiers	12%	26%	27%	31%	22%
Availability	7%	8%	3%	0%	6%
Delivery notification	5%	5%	9%	16%	6%
Price	4%	5%	2%	0%	4%
Product knowledge	2%	2%	2%	0%	2%

Percentage of Customers Responding

tively influence buying behavior, is critical. Figure 14-6 illustrates how and where these satisfiers make a difference. Policy issues, development and training, support mechanisms, and process design should all consider and seek to perpetuate these satisfiers. For example, if superior customer service is an important satisfier, service policies should focus on providing customers a quick, relevant, and sensitive response to their inquiries. Support mechanisms should ensure that customers calling in do not get put on hold for long periods of time.

4. *Identifying and removing dissatisfiers.* Dissatisfiers are the other side of the coin. The questions here are, "What product, service, and/ or support problems have you (the customer) encountered?" and "What are the obstacles or barriers to us doing more business together?" The objectives here are to identify and then change the business systems in a way that prevents or significantly reduces occurrences of the identified problems that are having a substantial negative effect on business and to work to overcome the obstacles or barriers to doing more business. See Figures 14-7 and 14-8.

5. *Building an early warning system.* One of the reactions to an understanding of what dissatisfiers exist in a business is to work to eliminate those dissatisfiers. The reality is that in most environments the best you can hope to achieve is a significant reduction in the frequency of occurrence of those problems. An early warning system keys off of the problems that have an impact on customer loyalty and prompts special and immediate attention to a customer when a loyalty-damaging problem occurs. The intent is to practice damage control immediately so that the customer is retained at least at the current loyalty level. When you are contacting customers on a regular basis through your IAM program, this early warning system allows you to leverage these regular contacts to address and minimize damage to the relationship caused by these problems.

Figure 14-7. Service and support problems: account/customer loyalty analysis.

Service and support problems	Complacent	At-risk	Defector	Total
Lack of communication	10%	22%	23%	11%
Delayed shipments	10%	6%	8%	6%
Lack of sales rep contact	5%	4%	0%	3%
Customer service	3%	4%	0%	2%
Damaged product	2%	3%	0%	2%
Lack of follow-up	2%	3%	0%	2%
Pricing	1%	5%	0%	2%
Product availability	1%	2%	0%	1%

Percentage of Customers Responding

The preceding five applications are designed to drive customer loyalty levels up by focusing on what is being done right that makes a positive difference and on what is being done wrong (or not being done) that has a negative impact, by building the overall IAM system in a way that is aligned with loyalty, and by providing economic justification to support the change.

Summary: Key Requirements of a Customer Loyalty Study

The following are the requirements for a customer loyalty study that provides the value and supports the economics described herein:

- Categorizes customers and revenue into one of four different loyalty segments
- Highlights at-risk and defector revenue losses or potential losses
- Determines differentiating satisfiers and their effects on loyalty
- Determines problem areas (product, service, and support) and their effects on loyalty

Figure 14-8. Barriers to doing more business: account/customer loyalty analysis.

Barriers	Secure	Complacent	At-risk	Defector	Total
Lack of 24-hour support	5%	7%	7%	8%	6%
Product selection	11%	11%	17%	17%	12%
Distance (location)	6%	7%	5%	17%	7%
Lack of volume discounts	5%	10%	11%	8%	9%
Product availability	1%	8%	11%	0%	6%

Percentage of Customers Responding

- Determines other obstacles or barriers and their effects on loyalty
- Quantifies customer loyalty's effect on business growth

As part of building IAM, a loyalty study provides the economics that drive the IAM investment. It provides significant input into the design of the business processes—support processes, the ongoing IAM process, and the IAM introduction process (see Chapter 10). It becomes a core component of the measurement system (see Chapter 13), and, last but not least, it is embedded in the account manager training, where it affects both knowledge and attitudes.

Note

1. Richard Farson, *Management of the Absurd* (New York: Simon & Schuster, 1996), p. 92.

15

Selecting an IAM Information System

As I was driving home from work one day, I remembered several discussions that had taken place during the day. They weren't particularly profound or insightful discussions, and they wouldn't ordinarily have been even very memorable discussions. The reason they kept coming back to me was that they were familiar.

The first conversation had occurred in the morning. I was on the telephone with some of the marketing staff of a new client. This included the vice president of direct marketing, one of her direct reports, and two marketing staff people. The topic of the conversation was their marketing and sales system and database. They expressed their frustration with the lack of progress, in particular their frustration with their information systems department. They said, "You need to help our I.S. people. They just don't get it. They just can't seem to understand what we want."

That afternoon I had a discussion with the information systems group that had responsibility for this project. They were also frustrated. "You need to help our marketing people," they said to me. "They know they want something, but they just don't know what they want."

So marketing was frustrated with systems and systems was frustrated with marketing. The natural question one might ask here is, Who was right? In a sense, they both were. Marketing had not defined what they wanted with enough clarity and enough specificity to allow systems to build it. For their part, systems did not understand functionally what needed to be done. Now, if you've ever seen this happen, I want you to stand up and shout, "Yes, that's the way it is!" My guess is that right now there is a large chorus of, "Yes, that's the way it is!" in companies across the country. The only way to avoid this problem is to approach this task in a methodical, tightly defined process that addresses the functionality issues while it builds a mutuality of understanding between systems and marketing.

The Software and Database Process

Let's first walk through an eight-step process specifically focused on IAM software and database development and then discuss specific areas of concern. The ideal software development process for IAM, as illustrated in Figure 15-1, is laid out in eight steps, with the predominant focus on the front end that culminates in the definition of requirements. The steps in the process are:

1. Define the IAM processes.
2. Define the optimization model.
3. Define requirements.
4. Conduct software fit analysis.
5. Assess software packages.
6. Select package.
7. Design modifications.
8. Implement.

In effect, three steps out of the eight-step process are dedicated to a definition of and an understanding of the systems requirements (steps 1, 2, and 3 in Figure 15-1). This focus is justified for the following reasons:

Figure 15-1. Software and database process.

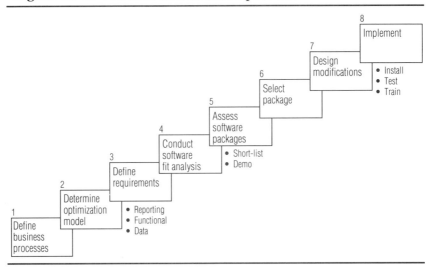

- The IAM business process itself is not tightly defined in most organizations. In some organizations it is a new process, in others it is a process undergoing significant change, and in still others it is a process with a significant amount of variability based on the orientation of individual account managers.
- There is typically ownership ambiguity and conflict around these requirement definition steps. In many organizations, it is simply not clear who (marketing or systems) has responsibility for defining the systems requirements.
- These are critical, make-or-break steps in the process. You cannot adjust or fine-tune a system when the requirements are incorrectly defined.

These issues will be illustrated as we walk through the process. It is important to remember that although to some degree these steps are sequential, this is not a completely linear process. In many cases, there is overlap in steps, and some steps are interchangeable.

The Make or Buy Decision

You will notice that this process assumes that, at least in part, a commercially available software package will be used. There may be isolated cases where there are unique requirements that justify a decision to develop an IAM system in-house, but in most cases buying a commercially available software package is the only reasonable decision. The factors influencing this decision are:

- *The concurrent development of the IAM process and the software selection.* In many organizations, IAM is being defined in a time frame that allows some adaptation of the process to fit into constraints within available packages. In most cases these trade-offs can be made with little discernible effect on performance and overall functionality. In fact, available packages have usually been developed in, or for, organizations that are ahead of the curve in automating IAM and sales processes.
- *The limited number of unique functional requirements.* In most companies, you can find requirements that are unique to that company. However, in most organizations, a high percentage (usually 80 percent or more) of their functional requirements are fairly standard and are needed by many other companies and available in many software packages.
- *The large number of available software packages.* There are literally hundreds of packages available today that provide—to varying

degrees and with varying functional or industry perspectives—
IAM functionality. See the appendix for a partial list of available software packages and vendors.

- *The significant amount of flexibility in many commercially available
  packages.* Many packages, in particular the higher-end packages, have a high degree of flexibility, offering such features as
  screen-painting tools, user-defined data elements, report-gen-
  erator tools, and data-interchange tools. This flexibility further
  reduces any performance or functionality trade-offs that are
  caused when the process is adapted to fit into available software constraints.

- *The economics of building and maintaining IAM software in-house.*
  In most cases these economics simply do not support a "make"
  decision, although this factor can be deceiving. Software development projects are notorious for being underestimated on the
  front end, and estimates frequently do not consider the ongoing cost to maintain the software.

The cumulative effect of these factors can be overwhelming.
When companies go into this decision assuming that they will find
an available package that meets their requirements and have applied
an appropriate amount of rigor to the definition of requirements and
the subsequent selection, they find a package that works effectively
for at least a substantial portion of their requirements.

The Software Development Process

As a preface to the development process, the software development
team is constructed. An ideal team provides multiple perspectives
including marketing, sales, IAM, customer service and support, sales
and marketing management, and systems development and training.
(See Figure 15-2.)

The front end of the process, steps 1 through 3, requires a heavy
marketing and sales orientation and a requisite investment of those
team members' time. In steps 4 through 8 the orientation is more
balanced between sales, marketing, and systems. In fact, some steps
are best managed if systems takes a lead role.

Step 1: Define the IAM Process

This step brings some clarity to the key strategic and tactical components of the IAM process. It answers the following questions:

Figure 15-2. Team members and perspectives they can contribute.

Team Members	Perspectives
• Director of sales and/or marketing	• Marketing
• Sales manager/supervisor	• Sales management
	• Marketing management
• Account managers (1-3, including field and phone)	• Sales
	• Account management
• Customer service manager	• Customer service and support
• Systems analyst and project manager	• Systems development
• Systems developer	
• Systems trainer	• Systems training

• What level of internal communication is necessary?

—Are there support teams (presale, postsale, and customer service)? In some situations, account managers will pass detailed customer and transaction information to support teams to give them the customer information they need to answer technical questions and/or to solve service problems.

—Is electronic communication with product and marketing groups necessary? In some organizations product and/or marketing groups develop communication campaigns and make them available to customers. In these situations it may be efficient to allow account managers to electronically pass their account lists to product/marketing management to facilitate these campaigns.

• What is the basic structure of customer accounts and the nature of your company's relationships within that structure? Do you have multiple levels of decision makers or separate entities within accounts that make independent buying decisions? Your IAM software should accommodate the structure of your accounts. This may require a system that allows many individual names within an account structure, allows you to identify buying process roles for individuals, and/or allows you to identify multiple decision-making groups within an account.

• What are the steps in the selling process? What are the core tactics for these steps? Are there data-gathering steps? Are there data feeds from other systems into the IAM system? How and where are service issues and support handled?

• What is the basic IAM structure—account management teams (e.g., inside and outside reps who work together to manage customer relationships), single account ownership inside, or single account ownership outside? If account managers are working in teams, they will need to, through the IAM system, access each other's notes, contacts, and other information for accounts that they co-manage.

• What is the value proposition to the market? In some cases this may affect the IAM process; in others it may not. When it does affect the process, it has a corresponding affect on the IAM software. For example, a value proposition of providing one-stop shopping for customers has an impact on data, access, and functional requirements.

Step 2: Define the Optimization Model

Because of the power and flexibility inherent in the concept, IAM fits into a lot of market situations. The variability and uniqueness in any given market situation can have a significant effect on how you manage, measure, and continually improve your sales and marketing effort. The critical issues here are developing an understanding of which factors have the most positive impact in the marketplace, then being able to measure the factors, and, finally, being able to modify appropriate business processes to drive those factors.

Consider the concept of a ''breakpoint,'' introduced in the book *Business Process Reengineering* (1993), by Henry J. Johansson and others: ''A Breakpoint is the achievement of excellence in one or more value metrics where the marketplace clearly recognizes the advantage, and where the ensuing result is a disproportionate and sustained increase in the supplier's market share.''[1] The questions here are, in sequence: How do we add value? How do we optimize the business? What are the breakpoints—what will we measure to evaluate our effectiveness? Then in subsequent steps, what are the reporting requirements, functional requirements, and data requirements to support these breakpoints (these requirements are based on the optimization model and the value proposition)? These requirements, if defined correctly based on the foundation set here, significantly increase the probability of making the best software and database decisions (although there are no guarantees). The most common optimization models we see in IAM are as follows. The measurements identified within each model are not necessarily mutually exclusive to that model. While many of the measurements are meaningful in many of these models, they are absolutely essential in the optimization models identified below.

• *Depth of relationship.* In a sense, this is the purest IAM optimization model. In it, account managers have responsibility for a relatively small number of large accounts. The market plan perspective is almost totally bottom-up; that is, the customer contact plan is literally the sum of individual customer plans. Breakpoint metrics include account penetration and share of customer. In all IAM models a focus on individual customers is an important thing, but in this model a focus on individual customers is the only thing.

• *Contact Productivity.* In some IAM environments, account managers take responsibility for a large number of usually smaller accounts (in some businesses more than 1,000 accounts) and have to deal with some degree of "churn"; that is, accounts moving in and out of their customer module. Frequently in this type of environment the breakpoint measurement is contact productivity, as reflected by time with customers and number of decision-maker contacts.

• *Home run productivity.* In some industries and in some product categories customers buy infrequently; there are long lead times to drive a decision and close the business; and the focus, energy, and investment in any given account significantly increases when a specific opportunity has been identified. This model is more likely when the product line includes large, budgeted, capital-expense products such as mainframe computers, factory automation equipment or systems, and construction equipment. The measurements are the number of identified opportunities and closure rate.

• *Contact integration.* In some environments the business can be optimized by increasing customer contacts while optimizing the contact mix. These are environments where there is a sales team (inside and outside account managers), an array of technological tools with which to contact customers, customers with access to and capability in technology, and frequent contact with customers. The breakpoint is a balance between the customers' perception of value from the contacts, the overall contact level or volume to customers, and the overall contact cost-to-revenue ratio.

• *Proposal generation.* This could be characterized as a marketplace where it is important to keep many irons in the fire. This is typically a market where the product is undifferentiated, bought periodically in high volume, and purchased by a purchasing agent through a bid process. Measurements would include proposals per account manager, proposals per account, and the closing ratio.

• *Campaign management.* In this model account managers have responsibility for a large number of accounts in a few different market segments. They need to be able to optimize the business by defining campaigns that are targeted at groups or segments of accounts in the module with similar needs. These campaigns can provide significant leverage and allow the account manager to very effectively serve the needs of a large set of customers. Breakpoints would include measures of campaign economic effectiveness and perceptions of customer value delivered by campaigns.

Now let's talk about why these IAM optimization models are relevant in a chapter about selecting and developing software. This step is so critical (and unfortunately, so frequently not completed) because it allows you to determine the most important functional requirements. If you are in a depth of relationship model and your software only allows five contact names per account, you are in trouble. In a depth of relationship model, you need a software solution that allows an unlimited number of contact names per account. If you are in a contact integration model and the software only allows one account manager to own the account, you have a problem. In a contact integration model, you need the capability to track multiple account owners or team ownership of an account. Knowing how you will optimize allows you to define how you will measure your IAM program, what your reporting requirements are, and what some core functional requirements are. Figure 15-3 highlights some key requirements for different optimization models.

Step 3: Define Requirements

Now that you have an understanding of the basic business process and an understanding of the optimization models and the key performance measurements, you are able to define the requirements, which include reporting requirements, functional requirements, and data requirements. Although these are presented here in sequential steps, they are much more interactive than sequential. Not only do reporting requirements suggest functional requirements; functional requirements suggest reporting requirements. Categories of management reports would include the following:

• *Productivity reporting.* This reporting provides individual account managers and management with the ability to evaluate all elements of productivity and their interaction with each other. It is typically based on the productivity equations illustrated in Figure 15-4. The same model can be applied to management of individual productivity, team productivity, or total IAM productivity.

Figure 15-3. IAM optimization models.

Optimization Model	Critical Requirements
1. Depth of relationship	• Support a multi-level account structure • Unlimited contact names within an account • Multiple buying groups within an account • Track, report, and summarize product (and product line) purchases at individual, buying group, and account levels

2. Contact productivity	• Tools to analyze account modules/territories
	  - Demographic counts
	  - Selection tools
	• Account manager productivity reporting
	• Ability to track all activities that drive productivity

3. Home run productivity	• Ability to track multiple projects within an account • Track project teams for customer accounts • Track project teams within selling company • Track strategic decision-makers within accounts • Opportunity win/loss reporting and analysis
4. Contact integration	• Multiple account manager ownership of an account (inside and outside) • Real-time economic quantification of contact costs at an account level • Field and inside data synchronization • Easy access to customer contact leverage tools (e-mail, fax, mail)
5. Proposal generation	• Integrated proposal generator subsystem • Proposal in-process reporting • Proposal aging reporting • Proposal won/loss analysis • Proposal tracking and reporting at account manager level

6. Campaign management	• Tools to analyze account modules/territories
	  - Demographic counts
	  - Needs analysis
	  - RFM counts
	  - Selection tools
	• Ability to drive targeted segment campaigns (phone, mail, electronic)
	• Campaign performance tracking and analysis
	  - Response, revenue and customer
	  - Campaign P&L

Figure 15-4. Productivity equation.

Telephone Account Management

Number of $\times$ Calls $\times$ Contacts $\times$ Proposals $\times$ Orders $\times$ Average $=$ **Sales**
work hours   per hour   per call   per contact   per proposal   order size

Field Account Management

Number of $\times$ Contacts $\times$ Contacts $\times$ Proposals $\times$ Orders $\times$ Average $=$ **Sales**
days in field   per day   per call   per contact   per proposal   order size

---

• *Campaign performance.* In IAM, campaigns are run as a way for account managers to gain leverage within a set of customers with similar needs: knowledge of the customers' needs, knowledge of the applications of products that fulfill those needs, making a product offering (including packaging and positioning), and specific experience discussing the offering with multiple similar customers. Within most campaigns we expect to see a higher level of productivity and a higher level of sales results than in general calling activity.

• *Opportunity analysis.* How effectively does your IAM organization identify opportunities, make product and/or service recommendations, and close on these opportunities? Opportunity analysis reporting is intended to answer these questions, and, in addition, to help you understand the reasons for your answers. It would typically include:

- Number of opportunities identified
- Work-in-process reporting (opportunities identified and not closed)
- Opportunity reopening
- Won-loss reporting on closed opportunities, including reasons for lost opportunities

• *Customer profiles.* This report, or screen, provides detailed information about a specific customer account. In many cases the specific information included is market- and industry-specific. Standard categories of information are:

- Company name and address
- Business unit names and addresses
- Company and business unit demographics
- Individual names and demographic data (e.g., title, department)
- Individual role in decision-making process
- Company structure/organization chart

- Contact history
- Purchase history
- Competitive relationship
- Installed products
- Needs
- Objectives

• *Market profiles.* Market profiles are counts that tell you how many customers meet certain conditions, set of conditions, or combinations of conditions.

• *Account/market coverage.* In some cases it is important to monitor account coverage. In particular, in cases where you have built large customer modules or are running in a contact productivity optimization module, it is possible to have accounts that are not getting enough contact or any contact at all. This reporting provides information on frequency of account contact within a specific time frame.

The next step is to define the specific functional capabilities that should be performed on the system to create the screens and reports that drive the IAM process. These could include contact management, customer communications, internal communications, interfaces with other systems, calculations, special processes, and so on. In the definition of reporting requirements, the perspective is how IAM is monitored, evaluated, and managed by individual account managers, sales managers, and directors. In the definition of functional requirements, the perspective shifts to how the IAM function is performed.

It is helpful to think of these functional requirements in seven categories:

1. Customer communications and scheduling
2. Customer analysis and planning
3. Module analysis and planning
4. Opportunity management
5. Sales and marketing library
6. Account penetration and networking
7. Customer service and support

The detailed functional requirements are driven out of, and explicitly linked to, the processes that were defined in earlier chapters. Figure 15-5 provides an example of functional requirements and Figure 15-6 provides an outline for functional requirements.

The example in Figure 15-5 provides a reasonable level of detail for the definition of functional requirements for customer communi-

Figure 15-5. Functional requirements: customer communications and scheduling.

Schedule calls and follow-up calls (both phone and face-to-face)	Schedule other media contacts	Maintain contact history	Provide call guide support	Campaign scheduling, selection, and contact
• Schedule by time and date • Allow untimed calls within a date • Schedule calls for next available time slot • Provide call prompting/alarm feature • Provide calendar/ schedule display • Find available time slots • Provide option for automated rescheduling	• Schedule mail, fax, and e-mail contacts • Select from standard letter library • Allow predefined and "on-the-fly" letter personalization • Schedule multiple contacts at one time	• Time and date stamp contact history records • Enter and store unlimited, time-stamped comments at an individual customer level • Display contact history and comments in reverse chronological sequence	• Provide generic, campaign-specific, and contact-specific call guides • Select call guide when scheduling or making contact • Record free-form and coded call guide responses • Provide optional on-line linkage to sales and marketing library	• Allow selection of customers for a sales campaign by criteria; e.g., all attributes, buying history, contact history, and/or call guide responses • Automatically schedule phone or field contact for future prompt • Automatically schedule and generate mail, fax, and e-mail contacts • Create campaign history information, e.g., background and contact history

cations and scheduling. In this figure, the boxes represent major tasks and each of the bullet points defines a specific activity within the task. Providing a greater level of detail at this level does not necessarily promote a better software decision and, in fact, can inappropriately and prematurely narrow the selection of candidate software packages for assessment in step 5. A similar detailed list of functional requirements of the other six categories is then developed using Figure 15-6 as a guide for this list. Figure 15-6 identifies (graphically displayed as bullet points) the major tasks that are required for each of the seven functional categories.

After the reporting and functional requirements are defined, the data requirements are defined. At this point it is necessary to increase systems' involvement. In many cases the best results occur here when systems takes a lead role in defining data requirements. Marketing and sales is better prepared to define the more explicit data requirements (the requirements for the data elements that are visibly used in the IAM system), such as customer demographics, customer history data, and marketing performance data. Systems is better able to define the more implicit data requirements (the requirements for those data elements that are necessary to support system capabilities but are transparent to the user). These include data requirements suggested by reporting and functional requirements (for example, a telephone account manager productivity report suggests that it is necessary to track calls, contacts, and proposals at the account man-

'

Figure 15-6. Functional requirements outline.

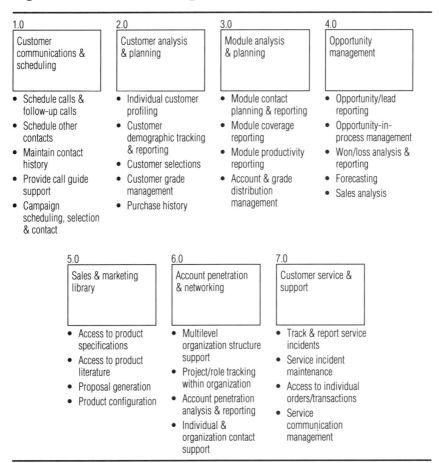

1.0 Customer communications & scheduling	2.0 Customer analysis & planning	3.0 Module analysis & planning	4.0 Opportunity management
• Schedule calls & follow-up calls • Schedule other contacts • Maintain contact history • Provide call guide support • Campaign scheduling, selection & contact	• Individual customer profiling • Customer demographic tracking & reporting • Customer selections • Customer grade management • Purchase history	• Module contact planning & reporting • Module coverage reporting • Module productivity reporting • Account & grade distribution management	• Opportunity/lead reporting • Opportunity-in-process management • Won/loss analysis & reporting • Forecasting • Sales analysis

5.0 Sales & marketing library	6.0 Account penetration & networking	7.0 Customer service & support
• Access to product specifications • Access to product literature • Proposal generation • Product configuration	• Multilevel organization structure support • Project/role tracking within organization • Account penetration analysis & reporting • Individual & organization contact support	• Track & report service incidents • Service incident maintenance • Access to individual orders/transactions • Service communication management

ager level) and the data requirements that are necessary to support structure and linkage needs (data elements that link together records in the database, such as orders to customers and individuals to buying groups within accounts).

The account structure is an important issue addressed when data requirements are defined. In business-to-business markets (except those where buying decisions are made simply, quickly, and by one individual, such as SOHO—Small Office/Home Office Market), it is necessary for the software to support a complex, multidimensional account structure. Bob Stone, in his book *Successful Direct Marketing Methods* (1994), discusses this multidimensional account structure: "Each account, or corporate buying unit, can have multiple locations. Each location is identified by a street address, and each location potentially has multiple buyer groups or groupings of individuals with the same functional requirements. A specific buyer group may be in sales, customer service, research, accounting, purchasing, or maintenance, for example, or it may be related to a new product, production line, market, or technology. Each buyer group is made up of various individuals. An integrated marketing and sales program, then, cultivates accounts at multiple locations around purchases that are being made at any one of those locations. It also identifies the opportunity to sell products and services across different buyer groups located at the same street address. This cross-selling is often facilitated by referrals from existing customers and by specific application briefs that tell how products and services are being used to solve problems."[2] (See Figure 15-7.)

In this structure customer grades are tracked at the buyer group level, communications are managed and tracked at the individual level, transactions like orders and quotes are linked to individuals, and characteristics are captured at all levels. It is important to remember that data requirements should address definition of the data, definition of the relationships between data elements, and definition of the data structure.

Figure 15-7. A corporate cross-selling model.

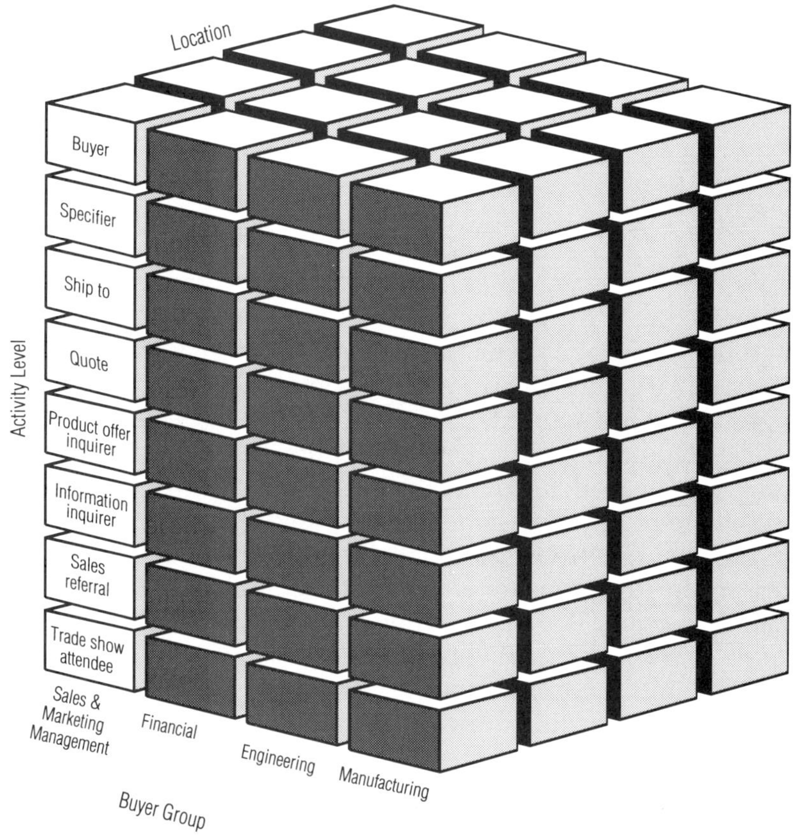

Step 4: Conduct Software Fit Analysis

This step is structured to allow a relatively quick fit analysis of a large number of packages to

- Increase understanding of the available options and potential trade-offs
- Provide a quantification of the fit between requirements and features in software packages
- Narrow the candidate software package group to three to five for further assessment and selection

The goal here isn't to find from three to five perfect software solutions, or even to find the three to five best available solutions. The goal here is to find from three to five good potential solutions out of the literally hundreds of different available packages that are usually categorized as account management, contact management, or sales automation software.

Narrowing this list is most efficiently done in two steps. The first is an initial screening. This initial screen is intended to eliminate the obvious "non-fits." This screen is a qualitative assessment that is done through networking, published reviews, reviews of product literature, directories, and discussions with associations. After the initial screen, which should have narrowed the list to twenty or fewer packages, a more detailed and quantitative assessment is done. The approach here is to

- Draft and send a request for proposal asking each candidate to respond in detail to each of the reporting, functional, and data requirements.
- Review and compile responses.
- Construct a requirements matrix. This matrix takes the requirements as defined in step 3 and sets them into a matrix with software packages to be evaluated in the fit analysis (see Figure 15-8).
- Conduct fit analysis (see Figure 15-8).
- Select the final candidates for short list.

In this step it is usually not necessary to have full demonstrations of the packages. However, if your application is particularly complex or has unique requirements, demonstrations may be of value.

Step 5: Assess Software Packages

At this point you have from three to five good candidate packages to select from. When most organizations get to this point, any one of the

Figure 15-8. ABC Company IAM software evaluation.*

Software Packages

Requirements	ConTech	Amaryllis	InfoAssistant	Outreach	Evergreen	World Class	Interconnect	Mediumistics	Contact Manager
Schedule mail, fax, and e-mail contacts	3	3	3	3	2	2	3	1	2
Select from standard letter library	3	2	2	1	3	2	1	2	3
Allow predefined and "on-the-fly" letter personalization	3	2	2	3	1	3	1	2	2
Schedule multiple contacts at one time	3	2	2	3	2	3	2	2	3

SCALE
3 = Complete support for function
2 = Partial support for function
1 = No support for function

*This is provided as an example and contains fictitious brands. It is not intended to reflect functional capabilities of actual software packages.

candidates is probably a reasonable choice from a functional perspective. Consequently, the issues in this step address, in addition to the fit to requirements, characteristics of the software and of the vendor that support a good design and implementation step. These issues include

- Size and experience of vendor
- Number of installations (similar to yours)
- Overall cost
- Design and installation support
- Design tools
- Training (technical and end-user)
- Technical support
- Maintenance
- New releases

The bottom line here is finding a vendor that can support you through a successful installation. I have seen examples where companies that have a similar IAM application and sell to the same market purchase the same software package but have completely different experiences. With the same software one was successful and one failed; the latter restarted with a different software package. The key here is often the vendor's personnel. Your individual contacts and support personnel from the vendor are as important as the overall strength and reputation of the vendor. Do you trust these people? Are they competent? Do they understand your issues? Do they listen to you? Do they provide value? These people are as important to you as your account managers are to your customers.

Step 6: Select Package

The result of your assessment is the selection of a package and a vendor to work with. This is a point where you need team consensus. While there are a large number of options, many of them reasonably good options, no package and no installation will be perfect. A common understanding of the anticipated trade-offs and team buy-in to the decisions will engender understanding and support during the installation.

Step 7: Design Modifications

Typically this is a configuration step (sometimes called tailoring or modifying) around a base packaged system. In this configuration, you actually define how IAM will work in your application, using the flexibility that is built into most good IAM packages. This is still an important step—one that shouldn't be overlooked or shrugged off as insignificant or too easy to cause problems. System elements or features that are modified or set up in this design include the following:

• *System parameters.* Most systems have some parameters that need to be set when the system is installed. Parameters include everything from passwords to systems alarms to language options.

• *Data tables.* These data tables vary substantially from package to package. A middle-of-the-road package might include tables for call or contact types, opportunity and status codes, title codes, user-defined data elements, and decision-making roles. These data tables provide flexibility and allow you to define the values or responses that are used in data elements in a way that is customized to your organization. Although these tables can be modified after implementation, it is preferable to thoroughly define and then load them before implementation. Doing so will provide better information for analysis, force the project team to address management and tracking issues at the right time in the IAM building process, and probably cost one tenth of what it will cost to set them up after implementation.

• *Processing.* The design options vary considerably from package to package. Low-end packages have limited or no processing options. Higher-end packages tend to have more flexibility in processing options, including screen formats (or screen painting), sequence or flow of screens and functions, and special calculations.

• *Reporting.* Reporting options include standard, custom, and semicustom reports.

• *Data interchange.* Many IAM packages provide a capability to export and import data in and out of the package. The most common necessary data interchange is between the IAM package and the order processing system. This interchange is required to provide purchase transaction and/or purchase history information to the account manager. The interchange is usually handled in one of three ways:

- A hot key allows the account manager to move from the IAM package to the order processing system with the press of one key. This option is usually the easiest, the least expensive, but is somewhat cumbersome for the account manager. It could have a negative impact on account manager productivity.
- A batch update is provided, using the import option to periodically pass order information into the IAM system database (usually done one to two times per day). This option is a little more complicated than the hot key option but in operation is seamless to the account manager. Its limitation lies in the timing or currentness of the purchase data. If the import is done once per day, purchase data could exclude up to twenty-four hours of purchase transactions. In environments where customers order frequently, this might be a concern.
- The IAM system is set up as a front-end system where the order is entered and then passed to the order processing system. This can be an elegant option, especially when using one of the higher-end, more robust IAM packages that is built around the customer (the term used to describe these systems is *customer-centric*). This option, however, is the most complex, most expensive, and most time consuming.

Step 8: Implement

The thoroughness with which the first seven steps are executed has a significant impact on the facilitation of this step. Regardless of the thoroughness of these steps, the following activities should be considered in implementation:

- *Testing.* This activity becomes increasingly important as the degree of system modifications increases. It should be conducted by both the systems support team members and account managers and use a sample data set that accurately reflects the actual data.
- *User acceptance/sign-off.* Systems and marketing have worked

closely together throughout this process. It might be tempting to let system acceptance by the users be handled informally, sometimes even implicitly (assuming that users have accepted the system simply because they have started using it). Resist this temptation. Execute a formal user acceptance sign-off at least one week before going live.

- *Set expectations.* I have yet to see an implementation that hasn't had some surprises and/or problems. Preparing account managers and management and locating system support time in the first few weeks moderates frustration levels and supports quick resolution of problems.

A Few Final Words of Caution

Before and during this process, be aware of the following traps:

- *A subtle and sometimes insidious "make" mentality.* It amazes me how frequently I still see the mentality that "it's not good if it's not built here," even in standard commercially available applications like IAM. This sometimes comes out in very subtle ways, such as holding commercial packages to a substantially higher standard or matching external costs to underestimated or underallocated internal costs.
- *Making the hardware decision prematurely.* Leveraging existing equipment does not always result in a cost savings, either short-term or long-term. This decision is best made in step 6 after a software selection has been completed.
- *Defining an overly complex solution.* This is not your last chance to define the perfect solution, so don't squeeze every possible anticipated need into the requirements. Be pragmatic. Define only the functionality and the data that you will use in the next six to twelve months. If you are like most organizations, you will be defining "phase 2" in six to twelve months. Save those futuristic requirements for the future.
- *Not visiting other similar sites.* A well-orchestrated software demonstration can be quite compelling. It can at times hide flaws in the product. Do not make your software selection based on a company's skill at demonstrating. Get out to a client site and see the software in an operating IAM environment.
- *Trying to build everything into the IAM package.* This is a corollary to defining an overly complex solution. Some software tools are used infrequently or used off-line. These tools do not need to be integrated into the IAM package. These tools include:

        —Segmentation and grading model(s)
        —Graphics and mapping software
        —Proposal generation

- *Not defining the data usage and economics.* What information would you like to have about your customers? This can be a dangerous question to ask. As a marketer, I would probably always want more information than would be practical to acquire and maintain. When defining data requirements, consider the following:

        —Availability of the data
        —Cost of acquiring the data
        —Ability and willingness of the account managers to capture the data
        —Accuracy of the data, once captured
        —Specific usage of the data (we usually recommend usage tied to a marketing and sales program within the next six months)
        —Tangible value of the data (linked to usage)
        —Cost to maintain the data

Notes

1. Henry J. Johansson, Patrick McHugh, A. John Pendlebury, and William A. Wheller III, *Business Process Reengineering* (New York: John Wiley, 1993), p. 113.
2. Bob Stone, *Successful Direct Marketing Methods* (Chicago: NTC Business Books, 1994), pp. 160–161.

16

The New Account Manager: A Day in the Life

[*The following scenario represents an IAM application. Although the company is not real, the described system is a composite of actual and envisioned successful account management programs. Integrated account management is not the latest "idea of the month." Nor is it just a set of tactics for generating sales. Rather, it is a strategy for doing business in an information-intensive age where time is precious, relationships are valued, productivity is a requirement, and customer retention is essential.*]

In early morning the weather turned and it started to snow. As on most days, Paul reached his desk at seven, avoiding the inevitable traffic buildup. It was cold.

Paul had been with Zetetic for almost ten years now. A great deal had happened in the computer industry in those ten years. A number of companies that had once been household names in the industry were no longer around; almost half of the dominant companies now were new. The biggest changes had taken place in Zetetic's end of the business—software. Almost everything was different now, from development right through to delivery. New versions were appearing every three months (on time, unlike back then!). Zetetic had pioneered the "transparent release installation" in the late 1990s. When a new or updated version of a software program was introduced, it was instantly installed in its existing user base, in a seamless, transparent manner. The assimilation into customer use was phased in gradually, new features replacing old in a timely manner.

Paul had been a member of the launch team for TRIP (Transparent Release Installation Program), and well remembered the hue and cry it evoked. TRIP produced its own breed of Luddite, predicting a twenty-first century where the need for personal contact in software business transactions would all but disappear. In reality, TRIP proved to be the exact opposite. With the ability to upgrade and assimilate becoming completely automatic and transparent, the need for reassurance and understanding grew accordingly. Far from sitting back and allowing it all to take place in some hands-off, uninvolved way, customers needed a high degree of reassurance that the technology not only did what it said it would and did it in an appropriate manner for their business, but, and much more importantly, that they would know how to apply the new technology to get the most value in their businesses.

These thoughts were prompted by Paul's upcoming call from Jack Purvis, one of Zetetic's outside representatives and Paul's partner on more than 150 accounts. Relatively new to the software industry and to Zetetic's method of account management, Jack had been with the company for almost six years and had never worked at an inside job, preferring the freedom of being out on the road. He was no hangover from the "smile and a shoeshine" days but just felt more comfortable being out there on the road. He got along easily and well with people, quickly forming relationships with those he did business with. Jack's own "database" when he joined Zetetic consisted of several tightly written school notebooks detailing his interaction with his customers over the years. With Jack's joining Zetetic and his introduction to the computer and its centralized database, a great many things changed for him. Used to working alone and being responsible for pretty well every aspect of the accounts he handled, Jack had some problems letting go and embracing the integrated marketing system when he was first introduced to it. Initially he had a problem with sharing the management of and responsibility for accounts. But, never one who could be accused of being a slow learner, he soon saw the benefits of the team approach and evolved into one of its most ardent advocates. Before long, the content of Jack's notebooks had become an invaluable addition to Zetetic's database. While Jack may not have been up to the same speed as some of his colleagues when it came to computers and technology, he certainly appreciated their ability to circumvent endless time-wasting meetings and cut to the heart of the matter. For him personally, it meant more time spent productively serving his customers.

As mentioned earlier, Zetetic's method of account management was new to Jack, and although this caused some initial problems, it wasn't long before Jack saw the advantages of the system. He really appreciated his new-found ability to handle a greater number of accounts. Before joining Zetetic, Jack had handled about twenty accounts on his own. Now, with help, he handled more than 150—and delivered more value and better service to Zetetic's customers. Pretty soon what had been "his accounts" in earlier conversation had become "our accounts." Of course, being somewhat of a pragmatist, Jack also appreciated the fact that he was making more money!

Sitting down at his desk, Paul booted up his computer. Monday's schedule appeared; he made sure his weekend changes had been made from where he had left work on Friday. First he checked his e-mail, finding just one item that needed attention immediately. Paul was in the habit of tackling the bulk of his e-mail during his lunch break. Of course, some of his customers knew this, so his lunch time e-mail traffic had grown accordingly.

He keyed into the database, first taking a quick glance at the entire day's schedule. He had scheduled thirty-five calls and had an additional ten calls "loosely scheduled"—pretty ambitious for a Monday. He quickly scanned the list, making sure that the updates he had made for the weekend had been recorded. He checked out the "Breaking News" page. There were one or two items that could be of interest, which he quickly transferred to his own file. He noticed nothing that would affect his conversation with Jack Purvis, except, of course, that e-mail he was about to take care of.

The e-mail was from Bill Dokes at Merchants, one of Zetetic's oldest and largest accounts, and one handled by Jack and Paul. Merchants was on Jack's schedule for a visit this week. Strictly routine, the call was one of their quarterly update calls with Bill in which they audited Bill's use of the software, ran the economic impact analysis for his software usage, and made him aware of the new releases that were available. In his e-mail, Bill Dokes explained that something unexpected had cropped up late Friday and he would be out of town for the entire week. He had tried to get hold of Jack, failed, and was asking Paul to pass along the word. He said he would be in his office until 8 A.M. Monday, before he left. Paul put a call through to him. Bill Dokes was one of his favorite people. "What a joy it would be," thought Paul, "if all my customers were like Bill!"

He answered his phone on the third ring, returning Paul's hello with his usual booming greeting. He had the wonderful knack of making a person feel as though there was no one else he would have preferred to talk with at that moment. It was certainly a great way for Paul to start the week! He said he had received Bill's message and would alert Jack. He mentioned the software update, and Bill asked him to send along some details. Then, noting that he had to scramble to catch a flight, Bill asked Paul to take down a name and telephone number. He quickly explained that the person at that number was someone he had spoken with over the weekend who was very interested in what Zetetic had to offer. He had given the person Paul's name and she was expecting a call from him. Paul thanked Bill, wished him a good week, and he was gone.

Keying in to the database Paul noted that Bill preferred product information to arrive by e-mail, not regular mail, and sent the software update information accordingly. He made a note to mention this to Jack when they talked. He quickly entered the name of his new prospect (Bill's referral) in the database. The software would automatically generate a letter to this new prospect, indicating in the letter that Bill had referred her and that Paul would follow up with a phone call within three days. It indicated in the database that Bill was the source for this new lead and also flagged Bill as the referrer. The system generated a thank-you letter to Bill. These system capabilities allowed Zetetic to track referral business and referral programs over the course of a year. It wasn't long before Zetetic learned that referral business was some of its most profitable business. Its referral-generating programs were highly successful, and the system support for these programs made it easy to track. What surprised Paul was that the act of referring a new prospect seemed to increase the profitability in the customers who did the referring. It was as if, now that they made a referral, they were more committed to Zetetic.

Paul had one more thing to do before fielding Jack's call and that was to set up the letter campaign to provide information on the release of the new file-saver software. He quickly reviewed the product specs fact sheet and the accompanying letter. This week he was targeting Zetetic's sportswear retailers. He scrolled quickly through the target database, checking that it was coded to provide the mode of mailing preferred by the target audience. It looked like e-mail was well on its way to being the dominant choice, although it surprised Paul that so many people still found comfort in receiving the hard copy through the mail (there were a number of people who requested these updates in hard-copy mail and e-mail).

Paul then put the agenda for his call with Jack up on his screen. He punched a key and brought up the map showing where Jack was going to be that day. He made a note to ask Jack to call on Apex for a quick product demo. While it wasn't officially on his schedule for this Monday, Apex was within striking distance of where Jack was going to be. He hit another key and highlighted all Zetetic accounts within a twenty-mile radius of Jack's itinerary. Moving further into the database he punched another key, which showed accounts in this geography that had not yet started using the new software update—now out for almost two months—making a note of those he should mention to Jack.

He then moved on to work through the list of customers he serviced with Jack that were on the agenda for discussion, refreshing his memory by scanning quickly through the background data on each one. He took a look at their recent purchase records, then quickly moved on to any problems or complaints since Jack's last visit. He noted purchases were up again at Aquatex, and made a note to speak with Jack about a possible upgrade there.

At 7:30 Paul's phone rang. Slipping on the headset, he reached for the receiver and was met with the familiar greeting, "Hi, old buddy, just who are we going to surprise today?" Jack, like a great many people, was still astonished at the ability of the database to call up something that was news to the customer. After Jack had begun with his usual few minutes of personal banter, they got down to business.

"Well, Home Improv finally went public with that acquisition," said Paul. "I'm glad we've been tracking Homestyle on our radar for a while. What say we begin with Improv, since they are on our list for today"?

"Starting with Improv's fine by me," Jack responded.

Home Improv was one of the clients Jack and Paul managed, a medium volume chain of warehouse-size hardware-home improvement stores located throughout the Midwest that was very definitely in a fast-growth mode. They had just announced the acquisition of one of their competitors, Homestyle, a smaller, very aggressive chain headquartered in Michigan. Zetetic had been alerted to the takeover some weeks back; it had been finalized on Friday and transferred on to its database from Improv's database on Saturday. Homestyle seemed to be a perfect match for Zetetic's services, but, despite their very aggressive approach to the whole home improvement area, it had never even come close to getting a sale there.

"Jack, I think I see a way we can help with the transition and stay ahead of the curve with Improv on this," said Paul.

"What do you mean?"

"Take a look at Improv's sales figures; over 70 percent of them involved their Cad-Cam capability using our CADLINK software. I think we can demonstrate how CADLINK can make the transition easier for them. If you look at what Improv has been doing with customer input on design and compare it with Homestyle, you'll see what I mean. With CADLINK Improv can sit down with a customer, design the entire job the way the customer wants it—down to the exact color inside the cabinets. It can check the availability of every item, set a price, and agree on a plan and timing, all in less than thirty minutes. I think, thanks to CADLINK, we've kept Improv ahead. Homestyle may be using technology to help their customers, but it doesn't seem to be high on its list of priorities, and it certainly isn't using it as much as Improv to allow customer design. At Improv, customers can pretty much design the whole room, or whatever, by themselves; not so at Homestyle. And, Homestyle is still keeping all that stored information in the individual stores, not sharing it across all their stores."

"Even if Homestyle is working on an intranet system," Jack said, jumping into the conversation, "it doesn't look like it has introduced it into any of its stores yet. My meeting with Frank is to follow up on the fifty CADLINK upgrades he received last week. With Improv's strategy to be fully connected by the end of the year, including Homestyle would be a natural, and it could be a big opportunity for us. CADLINK would make it a win-win situation: Improv brings Homestyle into the fold, Homestyle gets Improv's connectivity, while customers get the added benefit of the combined information of both. The first thing we should do is try to look a little deeper at just how good a fit CADLINK is for Homestyle. On the surface it looks like a natural, but they're smart people and there must be some reason they're not using it. If you look at our notes on the database you'll see Homestyle's customer base is different from Improv's; even its store traffic configures a little differently than Improv's. We know the product lines they carry differ, but that isn't such a big deal. Let's pull up that cost benefit analysis we did earlier in the year for Improv. You got it? Let's see how it might apply here, and while we're at it, let's take a look and see if there is any information available on the demographics of Homestyle's customer base. I'll be calling Joe in purchasing at Improv later about setting up the electronic fund transfer to handle future new releases. Let me see if he has an idea of how the transition will roll out. Let's take a look at our contacts at Improv and Homestyle, and see if there is a way we can add value during the transition."

Paul hit the key and brought up his contact list at Home Improv. There was a total of fifteen. He hit the key again to highlight which of the fifteen had been on the team that originally selected the Cad-Cam software for Home Improv. He hit another key to bring up his Homestyle contacts. Hitting it again, he brought up their titles, departments, and previous job records. Interesting! Two of the six names had worked at Home Improv. He hit the key again and got their internal extension numbers.

"You're absolutely right, Jack. In the meantime, I'll contact the people at Homestyle and see what information I can get about their customer demographics and their store traffic. Then I'll call Frank (the V.P. of operations at Homestyle). Maybe you could call Fred over in their training unit and bounce some of our ideas off him. When I speak with Frank I'll ask if he can find out who is on the transition team before you get there. Maybe we can get involved. Let's make sure that we have a solid understanding of their needs, what CAD-LINK brings to the party, and the potential economic impact, before we go much farther. I'll get an e-mail to you later today on this."

"Good idea," said Jack. "Talking about upgrades, Carport's inventory system has a glitch that appeared since they installed the new QUIKINV. So far Carport's been pretty okay about it, but it's not getting the results it expected. There's something amiss with the forecasting component. While it doesn't seem to be a technical problem, Carport isn't seeing the benefit in inventory turns that it had anticipated and based its purchase decision on. Whatever the problem is, I want to get it sorted out now. I feel that if we don't resolve it soon it may jeopardize our ability in other Carport franchises. I alerted our tech guys over the weekend. They're going to get on to it first thing this morning."

"This may be an opportunity to take advantage of Autobahn's information," said Paul. "I'm scheduled to speak to Autobahn, out in Ohio, later today, and it has been using QUIKINV successfully since its beta days; maybe Autobahn's information could shed some light on what's happening at Carport. Autobahn gives us access to pretty well everything on their database, so it should be a big help. In fact, don't you have a good relationship with Ray over there, their I.S. guy? Why don't you talk to him before you go to Carport?"

"That's a good idea, Paul. I'll try to get hold of Ray before I go see Carport. While you were talking I put both inventory charts up on the screen. Take a look at what happened at both after installing QUIKINV. Look at where they're both using the software. Now check out who installed it and who trained them both. Pretty well identical. Now look at the results. There's no comparison, even allowing for the different purchase levels. I know people are tired of hearing about 'just-in-time' inventory maintenance, but our software system covers every supplier, every buying point, every shipping point, every receiving point, practically down to when each individual last ate. Carport's forecasting is so off, it's got to have something to do with how they're using it. That software was working perfectly when we installed it. I'm sure our service guys will figure it out. Anyway, I'll call them before I hit Carport. I'll let you know how it goes."

"Let me know if you need anything from Autobahn. I should be calling Rick over there about 3:30. Let's move on to Rohrbachs," said Paul.

Jack said, "I received an e-mail from Carla this morning putting the meeting back to Thursday. I spoke with her on Friday, and one thing we discussed was the new distribution software. I promised to send her the literature, so could you arrange to get that out today? When we meet on Thursday she might have had a chance to read what you send her. Maybe I'll bring along a demo and ask her if I can put some of their figures on it. It always helps when there is something familiar on the screen. We can talk tomorrow or Wednesday and figure out just what figures to put on there."

"Listen Jack, I've been thinking about the work we've been putting in on Aquatex and how it's really starting to pay off. Didn't you mention last week that your visit to Aquatex today is mainly to discuss setting up some product training sessions? Thinking about that, I thought it might be an idea to include our new file management product into the mix. I don't mean do it without telling them. Suggest it to Mary when you visit and see what she says. And, with the way their purchases have been going, we should talk about upgrading them. Let's try to touch base after your visit and we can talk about the upgrade."

"O.K., but did you forget that those training sessions are for some new hires, so I'm not so sure we want to add to the confusion by introducing a new product into the mix at that time. Maybe; let me bounce it off Mary. Let me know what happens with Condor. By the way, fax me that Fortune letter. I'll be talking to you later. Thanks, Paul."

"Catch you later Jack. Bye for now."

Paul put a quick call in to Joe Magrane at Apex.

"Good morning, Joe. Paul Mellon here."

"Paul, you were on my call list for today. Do you want to go first?

"O.K. I was just calling to say that Jack Purvis is going to be in the area this afternoon and is going to drop by to give you a demo of that new software I mentioned last week."

"That's what I was going to call about. By the way, thanks for faxing me the specs. I shared them with my boss on Friday. He got very excited and asked me to arrange a demo as soon as possible. If he is available this afternoon that would be perfect. I'll get hold of him, see if he's free at say 3:30. If he's not I'll put a red flag on the database."

"Great. I'll call Jack and alert him. I'm glad I called. If there is any other information you need just let me know. I hope it works out; the timing couldn't be better."

"For us too. I'll call if I need anything. Thanks, Paul."

After the call, Paul updated the database and put in a follow-up to review Jack's notes from his call when Paul did his planning tomorrow morning. "This is one that could happen quickly, and I want to stay close and keep it moving as well as it has up to this point," thought Paul.

Sometimes things happen that way, but not often enough. Paul's next call reminded him of that fact. He had decided to call Mike over at Autobahn to sound him out about using their information to help Zetetic determine what was causing the performance issues at Carport. Paul would need to ask him a few questions beforehand. Carport wasn't a competitor, so Paul didn't anticipate any problems. But he didn't get a chance to ask the questions.

"Paul, glad you called," said Mike. "Before we get to *why* you called I want to tell you, we have a problem. Well, it may not be a problem, but it could become one. One of our Senior VPs in marketing met someone from Celestine at a conference last week."

"That one in Seattle; we were there."

"Anyway, whoever he met did a good job. He got back at the weekend and looks like one of the first things he did was to e-mail me with a request for some comparative figures on Zetetic versus Celestine products."

"It's all on the database."

"I know, I just wanted to let you know in case you needed to update anything."

"Were there any particular areas where he was concerned?"

"Well, he was particularly impressed with Celestine's electronic promotion capabilities that were triggered from excess inventory counts."

"I'll take a look at the database right away and get back to you. I'll make sure that the promotion feature comparison sheets are up-to-date. I was calling you to talk about something else, but it can wait. I'll call you right back."

"Thanks, Paul."

Paul updated the database, just adding some new figures that had been posted over the weekend. He did a quick comparison check with Celestine and couldn't see anything to worry about. Zetetic was ahead on a feature-by-feature basis in pretty well every category. If anything, it was pulling away. But, you never know. Paul updated the database and put in a quick call to Mike. He said he'd let him know how it went.

Paul broke for lunch at 11:30, deciding, what with the snow still coming down outside, he'd grab a sandwich and eat at his desk while he caught up on his e-mail. He'd managed to make twenty-three calls since saying good-bye to Jack, and twenty-three was pretty good for a Monday morning. He zapped an e-mail to Jack, updating him and asking him to call back by 2 P.M. He finished his lunch, then keyed Condor's file up onto his screen. He had scheduled a call to Tom Mills for 1:30 P.M. to talk with him about the merits of CADLINK versus the competitor's product JOCAD.

Condor was another of Zetetic's customers in the hardware and home improvement business. Located on the East Coast, Condor was affected by the downturn in building. Like every company in the industry, its sales and earnings were hit. Condor was not as badly affected as some, mainly as a result of sticking to its mission of servicing the high end of the market. It had been very tempting to move out of the niche it had carved for itself, particularly during the downturn, but fortunately Condor had stuck to its knitting. When the recovery started, Condor was in a good position to profit from it.

Tom Mills was a recent arrival at Condor. Very aggressive, he moved quickly to make his mark. On Friday he had come to Jack and Paul to tell them that he would like to install 100 copies of CADLINK in Condor stores. This was something Jack and Paul had been trying to get Condor to do for more than two years. Although Condor was currently using JOCAD, a competitor's software, Tom said he had already made up his mind to switch to CADLINK. Although he wanted to move ahead as quickly as possible, he wanted a detailed proposal from Zetetic. It is always tempting to accept an order on the spot and question it later, but it was a trap Paul had fallen into in the past, with some pretty dire consequences. Tom's request came on Friday. Paul had thanked him and promised to get back with him on Monday.

Paul brought Condor up on his screen. He and Jack spent some time over the weekend going over Condor's database, reviewing Zetetic's history with the company. They had reviewed calls over the last six months, their installed products, recent purchases, Zetetic's ongoing comments, and any complaints or problems that might have occurred over those months. Clean as a whistle.

Paul and Jack then took a look at what they had on JOCAD. One of the strengths of Zetetic's account management software was its ability to monitor competitive products, highlight differences—both positive and negative, and relay them back to the account managers and their development group on a timely basis.

The obvious difference between CADLINK and JOCAD was price. There was no doubt that Tom Mills knew that he could save money sticking with JOCAD, but CADLINK provided a number of features that weren't included in JOCAD. But, Paul would be a lot happier knowing what particular features Tom had in mind and how CADLINK could address those needs and bring something extra to the party. He and Jack had done a pretty thorough feature-by-feature analysis of both products. Overall, the picture looked good for CAD-LINK. Of course, Tom Mills and Condor might have some plans of their own that they didn't know about.

One thing Paul and Jack did have was Home Improv's history. Home Improv's history with CADLINK was very impressive (and available to them). They didn't know Tom Mills's opinion of Home Improv, but whatever it was he certainly had to be impressed with their performance in the marketplace.

Tom picked up his phone on the third ring. After hellos, Paul said he and Jack were anxious to understand the incremental value of CADLINK relative to Tom's particular needs. Paul asked Tom to tell him what particular functional needs he had that he would want addressed by CADLINK. Paul hit paydirt. Tom listed eight specific features, five of which were differentiating features in Zetetic's product. As Tom talked through his needs, Paul made sure that he captured each one in the database. Tom had done his homework well—he really understood what he wanted and why. This needs information was just excellent and would be a helpful reference on the database. It could automatically be inserted into letters and proposals, and it was actually educational for Paul to listen to Tom describe how he would use CADLINK. This application information would help Paul get an even better understanding of the benefits of CADLINK, which would obviously help him in a number of contacts in the future.

Paul took Tom through the data. While they moved through it, he continued to ask questions to make sure he clearly understood what factors were important to Tom, what features would impact Condor's business, and how the decision would be made. He also pointed out that he and Jack felt it would probably make more sense if Condor waited for the release of the new version of CADLINK, due out in less than a month, because it addressed an additional feature on Tom's list and could be bundled with the new system training that the product group was working on. Paul suggested running a pilot, putting ten copies in one of Condor's stores.

Like a lot of the really good contacts in integrated account management, this one was interesting. Paul focused on understanding Tom's needs, asked a lot of questions, focused on providing value by helping Tom better understand how the software would support his needs, and then listened to Tom convince himself that CADLINK was exactly what he needed. Paul then provided the depth of understanding Tom needed to get a CADLINK decision made at Condor.

When Paul had finished, Tom thanked him for his and Jack's thoroughness and said he felt even stronger about CADLINK. He agreed with the idea of a pilot but said it was not his decision alone and asked Paul to put it all together in a proposal he could submit to the rest of his purchasing team.

Tom was one of those people who are difficult to read, particularly over the telephone, but Paul felt he had been impressed and believed he knew which way Tom would eventually go. Paul asked Tom several more questions before concluding their conversation: whether he preferred e-mail or regular mail, the names of the other members of the purchasing team and how best to reach them, and some further store details. Keying the information into his database,

Paul promised the information Tom requested would be sent by the end of the day.

Once off the telephone, Paul made the adjustments to the proposal, keyed in the names of those people at Condor that Tom had given him, and dispatched the proposal, using a combination of e-mail and regular mail. He also sent all the information to the appropriate people internally. He finished by sending an e-mail note to Jack.

Jack called at 2 P.M. Paul updated him on his morning and spent some time discussing his conversation with Tom Mills. He outlined what he had sent Tom. Paul then told Jack about Autobahn and said he wasn't worried but that if Jack thought of anything he should let him know. He also gave him the other updates.

The rest of the afternoon was, as usual, chaotic but relatively uneventful. The days always went by quickly, and Paul was still surprised when he looked at his contact counts at the end of the day. This Monday was no different. Paul pulled up the day's customer activity on the screen. It showed him that he had completed thirty of the thirty-five contacts he had scheduled for the day. Each of the five others he had attempted to reach and ended up sending out an e-mail or fax note letting these customers know that he would get back with them later in the week. In addition, he was able to contact six out of the ten other loosely scheduled calls. He had identified four new sales opportunities, closed on two opportunities, advanced the sales process on three others, and passed on two service problems to his support team. Additionally, he had sent out eight letters and a dozen e-mail messages. He had added one new account to the database (the referral from Bill) and had added fifteen new contact names from existing accounts. He was also able to bring up and review Jack's day. He was pleased to see that Jack had been able to make the call and do the software demonstration at Apex. Paul also noted with pleasure that Jack had posted two sales of training packages that they had been working for some time. It felt like a productive day: Zetetic's business and sales results looked good and Paul felt that he and Jack had added some real value to their customers.

When he looked up, the clock had moved past six. Paul slid the computer out of the dock, put it in the case, and headed for the door.

Epilogue

There are a number of integrated account management (IAM) examples referred to in this book—both identified and not identified. The impact of IAM in these examples has been profound. Companies applying these principles are providing increased value to their customers, increasing customer satisfaction and loyalty, and concurrently decreasing marketing and selling costs.

- *Shell's TeamTBA.* The TeamTBA case provides a classic example of the short-term results that are possible with IAM. In its first six months of operation, TeamTBA increased the number of active Shell dealer accounts by 24 percent and the number of Gold Accounts (those purchasing 75 percent of the Shell branded product lines) by 237 percent. In its first year of operation, TeamTBA took a business that lost approximately $8 million the previous year and turned a $400,000 profit. It did this while increasing overall sales by approximately $100,000 and while increasing customer satisfaction in sixteen of the eighteen key satisfaction indicators in the TBA industry.

- *Anonymous.* IAM is still growing, but there are a number of success stories. However, when I think of the positive results from the use of IAM, I think of a customer comment from 1992 after a client had installed an IAM program. This customer had increased its revenue with our client from $550 in 1990 to $32,950 in 1992. Their comment to our client was, "Your prices are not the cheapest, but to sacrifice the service and relationships it's just not worth it."

Appendix
Software Packages and
Vendors

Following is a representative list of available software packages that may (or may not) fit your functional requirements. Specific information regarding software capabilities and vendor information is current with available information at the time this was written. This information is subject to change. For current information regarding any individual software package, please contact the vendor. Note: Inclusion (or exclusion) of a software package on this list should not be taken as a recommendation by the author (either implicit or explicit).

Vendor	Name	Type	Features
Symantec Corp.	ACT!	Personal Information Managers (PIMS) Word processing and text editing Mail/list management Time management Contact management	• Database • Word processing • Time management • Telemarketing functions • Contact profiles • Notes • Transaction history • Letter and memo writer • Unlimited searches • Reports • Tracks expenses
Action Plus Software	Action Plus Contact Suite	Account/contact management	• Contact management • Time management • Sales management • Invoicing • Inventory tracking • Database Synchronization • Word processing
Action Plus Software, Inc.	Action + Plus	PIMS contact management	• Unlimited profile database • Free-form, searchable notepads • Telemarketing scripts • Invoicing • Sales orders • Statements • Autodialing • Inventory • Graphic images • Word processing

Company	Product	Category	Features
ARI Network Services	ARISE	Account/contact management	• Mail merge • Spell checker • Appointment scheduling • To-do tasks • Electronic network messaging • Expenses • Goals • Project planning • Graphic images per contact • E-mail messages • Transmit fax
Franklin Quest Corp.	ASCEND	Account/contact management	• Configurable • Query tool • Microsoft Office integration • E-mail integration • Personal contact manager for Windows
Q & I Computer Systems, Inc.	Association Database SalesForce Automation Database	Account/contact management	• Sales force automation • Call centers • Companywide database
Aurum Software	Aurum-TeleTrak	Personal information managers Mail/list management Telephone management	• Lead tracking • Activity history • To-do lists • Lead fulfillment • Mass mailings • Questionnaire forms

Vendor	Name	Type	Features
CallBack Software	CallBack	Account/contact management	• Sales order creation • Quote generation • Campaign/event management
Abelson Communications, Inc.	CMOTOS	Account/contact management	• Integrates field sales, telemarketing, and customer service
WestWare, Inc.	Contact Ease	Sales analysis/reporting Contact management	• Unlimited contacts, people, and call-backs • Schedules • User fields • Direct link to DOS or Windows word processing
Bancom Systems, Inc.	Contact manager/Organizer system	Contact management	• Word processor • Direct mail • Telemarketing • Tracks personal activity items
DATANETICS	DATATRAC	Account/contact management	• Telemarketing • Customer service • Logging and acting on product complaints • Business activities • Schedules events or tasks • Generates correspondence • Chronological history of important events
Marketing and Sales Productivity Systems, Inc.	DOMINATE!	Account/contact management	• Multiuser customer applications to meet client's current and future sales and marketing needs • Modification training • Postinstallation • Support for a fixed fee

Company	Product	Category	Features
SourceMate	E-Power	Account/contact management	• Contact management system • Multiple contacts in large databases
Information Management Associates, Inc.	EDGE TeleBusiness Software	Mail/list management	• Direct marketing • Database marketing • Telemarketing • Account management • Customer service
Data Code, Inc.	Enterprise Series for Windows	Sales and marketing management	• Sales • Marketing • Customer data
Fastech, Inc.	FastTrack	Sale and marketing management	• Automates sales functions • Account profiling • Sales history • Order status • Promotions planning • Data synchronization
Interactive Micro, Inc.	Front Office	Account/contact management	• Sales and contact management software • Telemarketing commissions • Inventory • Job cost • Multiuser
Sirius Systems, Inc.	G2	Account/contact management	• Sales and marketing management
ELAN Software Corp.	GoldMine	Account/contact management	• Group calendaring • E-mail • Mail merge letters • Sale forecasting

Vendor	Name	Type	Features
ELAN Software Corp.	GoldSync	Account/contact management	• Lead tracking • Fax/merge • Point-to-point remote synchronization • Scheduled activities • Notes can be automatically transferred
Action Systems, Inc.	HEATSEEKER	Account/contact management	• Contact management • Account profiling and planning • Scheduling • Opportunity tracking
Canveon Systems, Inc.	Infotrac	Account/contact management	• Multiuser Windows contact database • History • Appointments • Documents • Forecasting • Activity reports • Data synchronization
Ruf Corp.	Integrated Marketing Software	Marketing	• Telemarketing • Database marketing • Marketing research • Mapping • Sales and customer service system • Fulfillment • Direct mail system
Janna Systems, Inc.	Janna Contact	Account/contact management	• Storage of letters, faxes, graphics, sound, and video • Shares contacts, documents, and schedules across work groups

Company	Product	Category	Features
Logic Design Corp.	LDC-Sales/Quote Management	Sales and marketing	• Lead management • Call history • Tickler function • Automatic lead assignment • Call scripts • Unlimited note pages • Form letter • Literature fulfillment • Mail management • Sales and marketing management reports • Generates price quotes
ENDPOINT! Marketing Information Systems	LEADS!	Account/contact management	• Companywide account opportunity • Contact management • Team selling • Automatic data synchronization cross-platform
PenUltimate, Inc.	Locomotion	Account/contact management	• PDA-based opportunity and contact manager • Integrates with ELAN's GoldMine
Marketforce	Marketforce	Sales and marketing management	• Field sales • Management reporting • Sales analysis • Telemarketing • Database/strategic marketing
Marketrieve Co.	Marketrieve Plus	Sales and marketing management	• Lead tracking • Forecasting • Sales and marketing analysis • Account management • Literature fulfillment • Opportunity management

Vendor	Name	Type	Features
Modatech Systems, Inc.	MAXIMIZER 3.0	Account/contact management	• Organizes contacts • Schedules • Correspondence • Phone calls • Expenses
Modatech Systems, Inc.	MAXIMIZER ENTERPRISE	Account/contact management	• Customizable sales strategy • Synchronizes reps
MEI Group	MEI+	Sales Planning/forecasting	• Multilingual • Contact management • Agenda • Opportunity management • Documents • Report generator • Proposals • Order entry • E-mail • Mail merge
New Horizons Development Group	MVP	Sales Planning/forecasting	• Customizable interfaces • Distributed database environment
ON! Contact Software Corp.	ON!Contact ENTERPRISE & Contact Client Management	Sales and marketing management	• Telemarketing management • List management • Query management • Sales cycle management
ONYX Software	ONYX Customer Center	Sales and marketing management	• Sales force automation • Service • Technical support • Quality assurance • Marketing

Company	Product	Category	Features
MFJ International	OverQuota	Sales management	• Share information on accounts, customer needs, and company commitments • Tracks selling process
OAC, Inc.	Perfect Business Solutions	Account/contact management	• Automatic database synchronization • Integrates with corporate systems • Four-week "turnkey" for success
Astea International, Inc.	PowerSales	Account/contact management	• Data synchronization • Automated sales and marketing functions
Soft Solutions, Inc.	PowerTrax	Contact management	• Password-protected list of contacts • Graphical environment • Links fields to pop-up menus of predefined titles and key words • Word processing • Calendaring • Reminders for each contact
Prism Systems, Inc.	Prism Sales Focus	Account/contact management	• Customizable home office to field account management systems • Calendar/time/activity planning • Corporate/rep data exchange • Multiple contacts/follow-up • History/products analysis
Prism Systems, Inc.	Prism Sales Management System	Sales and marketing management	• Account/activity/product management • Call reporting • Automatic corporate/rep data exchange with lead dissemination
Salesoft, Inc.	PROCEED	Sales and marketing management	• Modular system • Sales force • Sales management

Vendor	Name	Type	Features
ProTrak International, Inc.	ProTrak Relationship Management System	Sales and marketing management	• Tracks sales, marketing, client servicing • Follow-up tickler • Activity history • Link to word processor • Notebook • Multioffice options
Information Management Consultants, Inc.	PURSUIT for Windows	Account/contact management	• Access-based • Microsoft Office compatible • Network Ready • Customer-tracking system
RealWorld Corp.	RealWorld Accounting and Business Software	Account/contact management	• Accounting and business software • Selection of add-on enhancement for vertical markets
SaleMaker Corp.	SaleMaker	Sales and marketing management	• Integrated marketing and sales opportunity management software for headquarters and field sales applications
Data Systems Support	Sales Information Response System (SIRS)	Account/contact management	• Integrated sales and marketing productivity system
SalesPro International	Sales Producer	Sales and marketing management	• Contact • Correspondence • Sales cycle management • Client/prospect profiling • Activity tracking • Sales management • Ad-hoc reporting

Company	Product	Category	Features
SalesPro International	Sales Producer Banking	Sales and marketing management	• Client/prospect profiling • Contact and correspondence management • Export/import among users • Mainframe read
Prism Systems, Inc.	Sales Rep's Secretary	Account/contact management	• Automated on-line phone book • Calendars • Reminders • Activity planning • Customer tracking/history • Products • Correspondence module
Metropolis Software, Inc.	Sales Synergy & Metropolis Distribution Engine	Account/contact management	• Information sharing based on customizable rules
TRITECH Information Systems	Sales TRAXX-Q	Contact management	• Tracking and managing leads, projects, multiple contacts • Multiple selling situation • Quotations • Fulfillment • Forecasting
Sierra Software Innovations	SALESBASE 2.5	Account/contact management	• Opportunity management system for the large field sales force
SalesBook Systems	SalesBook	Account/contact management	• Front-to-back sales automation • Based on opportunity management model
Advanced Concepts, Inc.	SalesCTRL	Account/contact management	• Account management • Lead tracking • Database marketing

Vendor	Name	Type	Features
Saleskit Software Corp.	SalesKit	Sales management	• Customer service • Telemarketing • Field sales • Report generation • Automated tasks • Exchange information with corporate divisions • Creates unique screens • Customer database formats • Order status • Sales plans • Sales histories • Order tracking • Inventory status • Financial information • Customer phone lists • Market share analysis
SalesKit Software Corp.	SalesKit 5.0 for Windows	Sales and marketing management	• Formal opportunity management methods • Integrates with corporate systems • Permits customization by nonprogrammers
Scopus Technology, Inc.	SalesTEAM	Sales management	• Buyers in multiple sites • Multiparticipant decision making • Reports • Lead management • Contact management • To-do lists • Fulfillment operations • Prospect qualification quotes

Company	Product	Category	Features
			• Forecasts • Negotiations • Follow-up lists • Deal change notification
Scopus Technology, Inc.	SalesTEAM	Account/contact management	• Direct marketing management • Telesales • Telequalifying • Account and opportunity management • Sales process automation
Aurum Software	SalesTrak	Sales and marketing management	• Opportunity management • Quotation forecasting • Data synchronization
Profidex Corp.	SCAMP	Sales analysis/reporting Sales management	• Scripting • Letters • Label generation • Refines fields by user • Calendar • Notebook facilities
Profidex Corp.	SCAMP	Sales analysis/reporting Sales management	• Telemarketing • Sales force automation • Contact management • Market research applications • Scripting • Letter • Label generation • Refines fields by user • Calendar and notebook facilities

Vendor	Name	Type	Features
Cognitech Corp.	Sharkware Professional	Account/contact management	• Calendar • Harvey Mackay methodologies
Simin Business Systems	Simin	Account/contact management	• Sales force automation • Quoting • Order entry • Forecasting • Literature processing • Work flow • Rep management
Paul Guggenheim & Associates, Inc.	SMARTS	Sales and marketing management	• Lead tracking • Sales analysis • Budget/forecasting • Mail merge • Telemarketing • Automatic lead generation • Sales force automation
SNAP, Inc.	SNAP	Sales analysis reporting	• Lead entry and analysis • Marketing analysis • Account and territory management • Direct mail processing • Telemarketing • Product forecasting • Integrated word processing • Standard and customer reports • Electronic list loading modules

Company	Product	Category	Features
Business Software, Inc.	Softsell	Account/contact management	• Customer histories • Pop-up scripts • Form letters • Auto dialer • Reports
Saratoga Systems	SPS	Account/contact management	• Account/contact • Opportunity management software
Softek Business Systems, Inc.	SPS	Account/contact management	• Customer profile • Notes • Contacts • Telemarketing • Sales leads • E-mail • Directions • To-do lists • Expense • Literature • Bi-directional • Direct mail
SuperOffice Corp.	SuperOffice 3.0	Account/contact management	• Mac and Windows • Opportunity management • Sales tracking • Links with third-party word processors and spreadsheets
Gateway Systems Corp.	SYNERGIST Sales Portfolio for Windows	Account/contact management	• Remote sales force automation • Information synchronization

Vendor	Name	Type	Features
Tektron, Inc.	TakeControl Marketing		• On-line contact management • Inbound and outbound calling • Opportunity management • Strategic planning • Electronic fulfillment and letter merge • Productivity tools • Reports and graphs • Lead generation and qualification • Account management • Relationship building • Activity reports • Forecasting • Sales and service analysis • Database marketing campaigns • Call management • Response tracking • Campaign analysis • Electronic fulfillment • Letter merge • Productivity tools • Reports • Graphs • Database marketing • Marketing campaigns • Inbound and outbound calling • Response tracking • On-line library • Merges and cleans lists • Tracks leads • Maintains mailing lists • Coordinates fulfillment with calling process

Company	Product	Category	Features
TeleMagic, Inc.	TeleMagic Enterprise	Account/contact management	• Customizable contact management software for companywide usage
TeleMagic, Inc.	TeleMagic Professional	Account/contact management	• Two-level relational database • Contact management designed for individuals and/or small work groups
Appintec Corp.	TeleMagic/400	Account/contact management	• Contact and activity management system • Quick access to information
Information Management Associates, Inc.	TELEMAR	Account/contact management	• Database marketing • Telemarketing • Account management and fulfillment • Execute targeted direct mail and calling campaigns • Import/export capability for list management • Reporting system
Information Management Associates, Inc.	TELEMAR/PC	Account/contact management	• Windows-based notebook account, contact, and opportunity management system
TeleVell, Inc.	TeleSell Salesperson	Account/contact management	• Windows-based • Integrated, fully relational database
TeleVell, Inc.	TeleSell Salesperson Module		• Organizing prospects • Tracking leads • Preparing targeted letters and proposals • Updating mailing lists • Action items • "Quick-icons"

Vendor	Name	Type	Features
TeleVell, Inc.	TeleSell Telemarketing Module	Sales analysis/reporting	• Qualify leads • Survey customers • Unlimited questions • Answers per question • Unlimited campaigns • Unlimited calls per campaign • People per company • Million companies
Information Management Associates, Inc.	The EDGE TeleBusiness Software System	Account/contact management	• UNIX-based application development package • Creates customer telebusiness software applications
Fairfield Management Resources, Inc.	The Relationship Management System	Account/contact management	• Call history • Customer and prospect database • Pipeline tracking • Sales plans • Sales reports • Tickler • Open architecture • Client/server technology • Object-oriented design • Platform independence • Standard SQL database
Evergreen Ventures Corp.	The Sales Associate	Account/contact management	• Design own contact management/sales system
Marketware Software	Total Manager for Windows	Contact management	• Database management • Supports 96 fields of information • Tracking system • Contact history • Notepad

Company	Product	Category	Features
			• Auto dialer • Calendar • Calculator • Unlimited telemarketing scripts • Dynamic agenda • Week-at-a-glance • To-do lists • Direct mail capability • Report writer • Letter generator • Built-in word processor
Unitrac Software Corp.	UNITRAC	Sales and marketing management	• Account management • Telemarketing • Customer service
Unitrac Software Corp.	Unitrac for SQL Windows	Sales analysis/reporting	• Prospect/client tracking • Telemarketing • Statistical inquiry • Territory management • Lead source analysis • Automated correspondence • Mailing label generation • Tickler file management
Uptrends Management Software, Inc.	UPTRENDS	Account/contact management	• Time management system for individual and group scheduling
The Vantive Corp.	Vantive Sales	Sales and marketing management	• Targeted campaign development • Inbound/outbound call management • Sales opportunity qualification • Routing and management • Marketing fulfillment • Performance reporting

Vendor	Name	Type	Features
Soft Engineering, Inc.	Victor Sales Manager, Etc.	Sales and marketing management	• Sales • Services • Administration • Marketing activity
Market Power, Inc.	Visual MATRIX	Sales management	• Lead tracking • Contract management • Opportunity management • Team selling • Sales funneling • Sales cycle tracking and analysis • Sales pipeline management
Market Power, Inc.	Visual MATRIX	Account/contact management	• Lead tracking • Forecasting • Sales funneling • Sales cycle analysis • Data distribution/communications • Contact opportunity • Pipeline management
WinApps	WinContact	Marketing (direct)	• Contact management • Telemarketing, sales automation • Database design • Mail messaging • Direct mail • Fax • Auto dialing module

Index

[Page numbers in *italics* refer to illustrations.]